Frommer's®

Dubai

1st Edition

by Shane Christensen

Here's what the critics say about Frommer's:

"Amazingly easy to use. Very portable, very complete."

—*Booklist*

"Detailed, accurate, and easy-to-read information for all price ranges."
—*Glamour Magazine*

"Hotel information is close to encyclopedic."

—*Des Moines Sunday Register*

"Frommer's Guides have a way of giving you a real feel for a place."
—*Knight Ridder Newspapers*

WILEY

Wiley Publishing, Inc.

About the Author

Shane Christensen wrote *Frommer's Dubai* after living in the rapidly expanding emirate for 2 years. He has written extensively for Frommer's, and is the author of *Frommer's Grand Canyon,* co-author of *Frommer's Mexico,* and an original co-author of *Frommer's Argentina & Chile.* A native of California, Shane is now based in New York City.

Published by:

Wiley Publishing, Inc.

111 River St.
Hoboken, NJ 07030-5774

ISBN 978-0-470-28195-6

Editor: Anuja Madar
Production Editor: Lindsay Conner
Cartographer: Andrew Murphy
Photo Editor: Richard Fox
Production by Wiley Indianapolis Composition Services

Front cover photo: Jumeirah Beach Residence: Dubai Marina, Man on beach with camel
Back cover photo: Dubai: Small racing dhows

For information on our other products and services or to obtain technical support, please contact our Customer Care Department within the U.S. at 800/762-2974, outside the U.S. at 317/572-3993 or fax 317/572-4002.

Wiley also publishes its books in a variety of electronic formats. Some content that appears in print may not be available in electronic formats.

Manufactured in the United States of America

5   4   3   2

Contents

List of Maps

Acknowledgments

I would like to thank Trudee Christensen for the significant time she helped me with research, my editor Anuja Madar for her insights and guidance while preparing this book, and the following UAE experts for their recommendations of what's best in Dubai: Julia and John Moon, Shezan Amije, Heather Wipperman, Karri Zaremba, Shervin Limbert, Anna-Mari Jonker, and Aparna Verma.

An Invitation to the Reader

In researching this book, we discovered many wonderful places—hotels, restaurants, shops, and more. We're sure you'll find others. Please tell us about them, so we can share the information with your fellow travelers in upcoming editions. If you were disappointed with a recommendation, we'd love to know that, too. Please write to:

Frommer's Dubai, 1st Edition
Wiley Publishing, Inc. • 111 River St. • Hoboken, NJ 07030-5774

An Additional Note

Please be advised that travel information is subject to change at any time—and this is especially true of prices. We therefore suggest that you write or call ahead for confirmation when making your travel plans. The authors, editors, and publisher cannot be held responsible for the experiences of readers while traveling. Your safety is important to us, however, so we encourage you to stay alert and be aware of your surroundings. Keep a close eye on cameras, purses, and wallets, all favorite targets of thieves and pickpockets.

Other Great Guides for Your Trip:

Frommer's Egypt

Frommer's Morocco

Frommer's Israel

Frommer's Star Ratings, Icons & Abbreviations

Every hotel, restaurant, and attraction listing in this guide has been ranked for quality, value, service, amenities, and special features using a **star-rating system.** In country, state, and regional guides, we also rate towns and regions to help you narrow down your choices and budget your time accordingly. Hotels and restaurants are rated on a scale of zero (recommended) to three stars (exceptional). Attractions, shopping, nightlife, towns, and regions are rated according to the following scale: zero stars (recommended), one star (highly recommended), two stars (very highly recommended), and three stars (must-see).

In addition to the star-rating system, we also use **seven feature icons** that point you to the great deals, in-the-know advice, and unique experiences that separate travelers from tourists. Throughout the book, look for:

Finds	Special finds—those places only insiders know about
Fun Fact	Fun facts—details that make travelers more informed and their trips more fun
Kids	Best bets for kids and advice for the whole family
Moments	Special moments—those experiences that memories are made of
Overrated	Places or experiences not worth your time or money
Tips	Insider tips—great ways to save time and money
Value	Great values—where to get the best deals

The following **abbreviations** are used for credit cards:

AE	American Express	DISC	Discover	V	Visa
DC	Diners Club	MC	MasterCard		

Frommers.com

Now that you have this guidebook to help you plan a great trip, visit our website at **www. frommers.com** for additional travel information on more than 4,000 destinations. We update features regularly to give you instant access to the most current trip-planning information available. At Frommers.com, you'll find scoops on the best airfares, lodging rates, and car rental bargains. You can even book your travel online through our reliable travel booking partners. Other popular features include:

- Online updates of our most popular guidebooks
- Vacation sweepstakes and contest giveaways
- Newsletters highlighting the hottest travel trends
- Podcasts, interactive maps, and up-to-the-minute events listings
- Opinionated blog entries by Arthur Frommer himself
- Online travel message boards with featured travel discussions

The Best of Dubai

In Dubai, just about everything is meant to be the biggest and the best. And it's no joke: Here you'll find the world's tallest building, the largest man-made islands, the richest horse race, the biggest shopping festival, and soon the most extensive entertainment complex, the most massive mall, and the biggest hotel.

People who live here will tell you that Dubai is always changing—that's an understatement. Dubai is growing so fast that it hardly seems recognizable from one year to the next. The city's only competition these days seems to be with itself. Who can keep up? Construction cranes everywhere work relentlessly to continue raising a modern metropolis out of the desert sand.

Once completed, the Palm Island Deira will be twice the size as the Palm Jumeirah. Mall of Arabia will eclipse Mall of the Emirates, which is already the biggest shopping center outside North America. The 25-story Ski Dubai will soon be dwarfed in size by the Snowdome being built in Dubailand, which itself will house the largest collection of theme parks on the planet. Asia-Asia will take over as the world's largest hotel.

Each project is bigger, bolder, and significantly more expensive. The skyline is being filled with more architecturally daring high-rises. The land is being carved with new canals and marinas. The sea is being gifted with new artificial islands. In other words, nothing is constant. If Dubai has a core identity, it lies in its dynamic entrepreneurial spirit and not in its layout. Tomorrow there will undoubtedly be even more audacious plans to turn fantasy into reality.

1 Most Unforgettable Dubai Experiences

- **Doing a Desert Safari.** A journey into the timeless Arabian Desert will seem a world removed from modern Dubai, a chance to drive on the dunes, ride camels, eat authentic Arabic food, and watch belly-dancing under the stars. See p. 104.
- **Going to Wild Wadi.** This dazzling water park is pure fun, with rides and activities for kids and adults alike. It's the perfect place to cool off during Dubai's hot days. See p. 102.
- **Skiing in Dubai.** Unusual and utterly impractical, Ski Dubai is nevertheless one of the fantastic attractions in Dubai. Spend your day skiing, snowboarding, or throwing snowballs in freezing cold even as the outside temperature might be sizzling. See p. 105.
- **Taking a Dhow Cruise.** Cruising the Dubai Creek by day or night is an excellent way to view the old city up close and see the new city rising up in the distance. A dinner dhow cruise is an especially enchanting experience. See p. 103.
- **Shopping.** Dubai without shopping would be like Belgium without chocolate, as the two just go hand-in-hand. Wander Dubai's glittery tax-free malls, and don't forget to also

visit the traditional Eastern markets—especially the Gold Souk—where bargaining is expected.

- **Spending a Day at the Beach.** Most people are surprised by just how beautiful Dubai's beaches are, with powdery white sand and turquoise-colored water. There is a range of excellent public and private beaches in Dubai, with many offering watersports and activities for kids.

2 Dubai's Best Events & Seasons

- **Best Season in Dubai: Dubai Shopping Festival.** As long as you don't mind crowds, Dubai Shopping Festival is a thrilling time to visit the city, with people from around the world and special events taking place day and night. See p. 109.
- **Best Sports Event: Dubai World Cup.** The world's richest horse race, at the end of March, is the culmination of a 9-week horse-racing festival and brings in celebrities and jet-setters from around the globe. See p. 107.
- **Best Time to Come to Dubai: November to March.** Most people prefer the temperate days of "winter," and this is when the bulk of outdoor activities and special events take place.
- **Best Thing to Do in Summer: Stay Inside.** With extreme humidity and temperatures routinely more than 100°F (38°C), summer is too hot to be outside. This is the perfect time to visit the malls, and **Dubai Summer Surprises** is a 10-week festival offering deeply discounted hotel, restaurant, and store prices, as well as children's entertainment and educational activities. See p. 109.

3 Best Dubai Structures

- **Best Hotel Tower: Burj Al Arab.** Designed to resemble the billowing sail of an Arabian dhow, the iconic Burj Al Arab extends 321m (1,053 ft.) to the sky. See p. 68.
- **Best Skyscraper: Burj Dubai.** The world's tallest building, Burj Dubai dominates the skyline with its thin silver steel structure and can be seen for miles. See p. 14.
- **Best Man-Made Islands: The Palm Islands.** The three artificial islands shaped like palm trees sit off the coast of Dubai and are considered by some to be an Eighth Wonder of the World. See p. 14.
- **Best Traditional House: Heritage House.** Like other structures of its time, this 1890 Arabian home was made with coral and gypsum and has a central courtyard surrounded by rooms, some of which face the sea. See p. 101.

4 Best Things to Do for Free (or Almost) in Dubai

- **Take an Abra Ride on the Creek.** The traditional way to cross the creek is by water taxi, known as an *abra*. These little motorized boats connect Deira and Bur Dubai and have been ferrying passengers back and forth for decades. The price is negligible. See p. 104.
- **Go to the Beach.** Dubai has a number of excellent public beaches. They are clean, safe for swimming, and family-friendly.
- **Walk in Creekside Park.** Creekside Park offers waterfront pathways, botanical gardens, playgrounds,

picnic sites, and a children's educational theme park. See p. 103.

- **Window-Shop.** You don't have to spend any money to enjoy Dubai's incredible array of shopping, although I cannot promise that you won't decide to loosen your wallet. A walk through the souks (traditional markets) is as much a cultural as a shopping experience.

- **Visit Bastakiya.** There is no cost to walk through the historic quarter of Dubai, a fascinating (if idealized) representation of what Dubai looked like at the beginning of the 20th century. See p. 100.

5 Best Way to Spend a Day Outside Dubai

- **Desert Safari.** Sign up with a tour operator offering desert safaris close to Dubai. Options include half-day, full-day, and overnight excursions, and the most popular are evening dinner safaris. See p. 151.

- **In Sharjah.** Explore the traditional souks and Arabian homes in Heritage Area (p. 143), view the personal art collection of Sharjah's ruler at the Sharjah Art Museum (p. 144), and learn more about Islam at the Sharjah Islamic Museum (p. 144).

- **In Abu Dhabi.** Walk along the waterfront Corniche (p. 134), visit the extraordinary Emirates Palace hotel (p. 137), and see the enormous Sheikh Zayed Grand Mosque (p. 135). Abu Dhabi also has beautiful beaches, dazzling malls, and an impressive cultural arts center.

6 Best Splurge Hotels

- **Al Qasr** (© 4/366-8888; www.madinatjumeirah.com), Madinat Jumeirah. This extravagant resort in Madinat Jumeirah resembles an ornate Arabian palace. It sits on its own island surrounded by waterways, lush gardens, and the re-creation of ancient Gulf architecture. See p. 68.

- **Bab Al Shams** (© 4/832-6699; www.jumeirahbabalshams.com) is a serene desert resort located 45 minutes outside Dubai, ideal for escaping the busy city and immersing oneself in uninterrupted relaxation. Even when fully booked, the resort has the feeling of being mostly empty with an unobtrusive staff that caters to your needs. See p. 74.

- **Burj Al Arab** (© 4/301-7777; www.burj-al-arab.com), Jumeirah Beach. The famous luxury resort dominates the Dubai coastline, pampering guests in two-level suites with floor-to-ceiling windows overlooking the sea and a range of over-the-top amenities fit for kings and queens. See p. 68.

- **Fairmont Dubai** (© 4/332-5555; www.fairmont.com), Sheikh Zayed Road. Arguably the most refined hotel on Sheikh Zayed Road, the Fairmont houses some of the most upscale dining and nightlife options in town. Elegantly appointed guest rooms boast panoramic views of the city or the Gulf. See p. 66.

- **Grosvenor House** (© 4/399-8888; www.grosvenorhouse-dubai.com), Dubai Marina. The stylish tower overlooking the Dubai Marina blends Arabian touches with contemporary design. Guests have access to the excellent beach club at the nearby Le Royal Méridien. See p. 70.

- **Shangri-La** (© 4/343-8888; www.shangri-la.com), Sheikh Zayed Road. Gracious service is the hallmark of this spectacular hotel, which attracts business elites, visiting celebrities, and travelers with a strong sense of style. See p. 66.

7 Best Beach Resorts

- **Hilton Dubai Jumeirah** (© 4/399-1111; www.hilton.com), Jumeirah Beach. An excellent choice for families, the stylish Hilton features one of Dubai's most enticing beach clubs, spas, and selections of kids' activities. The city's trendiest restaurant, Bice, is located here. See p. 71.

- **Jumeirah Beach Hotel** (© 4/348-0000; www.jumeirahbeachhotel.com), Jumeirah Beach. Once you check in you'll want to stay put, as this outstanding resort features Jumeirah's most extensive beach club, health club, and kids' club, as well as an unbeatable selection of restaurants, bars, and cafes. See p. 71.

- **Le Méridien Mina Seyahi** (© 4/399-3333; www.lemeridien.com/minaseyahi), Jumeirah Beach. Kids and adults alike will love this sprawling beach resort, which offers fun-filled water- and land sports, sparkling pools, landscaped gardens, and a casual selection of restaurants and bars. See p. 71.

- **One&Only Royal Mirage** (© 4/399-9999; www.oneandonlyroyalmirage.com), Jumeirah Beach. This exquisite resort extends along 1km (¾ mile) of beautiful beachfront and sits amid 60 acres of flowering gardens and fountain-filled waterways. If you're looking for an ultra-refined beach vacation, stay at the Royal Mirage. See p. 73.

- **Ritz-Carlton** (© 4/399-4000; www.ritzcarlton.com), Jumeirah Beach. The elegant Ritz-Carlton enjoys a privileged view of the Arabian Gulf and features luxurious guest rooms that blend classic European and Arabic design. Service is outstanding. See p. 73.

8 Best Moderate Hotels

- **Arabian Courtyard Hotel & Spa** (© 4/351-9111; www.arabiancourtyard.com), Al Fahidi Street in Deira. This distinctly Arabian-style hotel sits across from the Dubai museum and is an excellent base for exploring the city's old quarter. See p. 61.

- **Orient Guest House** (© 4/351-9111; www.orientguesthouse.com), Bastakiya. Situated in a restored Arabian villa in the historic Bastakiya neighborhood, this boutique hotel offers 24-hour butler service, promising guests personalized attention. This is a distinct alternative to the city's predominantly high-rise hotels. See p. 63.

- **Novotel** (© 4/318-7000; www.novotel.com), next to the World Trade Centre. You'll discover one of the city's best values at this French-chain hotel, a simple yet stylish choice conveniently located off Sheikh Zayed Road. See p. 68.

- **Towers Rotana Hotel** (© 4/343-8000; www.rotana.com), Sheikh Zayed Road. You shouldn't expect luxury here, but you will find comfortable accommodations and friendly service in an excellent location on Sheikh Zayed Road. See p. 67.

9 The Most Unforgettable Dining Experiences

- **Al Nafoorah,** Emirates Towers (© 4/ 319-8088). Dubai's top Lebanese restaurant offers an opulent dining room leading to a lovely outdoor terrace facing the Dubai skyline. Service is as inspired as the cooking, focused on seafood and authentic Lebanese cuisine. See p. 91.
- **The Beach Bar & Grill,** One&Only Royal Mirage (© 4/399-9999). A personal favorite, this is where to come for an inspired lunch or romantic dinner on the beach. Fresh seafood and grilled steaks are served in the Moroccan-designed dining room or out on the beachfront deck. See p. 88.
- **Benjarong,** Dusit Dubai (© 4/343-3333). The Dusit Dubai's signature restaurant serves outstanding Royal Thai cuisine from a la carte or set-course menus. Service is among the best you will find in Dubai. See p. 85.
- **Bice,** Hilton Dubai Jumeirah (© 4/ 399-1111). The trendy Italian restaurant packs with a "who's who" of Dubai who come dressed to kill. Fortunately, the food is not lost on the scene, with outstanding classic Italian dishes prepared by Chef Andrea Mugavero. See p. 88.
- **The Exchange Grill,** Fairmont Dubai (© 4/311-8316). Few restaurants take steak as seriously as the Exchange Grill, modeled after New York's Oak Room. The chef serves 1855 USDA certified Angus as well as the world's most expensive beef, Mayura Station Gold Wagyu. Expect to spend a pretty penny, and to spend it in style. See p. 84.
- **Shabestan,** Radisson SAS (© 4/222-7171). Although Persian food is widely available in Dubai, Shabestan offers the best. The exotic dining room is reminiscent of a sultan's palace, and evenings bring live Persian music and a romantic ambience. See p. 80.
- **Verre,** Hilton Dubai Creek (© 4/ 227-1111). London-based Gordon Ramsay holds the most Michelin stars of any chef, and you can experience his impeccable modern European cuisine at Verre, an elegant dining space characterized by minimalist decor and refined service. See p. 76.

10 Best Shopping in Dubai

- **Best Boutique Mall: Emirates Towers Boulevard.** The elegant Boulevard features two floors of stylish shops, restaurants, and bars. It's smaller and more exclusive than Dubai's other shopping centers. See p. 113.
- **Best Shopping Center: Mall of the Emirates.** The largest shopping center outside North America offers world-class department stores and retail outlets, extensive dining and entertainment options, and Ski Dubai, the incredible indoor ski resort. Shop and ski, as they say. See p. 116.
- **Best Modern Souk: Souk Madinat Jumeirah.** This idyllic re-creation of an Arabian souk in the sprawling Madinat Jumeirah complex features boutiques selling Arabian art, sweets, jewelry, and upscale souvenirs. See p. 112.
- **Best Traditional Souk: Gold Souk.** The enormous gold souk features every size, shape, color, and quality of gold you can imagine. Jewelry is sold

by rows and rows of vendors, and bargaining is an important component of the shopping experience. See p. 112.

- **Best Persian Carpets: Persian Carpet House.** This trusted dealer sells

high-quality carpets from Iran, Afghanistan, Pakistan, Kashmir, and elsewhere in the region. Bargaining is expected. See p. 117.

11 Best Cultural Experiences

- **Bastakiya.** This restored historic neighborhood of meandering lanes, traditional Gulf houses, and ornate wind towers characteristic of early Dubai also has a number of restaurants, shops, and galleries. See p. 100.
- **Dubai Museum.** The Al Fahidi Fort-turned-museum represents Dubai life in its pre-oil days with re-creations of a souk, early Arabian homes, mosques, and date gardens. There are also exhibits of desert and marine life. See p. 100.
- **Jumeirah Mosque.** Although non-Muslims are typically not allowed to

enter mosques in the UAE, the beautiful Jumeirah Mosque is an exception. Cultural tours are offered 4 mornings a week through the Sheikh Mohammed Centre for Cultural Understanding. See p. 101.

- **Spice Souk.** This traditional market close to the Gold Souk offers a glimpse of Dubai as it once was, a place with winding alleyways of stalls packed with exotic fragrances, Arabic seasonings, herbs, perfume oils, and other delights. See p. 101.

12 Best Nightlife

- **Best Bar to Watch the Sunset: The Terrace.** The sun sets over the Dubai Creek and city skyline, which stretch out majestically before the Terrace deck, an excellent place to unwind after a day of seeing the sights. See p. 128.
- **Best Bar with a View: Vu's.** Appropriately named, Vu's offers a stunning panorama of the city from the 51st floor of the Emirates Towers hotel. See p. 127.
- **Best Champagne Bar: Cin Cin.** A beautiful crowd gathers to admire one another in this glamorous champagne and wine bar, with an equally exclusive cigar bar located next door. See p. 129.
- **Best Cocktail Bar: Buddha Bar.** A killer sound system plays the avant-garde lounge beats of the Buddha Bar

music series, as the jet-setting bargoers sip exotic cocktails in a mesmerizing setting. See p. 126.

- **Best Happy Hour: Barasti.** Western expatriates and visitors pack the beachfront deck at this casual hotel beach bar. Theme nights ensure that Barasti never gets dull. See p. 127.
- **Best Live Music Venue: Rock Bottom.** This is as close as Dubai comes to a dive bar, with live bands playing rock 'n' roll and party music into the wee hours. See p. 127.
- **Best Nightclub: The Apartment Lounge + Club.** Local and international DJs rock the house at Dubai's most exclusive club, a two-room "apartment" featuring a sleek martini-style lounge and a raging dance floor. See p. 125.

- **Best Outdoor Show:** *Jumana–Secret of the Desert* celebrates the history and culture of Dubai in a stunning outdoor show that takes place in the Al Sahra Desert Resort of Dubailand. See p. 124.
- **Best Pub: Irish Village.** Special events often happen at the Irish Village, where a large expatriate crowd packs the festive outdoor area every night of the week. See p. 128.
- **Best Wine Bar: Agency.** This chic wine bar houses roughly 400 types of wine, offering frequent wine promotions and tastings to the glamorous patrons. See p. 129.

2

Dubai in Depth

Dubai is a marvel for the senses, a city that surprises just as it impresses. Within just a few short decades, it has gone from being a relative backwater to the world's fastest-growing modern city. Everything seems possible here. Dubai's principal attractions are its white-sand beaches, glitzy malls, thrilling activities, and swanky nightlife. Indeed, Dubai is becoming a tourist magnet for people from all over the world. And it's not just tourism. The emirate has established itself as the region's major commercial center—promising political and economic stability, no corporate or income tax, and minimal red tape for those who invest here. I imagine its economic dynamism to be something like Manhattan a century ago, only Dubai has a lot more sunshine and a stunning coastline, too.

But for me what makes Dubai most interesting is not its proliferation of five-star beach resorts, high-end shopping centers, or fabulous nightlife, but rather the way in which ethnic and national groups from around the globe have congregated here to be part of a great urban experiment. With more than 150 nationalities living peacefully together, Dubai is by far the most open, tolerant place in the region. Its leaders have welcomed people of all backgrounds to participate in the emirate's growth, and demonstrated the vision and resources to embark on projects few cities could even dream of. In Dubai, grand ideas, shocking wealth, and the hard work of foreign labor are making this one of the most extraordinary urban cities of the 21st century.

1 Dubai Today

The modern emirate of Dubai, whose principal city is also called Dubai, is a land of contrasts. It sits squarely in the Arabian Desert, but has miles of beautiful coastline. Political and social turmoil stirs in parts of the broader Middle East, yet this is one of the world's most stable cities. Its Islamic heritage and Western orientation give it a unique position in the region, friendly with neighboring countries but largely sheltered from their troubles. The government is a constitutional monarchy with only limited democratic elements, while the economy is a vibrant capitalist system with staggering growth. Conservative communities live in harmony alongside liberal ones. Local

culture is protected, even as widely divergent customs from abroad are welcomed. Although Arabic is the official language, English is widely spoken. These contrasts reflect a city whose international outlook is grounded in the customs of contemporary Islam, a land characterized by its Arabian heritage and willingness to embrace change.

Dubai is a truly multiethnic society. Roughly half of its population of about 1.5 million (there are just more than 4 million people in the entire UAE, making Dubai the most populous emirate) hails from South Asia, a quarter from other Arab countries and Iran, and about 10% from the West and elsewhere in Asia. The

Emirati Food

It's difficult to find Emirati food in Dubai's restaurants. It's considered somewhat bland, and Arabic food here is heavily influenced by Lebanese, Moroccan, Tunisian, and even Iranian cuisine. Meals usually start with meze, Arabic appetizers such as hummus, tabbouleh, baba ghanouj, falafel, and kibbeh (ground meat with spices) served with pita bread and salad. Lamb, beef, and chicken are the favored meats, often accompanied by rice, spices, nuts (especially pistachios), dates, and yogurt. Muslims are forbidden from eating meat that has not been slaughtered in accordance with Islamic rituals (called halal), and they do not eat pork.

An authentic Emirati dish is roasted lamb stuffed with rice spiced with cinnamon, almonds, and pistachios. Although they're Lebanese in origin, *shawarmas* (lamb or chicken carved from a spit and served in a pita) are also tremendously popular. Seafood is a staple of the Emirati diet, and includes grilled *hammour* (a grouper fish), *chanad* (mackerel), and *beyah* (mullet). Main dishes may be served with unleavened Arabic bread, freshly baked in clay ovens, followed by fresh fruit such as dates, figs, and lemon and lime, as well as Arabic sweets. Fruit juices are often drunk with the meal, and Arabic coffee is served after.

During Ramadan, evening meals are usually enormous buffets. Unless you manage to swing an invitation to an Emirati's home for dinner, a good area to find cheap, authentic Arabic food is in Bur Dubai or Deira.

Indian, Iranian, and Pakistani communities are the largest. Among the Western population, British expatriates are most prominent. The local population makes up less than 15% of the total, making Emiratis a minority in their own land. But what is remarkable is their success in protecting their culture in the midst of such sweeping change. Dubai's new emphasis on its historic areas and cultural centers, as well as its promotion of traditional pastimes such as camel racing, falconry, and dhow sailing, represent a concerted effort to safeguard the local culture.

Religion (p. 16) and family life lie at the core of Emirati society. Relationships are strong not just within the immediate family but among the extended family, which often lives together. Respect for elders is a core value. Traditional song, dance, and poetry remain integral to the Emirati experience. Families still arrange marriages, which the bride and groom must agree to, and weddings are a significant cultural event that can last up to 2 weeks. They have become increasingly expensive, and the government has established a Marriage Fund to assist locals with affording the enormous wedding costs and dowries and encourage them to marry Emiratis rather than non-nationals. The bride typically moves in with the husband's family after marriage, but she does not take her husband's last name.

Emirati women may seem sheltered by some Western standards, but their role in the local society is changing. Unlike in some more traditional Islamic countries, women in Dubai drive and move around the city unescorted. They have equal educational opportunities and increasingly work outside the home. In UAE universities, 65% of students are women. With increased education and exposure to Western cultures, their readiness to commit to traditional roles as housewives is less certain. As in so many places, the younger generation is much more open-minded than the older one.

Up in Smoke

Shisha goes by many names, including narghile, hubbly bubbly, and hookah. This tradition is enjoyed not just at cafes and lounges throughout Dubai, but across much of the Middle East and South Asia. The pastime is gaining in popularity in Western countries as well, where chic hookah lounges have opened in cosmopolitan cities. *Shisha* is thought to have originated in India and Persia, gained in popularity during the years of the Ottoman Empire, and then spread across the Arab world. The earliest *shisha* was smoked in a coconut shell. The modern *shisha* water pipe works by water filtration and indirect heat, and is used for smoking flavored tobaccos. The tobacco comes in a variety of flavors such as apple, grape, and strawberry, and is meant to be shared with everyone at the table, usually over an afternoon coffee or following a nighttime meal. Politics, religion, and other social matters are often discussed over the calming influence of *shisha*. People may sit for hours chatting and smoking this aromatic pipe.

Emiratis are easy to recognize because of their national clothes. Local men wear an ankle-length white garment known as a *dishdasha* and a white or red-checkered headdress called a *gutra*. It is secured on the head with a black cord, the *agal*. Local women typically wear a full-length dress covered by a black *abaya,* and conceal their hair with a headscarf called a *sheyla.* Some women, particularly in the older generation, also cover their face with a veil. Both men and women are increasingly accessorizing their traditional dress to achieve greater individuality.

Dubai is the UAE's commercial center and the second-largest and wealthiest emirate in the federation, after the capital Abu Dhabi. There's a widespread misconception that Dubai's wealth comes from oil money. Unlike Abu Dhabi, which holds a staggering 10% of the world's proven oil reserves, Dubai's oil is quickly running out. Two decades ago, oil revenue made up half of Dubai's GDP; today it accounts for less than 5%. Dubai's engines of growth are fueled instead by the diversified economy, revolving around trade, manufacturing, and financial services. The strategic location explains its success as a business hub. It sits at a crossroads between the Far East, Asia, Africa, and Europe. More than 6,000 companies from more than 120 countries operate in Jebel Ali, Dubai's deepwater port and enormous free-trade zone for manufacturing and distribution.

Dubai's growth is phenomenal. Cranes and construction sites dominate the city, and the joke is that the crane is the national bird. Foreign labor is responsible for most economic activity. Job sectors tend to be stratified among nationalities, and few Emiratis work in the private sector, preferring instead lucrative public sector jobs. All Emiratis receive excellent government benefits, including education, healthcare, and access to financial resources. The foreign population does not have access to these same benefits, and living and working conditions for unskilled foreign workers can be onerous.

Tourism is an increasingly important source of revenue for Dubai. The number of visitors here more than doubled from 3 million in 2000 to 6.4 million in 2006, and tourism officials are aiming ambitiously for 15 million by 2010. The superlative hotels and entertainment options being established are meant to quiet any potential rivals. Dubai is an immensely easy city to travel in as long as you're not outside in the heat of summer, and services are excellent. Although Arabic is the official language, you can get by with English just about everywhere.

2 Looking Back at Dubai

Most of Dubai's history is known only to the desert and the sea. There's little information about pre-Islamic activity in this corner of the Arabian Peninsula. After the spread of Islam in the 7th century, the Umayyad Caliph invaded southeast Arabia and drove out the Sassanians, one of the great powers of the time. Several artifacts from the Umayyad period have been discovered in modern-day Jumeirah as a result of excavations carried out by the Dubai Museum (p. 100).

Few written records were kept before the 19th century, and much of the knowledge of Dubai's past was passed on orally between generations. Documented records of a Dubai village exist only after 1799. Those who first settled here did so around the creek. Traditional economic activity focused on fishing, pearling, herding sheep and goats, and cultivating dates and other small-scale agriculture. For centuries, this region was embroiled in dynastic disputes. It became known as the Pirate Coast because raiders from the modern-day emirates often attacked foreign ships and each other. Around 1830, a branch of the Bani Yas tribe—ancestors of the Bedouins who inhabited the harsh deserts around Abu Dhabi—left Abu Dhabi and settled a small fishing village at the mouth of the Dubai Creek. Dubai, under the Al Maktoum dynasty of the Bani Yas tribe that rules the emirate today, became one of seven sheikhdoms under British protection. It used British maritime protection to thwart attacks by the Ottoman Empire and competing sheikhdoms and to advance trade relations with neighboring states.

The advent of the pearling industry drove Dubai's growth, and by the 1870s, the emirate had become the main trading port along the Gulf coast. Dubai has always taken a laissez-faire attitude toward trade, and this liberal money-making posture attracted merchants from Iran, India, and elsewhere in the Arabian Peninsula. By the early 1900s, Dubai boasted the region's biggest trade markets. The dhow was the sailing craft that made trade possible, and the souk was the destination. You will see dhows continuing to operate along the creek today, as well as souks in Deira that still bustle with activity.

By the 1950s, Dubai had become a small but successful regional trading and fishing post, although its population was still not much more than 5,000 people. The pearling industry had died out in the 1930s, a result of World War I, the Great Depression, and the cultivation of cultured pearls elsewhere. The discovery of oil in 1967 and its production soon after generated a period of rapid development that forever altered Dubai. An influx of foreign workers, primarily from South Asia, led to exponential population growth.

Bedouin Beginnings

Bedouins are animal herders who travel the desert during the wetter winter months and move toward cultivated land in summer. Bedouin society is characterized by tribal, patriarchal order. Among the Arab-speaking tribes such as those that roamed the deserts of the present-day UAE, the head of the tribal structure was called the sheikh. Today, the rulers of each of the emirates are also called sheikhs.

In 1968, the U.K. announced, as a result of cutbacks in its foreign operations, that it would end its treaty relationships with the seven emirates, then called the "Trucial States" because of the truces that had been negotiated, as well as with Bahrain and Qatar. The nine entities tried unsuccessfully to establish an independent country, and Bahrain and Qatar went their own way. In 1971, Dubai joined Abu Dhabi, Sharjah, Ajman, Umm Al Quiwain, Fujeirah, and a year later Ras Al Khaimah to create the United Arab Emirates. This decision was especially important in ending a long history of border disputes between Abu Dhabi and Dubai, which had even led to war between the two in 1947.

Dubai's rulers sought to put Dubai on the map through a remarkable plan for development. The late Sheikh Rashid bin Saeed al Maktoum is credited with much of Dubai's rapid growth, focusing Dubai's energies on trade, diversifying the economy away from the shrinking oil supply, and building commercial infrastructure to attract investment. Rather than spending the oil money on palaces and weapons, as happened in some oil-rich states, he wisely channeled much of the revenue into new investments. Oil and trade remained the big industries, but in 1979 Dubai opened the Jebel Ali free zone to attract companies from around the world to do business here.

This expansionary vision has been continued by his son, Sheikh Mohammad bin Rashid al Maktoum, UAE Vice President, Prime Minister, and Ruler of Dubai. Sheikh Mohammad has pushed effectively to transform Dubai into the main trade, financial, and entertainment center of the region. He has encouraged competition among developers who come up with the most innovative projects. The Dubai government established new economic clusters based on its success with the Jebel Ali free zone, such as Media City, Internet City, Healthcare City, and the Dubai International Financial Center. In the past 5 years, it has focused increasingly on growth in the tourism and real estate sectors, as well. Now that Dubai's oil industry is all but exhausted, the emirate's economy is successfully diversified and booming.

Dubai's political system has been less dynamic, operating under the framework of a constitutional monarchy. The political relationship between the seven emirates developed as a loose federation rather than a centralized system. Each emirate has its own hereditary ruler and enjoys substantial autonomy. Dubai is the second-most powerful emirate after Abu Dhabi, and the other five emirates are substantially less wealthy and influential.

Under the government structure, the president of the UAE is the ruler of Abu Dhabi and the vice president is the ruler of Dubai. There's no universal suffrage or political parties in the UAE, where leaders are chosen by their dynastic positions. Democracy is slowly making an appearance into the political system, however. At the end of 2006, the UAE held its first-ever limited elections to select half the members of the Federal National Council (FNC), a 40-member consultative body with 20 members appointed by emirate rulers and 20 elected. One woman won election to the FNC and seven more women were appointed as council members.

3 Architecture

Long before traveling to Dubai, visitors' imaginations are often captured by the city's modern architectural wonders. While many may not be familiar with Arabian wind towers or courtyard houses, most have heard about the enormous sail-shaped Burj Al Arab, the indoor snow resort Ski Dubai, and construction of the world's tallest building, the Burj Dubai. When the World Trade Center was erected in 1979, it stood as the sole skyscraper in a mostly empty desert. Many observers scratched their heads, wondering what the point was of a high-rise in the still sleepy town. Even as late as 1990, most of Sheikh Zayed Road remained an empty sand pit. But today, the World Trade Center appears antiquated next to the sleek high-rises that stretch as far as the eye can see. It's estimated that up to a quarter of the world's construction cranes are located here, and Dubai's skyline may be the fastest growing in history. This wealthy emirate is home to some of the most innovative and ambitious architectural projects in the world, and the sky seems to be the limit for future developments.

Dubai's original architecture, dating from the late 19th century, was influenced by Iranian, Indian, and Islamic designs. The hot and humid climate, religious and social customs of the inhabitants, and available selection of construction materials were crucial considerations in building styles. The main features were simplicity, functionality, durability, and suitability for the climate. Early structures were made of stone, palm leaves, and palm tree trunks, with mud substituting for mortar. The majority of Dubai's first inhabitants lived in *barastis,* huts made with palm fronds. Later, the strongest available materials, coral stone from the sea and gypsum from the creek's salt marshes, were used for the emirate's four common structures—watchtowers, mosques, souks, and houses. Islamic emphasis on privacy and modesty factored into the design of courtyard homes, many of which were connected to wind towers for cooling in the summer months. Buildings were erected close together to create shaded and breezy pedestrian walkways.

With Dubai's oil discovery came an unplanned construction boom that created a hodgepodge of architectural styles.

Construction often paid little attention to traditional Islamic architecture or to the environment, and Dubai was not yet courting the world's attention by building the biggest and the best. Many glass towers were erected requiring enormous amounts of electricity to keep cool.

In recent years, builders have become more conscientious about both the environment and Arabic heritage. Master planning overseen by Dubai's rulers is leading to more harmonious development. The most efficient heat-resistant materials are increasingly used in construction, and more architects are incorporating traditional designs into their work. Madinat Jumeirah is an excellent example of a thoroughly modern development that celebrates Arabian style. Dubai's leaders are also making a serious effort at last to protect the emirate's architectural past, reconstituting the Bastakiya old quarter near the creek and opening museums and cultural centers to commemorate the early days. For more information about Dubai's early architecture, visit the **Architectural Heritage Society** (© **4/353-9765**) in Bastakiya. It's open Saturday to Wednesday from 8am to 1pm and again from 5 to 8pm.

To get a sense of the diversity and innovation of Dubai's architectural projects, I've picked five of Dubai's most fascinating architectural sights:

- **Bastakiya** (p. 100): This architectural heritage site is a complete restoration of one of Dubai's original neighborhoods settled by wealthy Persian merchants in the late 1800s. The buildings are historic, but the pristine quarter looks brand-new. You can walk along meandering lanes, see traditional Gulf courtyard houses with hand-carved wood doors, and marvel at the ornate wind towers that were used for cooling in the days before air-conditioning. The coral stone and cement wind towers, defined by double or triple wind openings, arched ends, and stepped recesses, once lined the Dubai Creek and cooled the residences using innovative air-current systems that passed from the wind towers to the floors below. Bastakiya also houses a museum, cultural center, restaurants, and a heritage hotel with an art gallery. The Al Fahidi Fort, which today is the Dubai Museum, was built in 1799 and is the city's oldest surviving structure.

- **Burj Al Arab** (p. 51): Created by architect Tom Wright to resemble the billowing sail of an Arabian dhow, the massive Burj Al Arab (which translates to "Arabian Tower") extends 321m (1,053 ft.) to the sky. The iconic structure, which rises from its own man-made island, dominates the Jumeirah Beach coastline, eclipsing the wavelike-shaped Jumeirah Beach Hotel just in front. The Burj is made of a steel frame exterior wrapped around a concrete tower, with white Teflon-coated fiberglass forming the building's white "sail." At night, the Burj is lit up in a spectacular show of changing colors. A helipad and glass-enclosed restaurant extend from the top. The expensive hotel (p. 68) features the world's largest atrium, and the opulent interior design includes 8,000 sq. meters (86,111 sq. ft.) of 22-carat gold leaf.

- **Burj Dubai:** Still under construction at press time but already the world's tallest building, Burj Dubai dominates the skyline with its thin silver steel structure that can be seen for miles. The final height remains a secret, but the project's construction manager, Greg Sang, says it will be greater than 700m (2,297 ft.); many predict it will be more than 800m (2,625 ft.). In designing the building,

lead architect Adrian Smith, of Skidmore, Owings, and Merrill, drew inspiration from traditional Islamic architecture, which uses stepped ascending spirals. The building will rise from a flower-shaped base—the flower is the *hymenocallis,* a white lily cultivated in the surrounding desert. At a projected cost of $4 billion, Burj Dubai will house one of the first Armani Hotels: 700 luxury apartments that, according to the developer, sold out within 8 hours of release; an outdoor swimming pool on the 78th floor; an indoor-outdoor observation deck on the 124th floor; and the world's fastest elevator. Corporate offices and retail outlets will fill most of the remaining floors, and the tower will be the centerpiece of the surrounding "Downtown Dubai" project.

- **The Palm Islands:** The largest artificial islands in the world sit off the coast of Dubai in the Arabian Gulf. Collectively, the Palm Islands are considered by some to be an Eighth Wonder of the World. Developed by UAE-based Nakheel Properties, this triad of islands includes the Palm Jumeirah, Palm Deira, and Palm Jebel Ali. Made with hundreds of millions of cubic meters of reclaimed land from the bottom of the Gulf, the islands are each designed in the shape of a palm tree with a trunk, fronds, and crescent, adding a total of 520km (323 miles) of coastline to Dubai. The Palm Jumeirah is the first island to have opened, and includes a 2km-long (1¼-mile) "trunk," 17 fronds, and an 11km (7-mile) crescent that surrounds the island, creating a breakwater. Residents are already moving into their luxury homes, and 30 beachfront hotels are being built, including an Atlantis Resort at the apex of the island's crescent. The

Palm Jebel Ali and Palm Deira, which will be much larger than the first island, are still under construction and will take another decade to complete. Bridges attach the islands to the mainland, and each will house multimillion dollar villas, luxury condos, private marinas, and retail and entertainment centers. Environmentalists worry about damage to surrounding marine habitats, and there's no doubt the enormous Palm Island projects have altered the ecology.

- **The World:** "The World," a series of 300 man-made islands 4km (2½ miles) off the coast of Dubai, is protected by an oval breakwater and situated to form the shape of a map. It was designed by UAE developer Nakheel Properties, which is also responsible for the Palm Islands project, at a cost of roughly $14 billion. Each of the islands ranges in size from 23,000 to 84,000 sq. m (247,569–904,168 sq. ft.), with 50 to 100m (164–328 ft.) of water between them, and are being sold at a mere $15 to $45 million. Although the developer won't release the names, it's reported that prospective buyers have included Brad Pitt and Angelina Jolie, Rod Stewart, and Tommy Lee. Reachable only by boat or helicopter, "the World" is a tourist and residential development with construction on the individual islands tailored to the owners' wishes. With land reclamation almost complete as of press time, the islands are being turned over to their new owners in 2008.

New projects seem to be announced every day. Here are a number of key developments underway:

- The **Arabian Canal** will link the Dubai Marina with the new **Dubai Waterfront,** facilitating the expansion of more waterfront communities. The $11-billion project envisions a 75km (47-mile) man-made waterway, which will flow inland from Dubai Waterfront, passing to the east of the new **Dubai World Central International Airport** before turning back toward Palm Jumeirah.

- **Bawadi** aspires to be the largest hospitality and leisure development anywhere. It will have a giant cluster of hotels, adding 60,000 guest rooms to Dubai with 51 new hotels. One of these will be **Asia-Asia,** the world's largest hotel expected to house 6,500 rooms. Part of the broader **Dubailand** project, Bawadi will create amusement centers, shopping malls, theaters, restaurants, and convention centers. It's also meant to become a model for the region of green and sustainable design.

- **Culture Village** may not become the Lincoln Center anytime soon, but its establishment will at last bring art and culture to Dubai in a serious way. The project envisions academies for the arts, music, and dance, as well as art and craft galleries and an outdoor amphitheater.

- Although the Burj Dubai is scheduled to open in 2008, **Downtown Burj Dubai,** which represents the area surrounding the world's tallest building, will not be ready until 2009. In addition to housing residences and offices, Downtown Burj Dubai will feature luxury hotels and the **Dubai Mall,** set to become the biggest shopping center on earth.

- At twice the size of Disney World, **Dubailand** intends to become the planet's largest entertainment complex, featuring resorts, sports and outdoor activities, health retreats, a huge shopping mall, and six theme parks. These will include Six Flags Dubai, Universal Studios Dubai, Paramount Studios Theme Park, Dubai Snowdome, and one of the world's largest water parks, among other attractions. About half these will be open by 2010. The Dubai Autodrome has already opened here.

- A multiuse project scheduled for completion by 2015, **Dubai Festival City** will add a new marina, golf course, residences, offices, and hotels, including the UAE's first W hotel. Festival Waterfront Center (also referred to as Dubai Festival City) is already open (p. 113) and is one of Dubai's largest malls.

- It's hard to imagine locals giving up their automobiles for a ride in the public tube, but the eventual opening of **Dubai Metro** should ease some of the city's spiraling congestion and quicken travel within the city. There will be two lines connecting the city's principal areas.

4 Religion

by Darren Humphrys

Islam is the official religion of the UAE and is integral to the local culture. The Arabic word "Islam" literally means "submission to God," and the core of the faith is the belief that there is only one God (Allah) who should be worshiped. And, in a line of prophets who included Adam, Abraham, Noah, Moses, John the Baptist, David, and Jesus, Mohammed was the last and most definitive. Muslims believe that Christianity, Judaism, and Islam are all essentially the same, but that the messages from the earlier prophets have been distorted and that Mohammed was chosen by God to revive, refine, and purify His message.

The main sources of Islam are the **Koran** (or Qur'an)—the revelations Mohammed received during his lifetime—and Mohammed's own actions, the **Hadith.**

Mohammed was born in Mecca (in present-day Saudi Arabia) in 570 and began to receive revelations from God, via the angel Gabriel, around 610. These continued until his death in nearby Medina in 632. The illiterate Mohammed would pass on each revelation to his scribes, who would then input them as a particular verse in the Koran. The Arabic word *qur'aan* means "recitation," and Muslims regard the holy book's contents as the word of God. The Koran's 114 chapters were not revealed in the order presented,

and in fact many were patched together from passages received by Mohammed at different times in his life. The year before he died, however, Mohammed finally recited in its entirety the order in which these original verses were to stay.

The Koran provided a basic framework for Islam, but it didn't go into specific detail: Of 6,616 verses, only 80 concerned issues of conduct. For more practical guidance, Muslims referred to Mohammed's actions and words while he was alive, even though he never claimed any infallibility beyond his intermediary status. The prophet's actions and words were remembered by those who knew him and passed down through Muslim communities.

The **five pillars of Islam** are drawn from the Koran and the Hadith, and are the basic religious duties and cornerstones of the faith.

- **Statement of Faith** *(shahadah)* "I testify that there is no god but God, and Mohammed is the Messenger of God." If you say this with absolute sincerity, then you have become, or are, a Muslim.

- **Prayer** *(salat)* Prayer must be performed five times a day, preferably within a mosque, though in the modern world many Muslims make this effort only for the midday prayer.

Since the Islamic calendar is a lunar one, the day, and the first prayer, begins at sunset. Prayers follow in evening, dawn, midday, and afternoon. The exact times for these are set in advance by the religious authorities and published in local newspapers. In the past, *muezzins* would climb to the top of the mosque's minaret and call the faithful to prayer, but today it is mostly pre-recorded and played over electronic speakers. Prayer involves specific rituals, the most important being the act of purification. This is achieved by rinsing out the mouth, sniffing water into the nostrils, and washing the face, head, ears, neck, feet, and (lastly) hands and forearms. Even if there is no water available, one must go through the actions.

- **Alms** *(zakat)* It is believed that alms-giving purifies the heart of greed, while receiving charity purifies it of envy. The Islamic tolerance toward begging is drawn from this.
- **Fasting** *(sawm)* Fasting takes place during Ramadan (see below), the ninth month of the lunar cycle.
- **Pilgrimage** *(hajj)* Every Muslim who has the means is bound by duty to make the pilgrimage to Mecca at least once in his/her lifetime. This usually takes place in the 12th month.

RAMADAN Ramadan—the ninth month of the Islamic lunar calendar—is when Mohammed received the first of his revelations from God. Muslims observe a strict fast during the entire month—originally modeled after similar Jewish and Christian practices—and use the time for worship and contemplation. During the day, all forms of consumption are forbidden including eating, smoking, drinking, and any form of sexual contact. However, this is only the outward show of what is intended as a deeper, spiritual cleansing and strengthening of faith. One Hadith says, "There are many who fast all day and pray all night, but they gain nothing but hunger and sleeplessness."

All Muslims who have reached puberty are expected to observe the fast. It is generally accepted that the elderly and the chronically ill are exempt, as are those who are sick or traveling, mothers who are nursing, and menstruating or pregnant women, all of whom are encouraged, for every day of fasting missed, to provide a meal for one poor person who is breaking their fast. Children are not required to fast, though some families encourage them to do so for part of a day or for a few days during the month.

At the end of the day the fast is broken with a light meal followed by the sunset prayer, which is then followed by an evening meal called the *iftar*. Muslims are encouraged to share *iftar* with family, friends, and neighbors as well as the poor and non-Muslims. The fast is resumed the next morning, traditionally when "you can plainly distinguish a white thread from a black thread by the daylight."

The last 10 days of Ramadan are considered especially important, and many Muslims retreat to their mosque or other community centers for prayer and recitations of the Koran. Laylat al-Qadr (the Night of Power) is a special night of prayer commemorating Mohammed's first revelation. It is believed that this is when heaven is open to the faithful and God determines the course of the world for the following year.

When the crescent of the new moon of the 10th month rises, Ramadan ends with Eid al-Fitr (Feast of Fast Breaking). The feast lasts for 3 days and is a time of both religious significance and social festivities.

Non-Muslims should be aware of the daytime fast taking place and attempt not to eat, drink, or smoke in front of those who are fasting. Many Dubai hotels offer in-house daytime meals to accommodate their non-Muslim guests, but restaurants

Practice What You Preach

Dubai is tolerant of other religions, and people are free to worship as they choose. There are a handful of Christian churches and a Hindu Temple in town. Religious tolerance does not extend to proselytizing, and trying to convert a Muslim to another faith is against the law. Those violating this law, even unknowingly, may be imprisoned or deported. Non-Muslims are not permitted entry to the mosques, except for the beautiful **Jumeirah Mosque** (p. 101).

that open during the day are typically cordoned off with curtains. Business activity is slower during Ramadan, and local labor laws require companies to shorten the working day by 2 hours during this period. Everything changes at sundown, however, when the city comes to life. Muslims pack restaurants throughout town for the breaking of the fast. Make a reservation, as getting a table can be difficult. After dinner, Dubai continues to sparkle, with shopping centers, *shisha* cafes, and Ramadan "tents" filling up in celebration of the holy month.

3

Planning Your Trip to Dubai

The most important factor to consider in planning a trip to Dubai is the climate. From mid-October to mid-April, while much of the northern world is buttoned up in the cold, Dubai is bathed in sunshine, blue skies, and moderate temperatures. This is high season here, and the time that most outdoor activities and special events occur. It's also the most expensive period. During the rest of the year, Dubai is hot. In summer, it is excruciatingly so. Think of Dubai's seasons in reverse: During the winter months, everyone spends their time outside, and in the summer months, folks stay put in the air-conditioned inside. The one benefit to coming during the off season is that prices drop, and if you're primarily coming to shop in Dubai's extravagant malls, the outside temperature may not matter much. But if you want to spend time at the beaches, theme parks, or in the desert, stay away during the sultry summer months.

Some travelers wonder whether Dubai is affected by the turmoil in some parts of the broader Middle East. The answer is no. Dubai is moderate politically, rich economically, and stable socially. The many national and ethnic groups inhabiting and visiting Dubai do so in harmony. In fact, Dubai is one of the world's safest cities. The one thing to remember is this is still an Islamic society, and as such there is an expectation that non-Muslims will respect local customs. That generally means not wearing provocative clothing or engaging in public displays of affection in places frequented by Emiratis. Dubai might remind you of Ibiza or Las Vegas in some of its beachfront resorts and nightclubs, but it's still a traditional society outside those Western enclaves.

For additional help in planning your trip and for more on-the-ground resources in Dubai, please turn to appendix A, p. 153.

1 Visitor Information

The **Department of Tourism & Commerce Marketing** (www.dubaitourism.ae) is officially responsible for all elements of Dubai's tourism sector. The **main office** is located at Baniyas Square (© 4/228-5000) and is open Saturday to Thursday 9am to 9pm and Friday 3 to 9pm. Another branch is located 40km (25 miles) south of Dubai on **Sheikh Zayed Road** going toward Abu Dhabi (© 4/883-3397), and has the same hours. The **airport branch** is located in Terminal 1 (© 4/224-5252) and is open 24 hours a day. Other tourism office branches are located in the following shopping centers: **City Center, BurJuman, Hamarain, Wafi,** and **Mercato.** These are generally open daily from 10am to 10pm.

The **Department of Tourism & Commerce Marketing** also has overseas offices promoting Dubai tourism. In the **United States:** 25 W. 45th St., Ste. 405,

New York, NY 10036 (© 212/575-2262); **U.K. and Ireland:** First Floor, 125 Pall Mall, London SW1Y5EA (© 44/207-839-0580); and **Australia and New Zealand:** Level 6, 75 Miller St., North Sydney, NSW2060 (© 61/2-9956-6620).

You can find extensive tourism information, including an interactive Dubai street map, at **www.dubaitourism.ae**. You can also find a useful Dubai map at www.world.maporama.com.

Destination-specific websites are:

- www.dubai.ae
- www.visit-dubai-city.com
- www.visitdubai.info
- www.godubai.com
- www.dubaicityguide.com
- www.dubaiforvisitors.com
- www.visitdubai.org
- www.visit-dubai.co.uk
- www.dubai-tourism.net
- www.tourismdubai.org

2 Entry Requirements

PASSPORTS
A passport is required for entry to the UAE. For information on how to obtain a passport, go to **"Passports"** in appendix A, p. 156.

VISAS
Nationals of Australia, Canada, Ireland, New Zealand, the United Kingdom, and the United States (as well as those of a number of other countries) do not require visas to visit the UAE for stays of less than 60 days. They will be granted a free-of-charge One Entry Visit Visa upon arrival. A penalty of AED 100 ($27/£14) per day is charged to visitors who overstay. For longer stays, travelers must obtain a visa before arrival in the UAE.

For information about visa requirements, visit www.dubaitourism.co.ae.

MEDICAL REQUIREMENTS
No health certificates are required for entry to the UAE, except for visitors who have been in an area infected by cholera or yellow fever during the past 14 days. However, an AIDS test is required for work or residence in the UAE, and testing must be performed after arrival. For more information, visit www.uaeinteract.org.

CUSTOMS
WHAT YOU CAN BRING INTO THE UAE
Every visitor to the UAE may bring in, free of duty, their personal effects and 400 cigarettes or 500 grams of tobacco. It is illegal to import drugs or pornography. After collecting your luggage at the airport, your bags will be X-rayed for inspection. There is also a duty-free sales outlet in the Dubai International Airport Arrivals hall. Duty-free allowances include 10 cigarette cartons, 100 cigars, 2 liters of spirits and 2 liters of wine (non-Muslim adults only), and perfume for personal use.

WHAT YOU CAN TAKE HOME FROM DUBAI:
Canadian Citizens: For a clear summary of Canadian rules, write for the booklet *I Declare,* issued by the Canada Border Services Agency (© **800/461-9999** in Canada, or 204/983-3500; www.cbsa-asfc.gc.ca).

U.K. Citizens: For information, contact **HM Customs & Excise** at © **0845/010-9000** (from outside the U.K., 020/8929-0152), or consult their website at **www.hmce.gov.uk**.

Australian Citizens: A helpful brochure available from Australian consulates or Customs offices is *Know Before You Go.* For more information, call the **Australian Customs Service** at © **1300/363-263,** or log on to **www.customs.gov.au**.

New Zealand Citizens: Most questions are answered in a free pamphlet available at New Zealand consulates and

Cut to the Front of the Airport Security Line as a Registered Traveler

In 2003, the **Transportation Security Administration (TSA;** www.tsa.gov) approved a pilot program to help ease the time spent in line for airport security screenings. In exchange for information and a fee, persons can be pre-screened as registered travelers, granting them a front-of-the-line position when they fly. The program is run through private firms—the largest and most well-known is Steven Brill's **Clear** (www.flyclear.com), and it works like this: Travelers complete an online application providing specific points of personal information including name, addresses for the previous 5 years, birth date, social security number, driver's license number, and a valid credit card (you're not charged the **$99 fee** until your application is approved). Print out the completed form and take it, along with proper ID, with you to an "enrollment station" (this can be found in over 20 participating airports and in a growing number of American Express offices around the country, for example). It's at this point where it gets seemingly sci-fi. At the enrollment station, a Clear representative will record your biometrics necessary for clearance; in this case, your fingerprints and your irises will be digitally recorded.

Once your application has been screened against no-fly lists, outstanding warrants, and other security measures, you'll be issued a clear plastic card that holds a chip containing your information. Each time you fly through participating airports (and the numbers are steadily growing), go to the Clear Pass station located next to the standard TSA screening line. Here you'll insert your card into a slot and place your finger on a scanner to read your print—when the information matches up, you're cleared to cut to the front of the security line. You'll still have to follow all the procedures of the day like removing your shoes and walking through the X-ray machine, but Clear promises to cut 30 minutes off your wait time at the airport.

On a personal note: Each time I've used my Clear Pass, my travel companions are still waiting to go through security while I'm already sitting down, reading the paper, and sipping my overpriced smoothie. Granted, registered traveler programs are not for the infrequent traveler, but for those of us who fly on a regular basis, it's a perk I'm willing to pay for.

—David A. Lytle

Customs offices: *New Zealand Customs Guide for Travellers, Notice no. 4.* For more information, contact **New Zealand Customs,** The Customhouse, 17–21 Whitmore St., Box 2218, Wellington (© **04/473-6099** or 0800/428-786; **www.customs.govt.nz**).

3 When to Go

The most important question to ask before traveling to Dubai is, "How hot is it?" From mid-October to mid-April, Dubai's weather is ideal with moderate temperatures and blue skies. From mid-April to mid-October, the climate becomes less bearable, with temperatures routinely exceeding 100°F (37°C) and humidity often hitting 95% or more from June through September. It's only slightly less hot and humid in the immediate surrounding months.

Another question to consider is whether to visit during Ramadan (the dates for which change each year based on the Islamic calendar). It's a fascinating period in Dubai but one in which businesses often have limited hours during the day, many restaurants don't open until night, and the majority of bars and nightclubs remain closed.

Dubai's Average Temperatures

	Jan	Feb	Mar	Apr	May	June	July	Aug	Sept	Oct	Nov	Dec
Avg. High (°F)	73	74	80	88	97	100	103	103	100	93	86	77
Avg. High (°C)	22	23	26	31	36	37	39	39	37	33	30	25
Avg. Low (°F)	58	59	63	69	76	80	85	86	81	74	67	61
Avg. Low (°C)	14	15	17	20	24	26	29	30	27	23	19	16

PEAK TRAVEL SEASONS

October to May is high season, with December and January the busiest months. Hotels also fill up for the Dubai Shopping Festival in February and the Dubai World Cup in March. The city is somewhat quieter during the heat of summer, when hotels and many other hospitality services reduce prices in order to lure more visitors.

CLIMATE

Dubai has a sub-tropical, arid climate and is sunny most of the year. Rainfall is infrequent, falling only in the winter months. The city is ill-prepared for downpours, and when they happen, chaos on the roads ensues but is short-lived. Flash floods are possible in the wadis (desert oases). Temperatures range from a low of 50°F (10°C) in January and February to a high of 120°F (49°C) in July and August. Even the sea is hot in summer, approaching 100°F (37°C). It's usually too hot to sit outside in the summer months, except in swimming pools that actually have to be cooled so they don't turn into nature-made Jacuzzis. Sandstorms are most common in March and April, but can occur whenever the wind kicks up.

CALENDAR OF EVENTS

For an exhaustive list of events beyond those listed here, check http://events.frommers.com, where you'll find a searchable, up-to-the-minute roster of what's happening in cities all over the world.

January

Dubai Marathon. The event includes a full marathon, 10km (6.2 miles) road race, and 4km (2.5-mile) run. It starts at Za'abeel Park and finishes close to the Dubai World Trade Center. People of all ages and backgrounds participate. January 18. www.dubaimarathon.org.

Dubai Shopping Festival. Roughly three million annual visitors come for "DSF," as it's known locally, which takes place for 1 month between late January and February. DSF has evolved into an international tourist extravaganza in which more than 2,300 Dubai retail stores participate with impressive bargains and store giveaways under the theme "One World, One Family, One Festival." Everything is on sale at discount prices—gold, jewelry, perfume, haute couture, electronics, handicrafts, textiles, you name it—and there are numerous raffles and special events. This is a fun but crowded period in Dubai. www.mydsf.com.

February

Dubai Pet Show. "Best in Show" has nothing on the Dubai Pet Show, which takes place at the Nad Al Sheba Racing Club. Competitions at this popular family event include best pedigree, crossbreed best in show, waggiest tail, dog most like its owner, and, the grand finale, best fancily dressed dog. One Saturday in February. www.dubaipet show.com.

Terry Fox Run. This run, which takes place at locations around the world, commemorates Terry Fox's 1981 "Marathon of Hope." To date, more than $400 million has been raised worldwide for cancer research in his name. This non-competitive event welcomes walkers, runners, bikers, and those with wheelchairs. There is no fee to enter. One Saturday in February. www.terryfoxrun.org.

Dubai Tennis Open. This million-dollar event takes place at the tennis stadium at Dubai's Aviation Club and includes top seeds at the men's and women's tournaments. Andy Roddick took the men's title in 2008. Late February to early March. www.dubai tennischampionships.com.

March

Dubai International Jazz Festival. Within just a few years, Dubai's jazz festival has grown from a simple village event to a major annual attraction. The 10-day festival includes nightly concerts by internationally acclaimed musicians and takes place at major venues throughout the city. Ten days in March. www.dubaijazzfest.com.

Dubai World Cup. This $15-million event is the world's richest horse race, with $6 million going to the Group One Dubai World Cup race alone. It takes place at Nad Al Sheba and marks the finale of the Dubai Racing Carnival, a 9-week festival of top-class racing

beginning in late February. One Saturday in late March. www.dubaiworld cup.com.

April to May

Boat Racing. April and May bring a host of competitions to the Arabian Gulf, including sailing, traditional dhow, rowing, and powerboat races. For a schedule of events, visit www. minaseyahidubai.com.

June to August

Dubai Summer Surprises. Created to lure visitors to Dubai during the sultry summer months, "DSS" lasts for 10 weeks between June and August and includes steep shopping discounts and reduced hotel rates. Since kids are out of school, DSS has a particular emphasis on family events, including children's entertainment and educational activities. www.mydsf.com.

October

UAE Desert Challenge. This thrilling motor-sport event is the World Cup finale in cross-country racing. Top drivers from around the world compete. Other desert rally events take place at various locations in October and November. www.uaedesertchallenge. com.

October to April

Camel Racing. Camel racing is one of Dubai's most revered traditional sports. Robot camel jockeys (rather than child jockeys) now prod the desert animals forward at impressive speeds, with races taking place at Nad Al Sheba weekend mornings throughout the winter. The races cover as much as 10km (6.2 miles) in 18 minutes.

November

Horse Racing. The racing season starts in November and culminates in late March with the Dubai World Cup. Races take place at Nad Al Sheeba Racing Club and Jebel Ali Racecourse, usually on Thursdays and Fridays at

7pm. General admission and parking are free. www.emiratesracing.com.

December

Dubai Rugby Sevens. Sponsored by Emirates Airlines, this 3-day event starting at the beginning of the month is the first round of the International Rugby Board Sevens World Series. More than 1,750 players take part. The event is enormously popular with Western expatriates living in Dubai, and is accompanied by "Rugby Rock" concerts that liven up the crowd. www.dubairugby7s.com.

Dubai International Film Festival. This weeklong cultural event in mid-December showcases full-length feature movies, shorts, and documentaries from around the world, with an emphasis on Arab cinema. The event continues to grow in prominence and takes place at venues across the city. www.diff.ae.

Islamic New Year's Day. This holiday celebrates the Prophet Mohammad's emigration from Mecca to Medina to create the first Islamic state. December 29, 2008, and December 18, 2009.

4 Getting There & Getting Around

GETTING TO DUBAI
BY PLANE

Dubai International Airport (www.dubaiairport.com) serves more than 110 airlines from 160 countries. It has two terminals, with most international flights scheduled out of Terminal 1 (a free shuttle connects the terminals). Emirates Airlines (see appendix A, p. 158) is based here. The airport code is DXB.

Dubai International Airport has excellent duty-free shops in the Departure and Arrivals halls, as well as restaurants, car-rental agencies, hotel and visitor information desks, and exchange services. A dedicated lounge for unaccompanied minors and passengers with special needs is available in the Arrivals hall. The five-star Dubai International Hotel is also located in the Arrivals hall.

A second airport, Al Maktoum International, will open in phases starting in 2008, although it will initially handle only cargo.

Abu Dhabi International Airport (www.abudhabiairport.com) has two terminals, with most international flights clustered around a circular satellite in Terminal 1. Etihad Airways (see appendix A, p. 158) is based here. The airport code is AUH.

Abu Dhabi International Airport has a hotel, duty-free shops, restaurants, car-rental agencies, visitor information, and exchange services. It also offers banking services, healthcare, and VIP lounges. It can sometimes be less expensive to fly into Abu Dhabi than Dubai, and it's located less than 2 hours away from Dubai by car or bus.

Arriving at the Airport

IMMIGRATION & CUSTOMS CLEARANCE International visitors arriving by air must first pass through immigration. It's usually a long walk (10 min. or so) from the jetway to the Immigration hall. There are 32 passport control desks. After clearing immigration, visitors then pick up their luggage in the Arrivals hall before clearing Customs. All bags are X-rayed by Customs officials. The process of clearing immigration and Customs at Dubai International Airport is generally efficient, taking less than an hour total. Most Dubai officials speak at least some English.

In Abu Dhabi, international visitors arriving by air must first pass through immigration. It's a short walk from the jetway to the Immigration hall. After clearing immigration, visitors then pick up their luggage in the Arrivals hall before clearing Customs. The process of clearing immigration and Customs at Abu Dhabi International Airport is generally efficient.

Getting into Town from the Airport

Many international rental car agencies are located in the airport (see above). You will find them just as you exit Customs and enter the Arrivals hall.

A taxi is the simplest way to get from the airport to Dubai destinations and is relatively inexpensive. The Dubai Transport taxi stand is clearly marked as you leave the Arrivals hall. Expect to pay AED 35 to AED 50 ($9.50–$14/£4.80–£6.90), depending on how far you're going in the city.

The RTA airport bus (© 4/800-9090; www.rta.ae) runs every 30 minutes between the airport and Deira or Bur Dubai. The fare is AED 3 (80¢/40p).

Many international rental car agencies are located in the Abu Dhabi airport (p. 24). Etihad Airways passengers are entitled to free bus transfer to Dubai. Airport taxis into downtown Abu Dhabi cost AED 65 ($18/£8.95) and AED 250 ($68/£35) to Dubai.

LONG-HAUL FLIGHTS: HOW TO STAY COMFORTABLE

- Your choice of airline and airplane will definitely affect your legroom. Find more details about U.S. airlines at **www.seatguru.com**. For international airlines, the research firm Skytrax has posted a list of average seat pitches at **www.airlinequality.com**.
- Emergency exit seats and bulkhead seats typically have the most legroom. Emergency exit seats are usually left unassigned until the day of a flight (to ensure that someone able-bodied fills the seats); it's worth checking in online at home (if the airline offers that option) or getting to the ticket counter early to snag one of these spots for a long flight. Many passengers find that bulkhead seating offers more legroom, but keep in mind that bulkhead seats have no storage space on the floor in front of you.
- To have two seats for yourself in a three-seat row, try for an aisle seat in a center section toward the back of coach. If you're traveling with a companion, book an aisle and a window seat. Middle seats are usually booked

---

Tips Coping with Jet Lag

Jet lag is a pitfall of traveling across time zones. If you're flying north-south and you feel sluggish when you touch down, your symptoms will be the result of dehydration and the general stress of air travel. When you travel east-west or vice versa, your body becomes confused about what time it is, and everything from your digestive system to your brain is knocked for a loop. Traveling east is more difficult on your internal clock than traveling west because most peoples' bodies are more inclined to stay up late than to fall asleep early.

Here are some tips for combating jet lag:

- **Reset your watch** to your destination time before you board the plane.
- **Drink lots of water** before, during, and after your flight. Avoid alcohol.
- **Exercise and sleep well** for a few days before your trip.
- If you have trouble sleeping on planes, **fly eastward on morning flights.**
- **Daylight** is the key to resetting your body clock. At the website for **Outside In** (www.bodyclock.com), you can get a customized plan of when to seek and avoid light.

last, so chances are good you'll end up with three seats to yourselves. And in the event that a third passenger is assigned the middle seat, he or she will probably be more than happy to trade for a window or an aisle.

- To sleep, avoid the last row of any section or the row in front of an emergency exit, as these seats are the least likely to recline. Avoid seats near highly trafficked toilet areas. Avoid seats in the back of many jets—these can be narrower than those in the rest of coach. Or reserve a window seat so you can rest your head and avoid being bumped in the aisle.

- Get up, walk around, and stretch every 60 to 90 minutes to keep your blood flowing. This helps avoid **deep vein thrombosis,** or "economy-class syndrome." See the box "Avoiding 'Economy Class Syndrome,'" p. 29.

- Drink water before, during, and after your flight to combat the lack of humidity in airplane cabins. Avoid caffeine and alcohol, which will dehydrate you.

GETTING AROUND
BY CAR

Driving is an economical way to travel in Dubai. If you're visiting from abroad and plan to rent a car, keep in mind that an international driver's license or a temporary Dubai license is required. Some rental car companies are able to help arrange international or temporary Dubai licenses for visitors.

Most rental cars are new, automatic, and air-conditioned. Rates vary considerably, and are usually cheaper when booked in advance online. Comprehensive insurance is essential (including personal accident coverage). For listings of the major car-rental agencies in Dubai, please see appendix A, p. 159.

Dubai's roads are excellent, if increasingly crowded. Traffic signs are well marked and written in both English and Arabic. Speed limits range from 60 to 80kmph (37–50 mph) on city roads, and from 100 to 120kmph (62–75 mph) on highways. Seat belts are mandatory, as is use of hands-free devices when using a cellphone behind the wheel. Children 9 and under are not allowed to sit in the front seat. Anyone involved in a traffic accident must wait at the scene until the traffic police arrive to make a report. Call ℂ **999** to report the accident.

There are four bridges and a tunnel linking the two sides of Dubai on each side of the Dubai Creek. Traffic along Sheikh Zayed Road and the Maktoum Bridge is exceptionally heavy during rush hour. An eight-lane highway, which is Sheikh Zayed Road in Dubai, heads southwest toward Abu Dhabi, which takes between 90 to 120 minutes to reach depending on how fast you drive.

Although Dubai's roads are in good shape, standards of driving are poor. Traffic accidents are a leading cause of injury and death in the UAE. Local drivers in particular often drive at very high speeds. Unsafe driving practices are common, particularly on inter-city highways such as Sheikh Zayed Road. On highways, unmarked speed bumps and blowing sand create additional hazards. Some visitors find it's simpler to take taxis rather than deal with renting a car and driving themselves.

Paid parking is available in most areas of Dubai. Look for the "pay and park" meters that require either AED 1 or AED 2 (25¢–50¢/15p–30p) per hour. Parking meters generally operate Saturday to Thursday from 8am to 1pm and again from 4 to 9pm; Friday is usually free. Valet parking is offered at most hotels, where many restaurants and bars are located.

Gasoline, referred to as "petrol" in Dubai, is available at stations operated by Emarat, EPPCO, and ENOC. Gas is less expensive in Dubai than in most Western countries.

BY TAXI

Dubai taxis are safe, clearly marked, and relatively inexpensive. They're the most common form of transportation for those without cars. It's generally easy to flag one off the street, or you can order one from **Dubai Transport** (© 4/208-0808; www. dtc.dubai.ae). The fare is AED 3 (80¢/ 40p) for pickup followed by AED 1.60 (45¢/20p) per kilometer. Ordering a taxi through the dispatcher costs only AED 3 (80¢/40p) extra. Dubai has seven taxi companies offering fixed metered rates. Most taxis are air-conditioned Toyota Camrys. A fleet of taxis with pink roofs that are for women and driven by women was initiated in 2007. To book one, contact the Dubai Transport Corporation (© 4/208-0808; www.dtc.dubai.ae).

5 Money & Costs

The monetary unit of the UAE is the dirham (designated as Dhs. or AED, which stands for Arab Emirate Dirham), which is divided into 100 fils. Bills come in the following denominations: 5 (brown note), 10 (green), 20 (light blue), 50 (purple), 100 (pink), 500 (blue), and 1,000 (burgundy). The notes are written in English on one side and Arabic on the other. To see examples of the different dirham notes, visit the "currency" section of www.centralbank.ae. There are three

What Things Cost	AED	US$	UK£
Bottle of house wine in restaurant	200	54.50	27.60
1.5-liter bottle of water in restaurant	12	3.25	1.65
Cappuccino	15	4.10	2.05
Midsize car rental per day	350	95.35	48.25
Cinema Ticket	35	9.50	4.80
Imperial gallon of gas (petrol)	6.25	1.70	0.85
Pint of beer	28	7.60	3.85
Postcard	3	0.80	0.40
Taxi for 10km (6-mile) journey	20	5.45	2.75
Entry to Wild Wadi	120	32.70	16.55
Entrance to Dubai Museum	3	0.80	0.40
18-hole golf at Dubai Creek Club	760	207.00	105.00
18-hole golf at Emirates Golf club	825	225.00	114.00
2-hour lift ticket at Ski Dubai	150	41.00	21.00
Admission to Wild Wadi	180	49.00	25.00
Abra (water-taxi) ride	10 fils	0.02	0.01
1-hour creek cruise	65	18.00	8.95
Dinner desert safari	300	82.00	41.00
Scuba dive (1 tank)	400	109.00	55.00
Full-day dhow cruise Musandam	200	54.50	27.60
Seven-course tasting menu at Verre (without wine)	495	135.00	68.00
Fast food *shawarma*	4	1.10	0.55
Suite at the Burj Al Arab	6,000	1,635.00	828.00
Room at Arabian Courtyard	750	204.00	103.00

types of silver coins written in Arabic representing 25 fils, 50 fils, and 1 dirham.

The dirham is pegged to the U.S. dollar at $1=AED 3.67. The exchange rate with the British pound at press time was £1=AED 7.25. For up-to-the-minute currency conversions, visit www.oanda.com.

Dubai is increasingly expensive, with inflation on the rise. Hotel prices have roughly doubled in the past 5 years, and the price of everything from food to entertainment continues to climb. It is difficult to find a moderate hotel for under $200 in the high season (luxury hotels often go for $400 and up), and a three-course dinner without alcohol will cost about $40 per person. Taxis remain relatively inexpensive.

Cash is the prevalent means of paying in Dubai, although credit and debit cards are widely accepted. This is the case just about everywhere except in the souks. ATMs are prevalent throughout the city, available not just in banks but in many supermarkets and shopping centers, as well. Most accept a wide range of cards, including those linked to the Plus system, American Express, Global Access, MasterCard, and Visa. Currency and traveler's check exchange is possible in most banks, exchange houses, and many hotels.

6 Health

STAYING HEALTHY
GENERAL AVAILABILITY
OF HEALTHCARE

Modern medical care and medicines are widely available in Dubai and the UAE's other principal cities, but may not be in outlying areas. Your hotel concierge or consulate is also a good place for a list of recommended doctors and specialists.

Dubai's healthcare network includes four government hospitals that provide care at relatively low costs, and a number of expensive private hospitals and medical clinics. Emergency care in the government hospitals is free regardless of nationality.

Dubai Healthcare City (www.dhcc.ae) aims to become the preeminent healthcare services center in the region. It's designed as an integrated center for clinical and wellness services, medical education, and research, and has teamed up with the Harvard Medical School. It includes a network of hospitals, clinics, doctors, pharmacies, and wellness centers.

Some general tips: Take a sufficient supply of your prescription medicines. It's a good idea to carry a copy of the prescriptions or a letter from your doctor, and to write down the generic names of those prescription drugs. Non-prescription medicines that travelers should consider packing include aspirin or other pain reliever, antihistamine, Imodium or other anti-diarrheal, re-hydration mixture, antiseptic, multivitamins, bandages, sunscreen, and Chap Stick. It's also wise to take a spare pair of glasses and contacts with you.

COMMON AILMENTS

DIETARY RED FLAGS   Food is generally safe throughout Dubai. Be cautious about eating raw salads and *shawarmas* (meat cooked on a spit and served in a pita) in older cafes and restaurants in the old quarter (Deira and Bur Dubai). The city's tap water is potable, but many people prefer to drink bottled water.

BUGS, BITES & OTHER WILDLIFE CONCERNS   There are few mosquitoes in the city of Dubai. Mosquitoes are more common around wadis, the desert streams (oases) that fill after the rains, and around date groves. They're most likely to find you in the evening if you're camping in the desert. There's no risk of malaria in the UAE.

There have been sightings of the Australian redback spider in Dubai, which is a potentially lethal but non-aggressive

Avoiding "Economy Class Syndrome"

Deep vein thrombosis, or as it's known in the world of flying, "economy-class syndrome," is a blood clot that develops in a deep vein. It's a potentially deadly condition that can be caused by sitting in cramped conditions—such as an airplane cabin—for too long. During a flight (especially a long-haul flight), get up, walk around, and stretch your legs every 60 to 90 minutes to keep your blood flowing. Other preventative measures include frequent flexing of the legs while sitting, drinking lots of water, and avoiding alcohol and sleeping pills. If you have a history of deep vein thrombosis, heart disease, or another condition that puts you at high risk, some experts recommend wearing compression stockings or taking anticoagulants when you fly; always ask your physician about the best course for you. Symptoms of deep vein thrombosis include leg pain or swelling, or even shortness of breath.

insect similar to the black widow. They seldom leave their webs and bites are uncommon. Antivenin is available.

RESPIRATORY ILLNESSES Respiratory illnesses are common in Dubai and elsewhere in the Gulf. One in three people suffer from allergies here, triggered by pollution, airborne dust, and sand.

SUN/ELEMENTS/EXTREME WEATHER EXPOSURE Dubai's sun is extremely intense. The UV rays are most dangerous from May to September, which are the hottest months. Avoid excessive sun exposure, especially when visiting the beach. Adequate sunscreens, sunglasses, and some form of head protection (such as a hat or visor) are important. Heat stroke and heat exhaustion are always a risk in high temperatures. It's important to drink plenty of water, and try to stay out of the sun during the middle of the day.

WHAT TO DO IF YOU GET SICK AWAY FROM HOME

The most frequented hospitals among Western expatriates and visitors are the

American hospital (p. 154) and Welcare Hospital (p. 154). They have extensive inpatient and outpatient services and English-speaking doctors. Check with your insurance company before receiving treatment to ensure coverage. You may need to pay all medical costs upfront and be reimbursed later. Note that emergency services are free regardless of nationality at all UAE government hospitals (such as Al Wasl, Al Bahra, Al Maktoum, Rashid, and Dubai Hospital), but not in private hospitals.

Your hotel concierge or consulate is also a good place for a list of recommended doctors and specialists. English-speaking physicians are easy to find. Generic equivalents of common prescription drugs are generally available in Dubai. For a list of 24-hour pharmacies in Dubai (which rotate on a daily basis), call ✆ 4/223-2323, or consult the "Pharmacies on Duty Section" of www.dubaipolice.gov.ae.

We list **additional emergency numbers** in appendix A, p. 154.

7 Safety

STAYING SAFE

Crime is generally not a problem for travelers to the UAE. That said, you should

not leave wallets, purses, or credit cards unattended. Pickpocketing has been reported in the souk areas. Although vehicle break-ins in the UAE are uncommon, travelers should ensure that unattended vehicles are locked and valuables are not left so they're easily visible.

Traffic accidents are a leading cause of injury and death in the UAE (p. 26). Drinking and driving is illegal no matter how little alcohol is consumed, and doing so will result in jail and stiff fines. Drinking in public places not licensed for alcohol will also result in fines. Drug importation, drug use, and even being involved in drugs by association will result in jail. Pornography is also illegal.

Women should face few safety concerns in Dubai. In contrast with some countries in the region, women enjoy the same rights as men and can dress as they please. However, some modesty in dress is preferred out of respect for the local culture.

As a result of broader turmoil in the Middle East, the U.S. Department of State advises the following: "Americans in the United Arab Emirates should exercise a high level of security awareness. The Department of State remains concerned about the possibility of terrorist attacks against U.S. citizens and interests throughout the world. Americans should maintain a low profile, vary routes and times for all required travel, and treat mail and packages from unfamiliar sources with caution. In addition, U.S. citizens are urged to avoid contact with any suspicious, unfamiliar objects, and to report the presence of the objects to local authorities. U.S. Government personnel overseas have been advised to take the same precautions. In addition, U.S. Government facilities may temporarily close or suspend public services from time to time as necessary to review their security posture and ensure its adequacy."

In the local culture, it is considered impolite to show the soles of one's shoes. Practically speaking, that means avoiding sitting in a way that results in the bottom of your shoes pointing at someone else. In the local culture, it's also important not to eat or offer food or other items with the left hand, which is considered unclean. One should not take photographs of locals, particularly of women, without permission. Public displays of affection are considered taboo.

Homosexual practices are prohibited in the UAE, and as a result there are no openly gay or lesbian spots in town.

Israeli nationals are not allowed entry to the UAE.

8 Specialized Travel Resources

TRAVELERS WITH DISABILITIES
Dubai continues to improve services for travelers needing special assistance. Most public places have handicapped parking and elevators rather than just stairs, shopping centers have wheelchair access, and many international hotels offer guest rooms and other facilities for disabled travelers. These include City Centre Hotel, Crowne Plaza Dubai, Hilton International Dubai, Hyatt Regency Dubai, Jebel Ali Hotel & Golf Resort, the Jumeirah Beach Hotel, JW Marriott Hotel, Metropolitan Palace Hotel, Oasis Beach Hotel, Radisson SAS Hotel Jumeirah Beach, the Ritz-Carlton Dubai, and Renaissance Hotel Dubai.

The Dubai International Airport has dedicated desks between rows A and B in the Departures hall for passengers with special needs. Electric carts are available to shuttle passengers to/from the Sheikh Rashid Departures concourse, where there are special lounges for disabled travelers near gates 9 and 22. There's a dedicated lounge for disabled travelers in the Arrivals hall, and the Dubai International Airport Hotel has guest rooms for disabled passengers, as well. **Dubai Transport** (© 4/ 224-5331; www.dubaitransport.gov.ae)

Dubai's Darker Side: Trafficking in Persons

According to the U.S. Department of State, the UAE is a destination country for men and women trafficked for the purpose of involuntary servitude and commercial sexual exploitation. Many female domestic servants traveling from other countries face conditions of involuntary servitude, as do some men who come to the UAE to work in the construction industry. Women from some parts of Eastern Europe, Africa, and Asia are reportedly trafficked to the UAE for commercial sexual exploitation. For more information, visit www.state.gov.

has a couple specially designed vans for visitors needing assistance, which can be ordered in advance. For more information about wheelchair-accessible locations and other services for travelers with special needs, visit the "Simply Accessible" section of www.dubaitourism.co.ae.

FAMILY TRAVEL

Family lies at the core of Emirati culture, and children are welcomed just about everywhere. It's widely considered a very safe and friendly city for families. Most hotels offer kids activities and babysitting services. Many restaurants have children's menus and some have special family areas. Amusement centers, water parks, shopping center arcades, and beaches are ubiquitous in Dubai. Children's City (p. 102) and the Dubai Zoo (p. 102) cater specifically to kids. The best time for children to enjoy the city is from mid-October to mid-April, when the temperatures are moderate, facilitating outdoor activities. For 10 weeks between June and August, "Dubai Summer Surprises" focuses on children's entertainment and educational activities at shopping malls and other indoor venues. To locate accommodations, restaurants, and attractions that are particularly kid-friendly, refer to the "Kids" icon throughout this guide.

For a list of more family-friendly travel resources, turn to the experts at frommers.com.

WOMEN TRAVELERS

There are a few things women travelers will want to be aware of. Women have all the same legal rights as men and are free to dress as they please, although modest attire is encouraged out of deference to the local culture. Many public places offer special sections for women as well as special hours during which only women are allowed, which is intended to show respect for women's privacy. This may include banks, post offices, libraries, city parks, and even some health clubs and spas.

Emirati men often do not directly address foreign women, which is also meant as a sign of respect in the local culture. They may stare, however, and this is usually a result of curiosity rather than rudeness. Sexual harassment is officially censored, and the Dubai government punishes offenders by "naming and shaming" them. Although women should feel safe traveling alone, they should be cautious about visiting lower-end hotels or nightclubs where prostitution may be an issue and single women are sometimes propositioned. For general travel resources for women, go to frommers.com.

STUDENT TRAVEL

Students holding ISIC, ITIC, or IYTC cards can often get discounts of up to 25% off published rates at Dubai hotels. Dubai also has one youth hostel in the Al Ghusais area at 39 Al-Nahda Rd. (© 4/ 298-8151), between Al Mulla Plaza and the Al Bustan Center. Dorm rooms cost AED 50 to AED 165 ($14–$45/ £6.90–£23) per night, including breakfast, with YHA membership (AED 150/$41/£21) per year).

Check out the **International Student Travel Confederation (ISTC)** (www.istc. org) website for comprehensive travel services information and details on how to get an **International Student Identity Card (ISIC)**, which qualifies students for substantial savings on rail passes, plane tickets, entrance fees, and more. It also provides students with basic health and life insurance and a 24-hour help line. The card is valid for a maximum of 18 months. You can apply for the card online or in person at **STA Travel** (*©* **800/781-4040** in North America, 132 782 in Australia, or 0871 2 300 040 in the U.K.; www.statravel.com), the biggest student travel agency in the world; check out the website to locate STA Travel offices worldwide. If you're no longer a student but are still under 26, you can get an **International Youth Travel Card (IYTC)** from the same people, which entitles you to some discounts. **Travel CUTS** (*©* **800/592-2887;** www. travelcuts.com) offers similar services for both Canadians and U.S. residents. Irish students may prefer to turn to **USIT**

(*©* **01/602-1904;** www.usit.ie), an Ireland-based specialist in student, youth, and independent travel.

VEGETARIAN TRAVEL

It's relatively easy to maintain a vegetarian diet in Dubai. Almost all restaurants across the ethnic gamut offer vegetarian selections. The many Indians living here, many of whom do not eat meat for religious reasons, ensure plenty of vegetarian options in the emirate's often inexpensive Indian restaurants. Other Asian restaurants tend to focus on vegetarian dishes, and in Lebanese and Arabic restaurants, meze (appetizers) are usually meat-free. Some of the best restaurants serving vegetarian dishes are Asha's (p. 78), Glasshouse (p. 79), the Noodle House (p. 86), Thai Chi (p. 81), and La Vigna (p. 80). The Lime Tree Cafe (p. 91) is the most popular vegetarian restaurant among Western expatriates living in Dubai.

For more vegetarian-friendly travel resources, go to frommers.com.

9 Sustainable Tourism

Sustainable tourism is conscientious travel. It means being careful with the environments you explore, and respecting the communities you visit. Two overlapping components of sustainable travel are **eco-tourism** and **ethical tourism.** The **International Ecotourism Society** (TIES) defines eco-tourism as responsible travel to natural areas that conserves the environment and improves the well-being of local people. TIES suggests that eco-tourists follow these principles:

• Minimize environmental impact.
• Build environmental and cultural awareness and respect.
• Provide positive experiences for both visitors and hosts.
• Provide direct financial benefits for conservation and for local people.

• Raise sensitivity to host countries' political, environmental, and social climates.
• Support international human rights and labor agreements.

Sustainable travel remains a fledgling industry in Dubai, but the local government is beginning to take a closer look at the advantages of eco-tourism. In April 2008, Dubai hosted the Global Travel and Tourism Summit with a focus on sustainability. **Al Maha Desert Resort & Spa** (p. 73) is an elegant eco-tourism desert resort owned by Emirates Airlines. There are many eco-friendly activities offered in Dubai, from snorkeling and scuba diving in the Gulf to hiking and camping in the Hajar Mountains.

(Tips) It's Easy Being Green

Here are a few simple ways you can help conserve fuel and energy when you travel:

- Each time you take a flight or drive a car greenhouse gases release into the atmosphere. You can help neutralize this danger to the planet through "carbon offsetting"—paying someone to invest your money in programs that reduce your greenhouse gas emissions by the same amount you've added. Before buying carbon offset credits, just make sure that you're using a reputable company, one with a proven program that invests in renewable energy. Reliable carbon offset companies include **Carbonfund** (www.carbonfund.org), **TerraPass** (www.terrapass.org), and **Carbon Neutral** (www.carbonneutral.org).

- Whenever possible, choose nonstop flights; they generally require less fuel than indirect flights that stop and take off again. Try to fly during the day—some scientists estimate that nighttime flights are twice as harmful to the environment. And pack light—each 15 pounds of luggage on a 5,000-mile flight adds up to 50 pounds of carbon dioxide emitted.

- Where you stay during your travels can have a major environmental impact. To determine the green credentials of a property, ask about trash disposal and recycling, water conservation, and energy use; also question if sustainable materials were used in the construction of the property. The website **www.greenhotels.com** recommends green-rated member hotels around the world that fulfill the company's stringent environmental requirements. Also consult **www.environmentallyfriendlyhotels.com** for more green accommodations ratings.

- At hotels, request that your sheets and towels not be changed daily. (Many hotels already have programs like this in place.) Turn off the lights and air conditioner (or heater) when you leave your room.

- Use public transport where possible—trains, buses and even taxis are more energy-efficient forms of transport than driving. Even better is to walk or cycle; you'll produce zero emissions and stay fit and healthy on your travels.

- If renting a car is necessary, ask the rental agent for a hybrid, or rent the most fuel-efficient car available. You'll use less gas and save money at the tank.

- Eat at locally owned and operated restaurants that use produce grown in the area. This contributes to the local economy and cuts down on greenhouse gas emissions by supporting restaurants where the food is not flown or trucked in across long distances. Visit **Sustain Lane** (www.sustainlane.org) to find sustainable eating and drinking choices around the U.S.; also check out **www.eatwellguide.org** for tips on eating sustainably in the U.S. and Canada.

Frommers.com: The Complete Travel Resource

Planning a trip or just returned? Head to **Frommers.com,** voted Best Travel Site by *PC Magazine.* We think you'll find our site indispensable before, during, and after your travels—with expert advice and tips; independent reviews of hotels, restaurants, attractions, and preferred shopping and nightlife venues; vacation giveaways; and an online booking tool. We publish the complete contents of over 135 travel guides in our **Destinations** section, covering more than 4,000 places worldwide. Each weekday, we publish original articles that report on **Deals and News** via our free **Frommers.com Newsletters.** What's more, **Arthur Frommer** himself blogs 5 days a week, with cutting opinions about the state of travel in the modern world. We're betting you'll find our **Events** listings an invaluable resource; it's an up-to-the-minute roster of what's happening in cities everywhere—including concerts, festivals, lectures, and more. We've also added weekly **podcasts, interactive maps,** and hundreds of new images across the site. Finally, don't forget to visit our **Message Boards,** where you can join in conversations with thousands of fellow Frommer's travelers and post your trip report once you return.

You can find some eco-friendly travel tips and statistics, as well as touring companies and associations—listed by destination under "Travel Choice"—at the **TIES** website, www.ecotourism.org. Also check out **Ecotravel.com**, which lets you search for sustainable touring companies in several categories (water-based, land-based, spiritually oriented, and so on).

While much of the focus of ecotourism is about reducing impacts on the natural environment, ethical tourism concentrates on ways to preserve and enhance local economies and communities, regardless of location. You can embrace ethical tourism by staying at a locally owned hotel or shopping at a store that employs local workers and sells locally produced goods.

Responsible Travel (www.responsible travel.com) is a great source of sustainable travel ideas; the site is run by a spokesperson for ethical tourism in the travel industry. **Sustainable Travel International** (www.sustainabletravelinternational.org)

promotes ethical tourism practices, and manages an extensive directory of sustainable properties and tour operators around the world.

In the U.K., **Tourism Concern** (www. tourismconcern.org.uk) works to reduce social and environmental problems connected to tourism. The **Association of Independent Tour Operators (AITO)** (www.aito.co.uk) is a group of specialist operators leading the field in making holidays sustainable.

Volunteer travel has become increasingly popular among those who want to venture beyond the standard group-tour experience to learn languages, interact with locals, and make a positive difference while on vacation. Volunteer travel usually doesn't require special skills—just a willingness to work hard—and programs vary in length from a few days to a number of weeks. Some programs provide free housing and food, but many require volunteers to pay for travel expenses, which can add up quickly.

For general info on volunteer travel, visit **www.volunteerabroad.org** and **www. idealist.org**.

Before you commit to a volunteer program, it's important to make sure any money you're giving is truly going back to the local community, and that the work you'll be doing will be a good fit for you. **Volunteer International** (www.volunteer international.org) has a helpful list of questions to ask to determine the intentions and the nature of a volunteer program.

ANIMAL-RIGHTS ISSUES

The Dubai Zoo is often criticized for the cramped conditions in which the animals are kept, particularly in the sweltering heat of summer. More than 800 animals are kept in a space of just 1.7 hectares (5 acres). Their situation should improve significantly with the zoo's pending move to Dubailand, where they will be spread out over 80 hectares (198 acres).

The Dubai municipal authority and the World Society for the Protection of Animals (WSPA) signed a memorandum of understanding in 2007 to share expertise and best practices in order to promote animal welfare and the humane treatment of animals. Dubai became the first emirate to adopt a humane stray control program with support from the WSPA. These initiatives came in the wake of problems with abandoned and neglected animals, often by expatriates leaving the country. A new law seeks to increase animal protection.

For information on animal-friendly issues throughout the world, visit **Tread Lightly** (www.treadlightly.org).

10 Packages for the Independent Traveler

Emirates Airlines (☎ 800/777-3999; www.emirates.com) offers airfare and hotel packages to Dubai originating in North America or Europe. The Dubai-based airline also teams up with **Arabian Adventures** (www.arabian-adventures. com) to offer adventure travel in and around the emirate.

Travel Wizard (☎ 800/330-8820 or 415/446-5252; www.travelwizard.com) offers luxury beach and desert package tours in and around Dubai. Tours ranging from 3 to 8 days include accommodations, breakfast, activities, and transportation to and from the airport. The 3-day "Dubai Stopover" package focuses on city sightseeing, while the 8-day "Tailor Made Dubai" tour splits its time between luxurious city and desert destinations.

Indus Travels (☎ 866/391-0475; www.industravels.ca) is a Canadian-based company offering customized small group and private tours to Dubai. Packages range from 4 to 8 days and may focus on sun and sand, deserts and mountains, or local culture and heritage. Indus Travel will also tailor itineraries to culinary, architecture, and other special interests.

Gate 1 Travel (☎ 800/682-3333; www.gate1travel.com) offers a "7 Day Dubai" tour that includes airport transfer, 5 nights accommodations, daily breakfast, and city sightseeing via an air-conditioned motorcoach. Airfare from New York or other departure cities can be arranged.

For more information on Package Tours and for tips on booking your trip, see frommers.com.

11 Special-Interest Trips

ACADEMIC TRIPS & LANGUAGE CLASSES

The **Sheikh Mohammed Center for Cultural Understanding** (www.cultures.ae), located in the Bastakiya old quarter of Dubai, offers city tours with a focus on history and culture. One excursion is the Jumeirah Mosque visit, which takes place four times a week as a fixed public tour (p. 101). Guests at the mosque participate in a talk on the UAE's official religion, Islam. Other activities include Arabic courses, UAE Culture and Dubai orientation courses, a Bastakiya walking tour, a cultural breakfast and lunch, coffee mornings, cultural question-and-answer sessions, and "story circle for children."

ADVENTURE & WELLNESS TRIPS

Desert Rangers (© 4/340-2408; www.desertrangers.com) is a Dubai-based operator offering specialized adventure travel in the desert. Among the thrilling options are desert-driving courses, camel trekking by night, rock climbing, canoe expeditions, deep-sea fishing, and desert balloon safaris.

Arabian Adventures (© 4/303-4888; www.arabian-adventures.com) will also custom design adventure travel in the desert surrounding Dubai.

Horse Racing Abroad (© 444/441-661 in the U.K.; www.horseracing abroad.com) offers a week holiday from the U.K. to the Dubai World Cup. Join the jet-set crowd that comes to Dubai each March for this world-renowned event. The adventure package includes 6 nights luxury accommodations, tickets to the World Cup, and round-trip airfare from London Gatwick, Birmingham, or Manchester.

Mountain High (© 4/394-6484; www.mountainhighme.com) is an outdoors organization focused on engaging the "mind and spirit." Established by Dubai resident Julie Amer, a British outdoors lover, Mountain High arranges mountain treks, biking trips, morning meditation sessions, dhow and kayak trips, snorkeling, and outdoor workshops on goal setting.

TEN Travel & Tourism (www.travel.theemiratesnetwork.com) offers half-day shopping tours of Dubai. The guided tours, which require at least 2 people and can start anytime of the day, include visits to major malls and souks, with tips on bargaining. Free pickup and drop-off service is provided anywhere in Dubai.

Reem Tours & Travel (© 4/272-7116; www.reemtours.net) also offers shopping tours of Dubai, including visits to luxury malls and traditional souks selling handicrafts, antiques, and carpets. The tour includes a visit to the Sharjah Central Souk, as well.

12 Staying Connected

TELEPHONES

Etisalat (www.etisalat.ae) is the UAE's main telecommunications provider. A second provider, **Du** (www.du.ae), recently began offering service. Local calls in Dubai are free, except to cellphones. Direct dialing is possible to most countries. Pay phones are common in Dubai, and require prepaid phone cards widely available in supermarkets, gas stations, and other shops.

The international country code for the UAE is **971,** and the city code for Dubai is **4. To call the UAE/Dubai:**

1. Dial the international access code: 011 in the U.S., 00 in the U.K., for example.

2. Dial the country code: 971 for the UAE.

3. Dial the city code: 4 for Dubai, and then dial the number.

To call within the UAE: For calls within Dubai, omit the city code. For calls to other emirates, first dial 0 and then the city code: 2 for Abu Dhabi, 3 for Al Ain, and 6 for Sharjah. For calls to Etisalat cellphones, it is necessary to first dial 050. For calls to Du cellphones, it's necessary to first dial 055.

To make international calls: Dial 00 to get an international line, followed by the country code and the phone number.

For directory assistance: Dial 181 for Etisalat, and 199 for Du.

Online Traveler's Toolbox

Veteran travelers usually carry some essential items to make their trips easier. Following is a selection of handy online tools to bookmark and use.

- **Airplane Food** (www.airlinemeals.net)
- **Airplane Seating** (www.seatguru.com, www.airlinequality.com)
- **Foreign Languages for Travelers** (www.travlang.com)
- **Online Shopping** (www.uaemall.com)
- **Maps** (www.mapquest.com)
- **Nightlife Information** (www.dubailook.com)
- **Restaurant Reviews** (www.timeoutdubai.com)
- **Take-Out Food** (www.roomservice-uae.com)
- **Time and Date** (www.timeanddate.com)
- **Travel Warnings** (http://travel.state.gov, www.fco.gov.uk/travel, www.voyage.gc.ca, www.smartraveller.gov.au)
- **Universal Currency Converter** (www.oanda.com)
- **Weather** (www.intellicast.com, www.weather.com)

For an operator: Dial 100.

CELLPHONES

Cellphones, commonly referred to here as "mobile phones" or "mobiles," are common in the UAE. Etisalat is the main network provider, and the prefix for calling Etisalat mobiles is 050 (rather than 4, which is the prefix for land lines in Dubai). If your own network provider does not allow roaming while in the UAE, you can use Etisalat's Wasel service. This allows you to use a prepaid Etisalat SIM card in your existing cellphone while in the UAE. A second cellphone network called Du (www.du.ae) recently began service in the UAE. The prefix for calling Du mobiles is 055. Both Du and Etisalat offer monthly or pay-as-you-go mobile service.

VOICE-OVER INTERNET PROTOCOL (VOIP)

If you have Web access while traveling, consider a broadband-based telephone service (in technical terms, **Voice over Internet protocol,** or **VoIP**) such as Skype (www.skype.com) or Vonage (www.vonage.com), which allow you to make free international calls from your laptop or in a cybercafe. Neither service requires the people you're calling to also have that service (though there are fees if they do not). Check the websites for details.

INTERNET & E-MAIL
WITH YOUR OWN COMPUTER

Emirates Internet and Multimedia (EIM) is responsible for Internet services in the UAE. Most Dubai accommodations have Internet access, and Wi-Fi is common in international hotels, but if you can't get service, you can connect to EIM's "Dial and Surf" service through your computer's modem using a regular phone or ISDN line. Just dial ✆ **4/500-5555** to gain access, and the fee will be billed to the phone line you are using. Call the EIM help desk (✆ **800-6100**) for more information.

WITHOUT YOUR OWN COMPUTER

Most international hotels in Dubai offer business centers with Internet access.

Note that certain websites are censored in the UAE.

For help locating cybercafes and other establishments where you can go for Internet access, please see "Internet Access" in appendix A, p. 155.

13 Tips on Accommodations

Dubai has one of the world's fastest-growing hotel scenes of any major world city. If the emirate's plans to become a global tourism hub continue to take hold—and they probably will—Dubai is expected to expand from roughly 6 million annual visitors today to more than 15 million within a decade. Authorities envision the need to construct an additional 70,000 to 80,000 hotel rooms to meet this demand. This helps explain the construction cranes in almost every corner of the city, as well as on the imaginative Palm Islands. Dubai is a city literally reaching into the sky and across the sea.

Most all of the hotels we include are officially designated with four or five stars, which should not be confused with the zero- to three-star scale that we use. Many of the world's top-name hotels are here, and some with multiple locations: Ritz-Carlton, Marriott, Raffles, Hyatt, Hilton, Fairmont, Sheraton, Sofitel, and One&Only, to name a few. The Jumeirah Group, overseen by Dubai's royal family, boasts some of Dubai's best-known resorts and hotels. These include the iconic Burj al Arab, which is so big it almost eclipses the horizon, the Jumeirah Beach Hotel, Emirates Towers, and the Arabian palace hotels inside Madinat Jumeirah. Jumeirah Group also owns the desert oasis resort, Bab Al Shams, whose only real competition is Al Maha Desert Resort & Spa. A visit to either is like a trip to heaven.

As if the so-called "seven star" Burj al Arab were not already sufficiently over-the-top, Dubai is building the world's largest hotel—Asia-Asia—which, with 6,500 rooms, will substantially surpass the current record holder MGM Las Vegas. Asia-Asia Hotel will be the centerpiece of a future resort called Bawadi, a long luxury strip with 31 hotels resembling Egyptian palaces, Hollywood, the U.K. Parliament, and apparently even the moon. These hotels will begin to open in 2010, and you can bet there will be many more along the way. Perhaps one day Las Vegas will be looking to Dubai for inspiration, rather than the other way around.

Most all of Dubai's entertainment revolves around the hotel scene. Because hotels are uniquely permitted to hold liquor licenses, the majority of the city's top restaurants and virtually all bars and nightclubs lie in hotels. The action is nonstop, except during Ramadan, when all Muslims are required to fast by day and non-Muslims are asked to be respectful of the holy month. Live music and dancing are not allowed during this period, so many bars and most clubs shut down temporarily. Eating during the day and drinking often still takes place in hotels during Ramadan, but discreetly. Year-round, visitors to Dubai are technically not allowed to drink outside the hotel they are visiting unless they get a liquor permit.

The most extravagant, and expensive, hotels in Dubai are the international resorts lining Jumeirah Beach, which stretches for miles along the Gulf. The beaches here are beautiful—soft golden sand fronts a blue-green sea, with water as warm as the Caribbean. These world-class resorts offer amenities equal to the best establishments in the world. Most of them have spas, health clubs, sports activities, and beach centers with extensive watersports, as well as wide-ranging dining and entertainment options. They are the reason one magazine characterized Dubai as "the new Ibiza."

The hotels lining Sheikh Zayed Road are also very impressive. To lure travelers and ensure that Dubai is internationally recognized as the region's tourist capital, the sleek accommodations lining Dubai's main thoroughfare compete for design, luxury, service, and amenities. Dubai's twin towers, known as Emirates Towers, first set the stage for the road's surrounding architectural splendor, and today the hotels and other high-rises spanning the skyline form an urban desert wonder. Business travelers tend to stay on Sheikh Zayed Road, but these hotels also have extensive services for visitors who are on holiday, and they lie just minutes away from Jumeirah Beach and the best sights of old Dubai.

The old town consists of Deira and Bur Dubai. It's not as glitzy as Jumeirah Beach or Sheikh Zayed Road, but it has much more local flavor. The best hotels here overlook Dubai Creek, but they're also the most expensive in the area. For travelers seeking more moderate accommodations, Deira and Bur Dubai offer the city's least expensive options. Be cautious when choosing other hotels in the area—some are used for prostitution and are simply not recommended.

Just as the guests to Dubai's hotels seem to come from every corner of the globe, so too do the staff. Service has improved markedly, but the limited English ability and lack of familiarity with Western expectations among some of the staffs occasionally means that service isn't quite up to par with other tourist hubs. This is more the case with inexpensive hotels than with the expensive, international ones. Nevertheless, you can always get by with English, and for better or worse don't need to speak a word of Arabic here. As you might expect, you will find a significant difference between the attention you will receive at a five-star hotel and one more modest in quality and price.

Dubai hotels are expensive and unfortunately getting more so, especially for U.S. travelers who face falling dollar value in currency exchanges. Hotel prices tend to drop 30% to 40% in summer (late June to Aug), but Dubai is so hot then you may feel like you should be the one paid to stay during those months. There are occasionally discounts around some of the festival periods, as well. European and other travelers are likely to find the prices a little more manageable, but still high. I strongly suggest that you check Internet promotional rates before booking. Most hotels will quote rates in dirhams but can easily convert that to dollars, pounds, or euros. Foreign credit cards are widely accepted. All rates are subject to a 10% municipality fee and 10% service charge.

For tips on surfing for hotel deals online, visit frommers.com.

4

Suggested Dubai Itineraries

It's possible to see most of Dubai's key sites and attractions in 3 days, but you'll have to move quickly and somewhat strategically. If this is the amount of time you have, I want to help you maximize your experience by providing a suggested itinerary. The increasing traffic in Dubai means that the most sensible way to explore the city is to focus on particular neighborhoods each day, walking when possible and taking taxis (by water and land) when necessary. I start you with a tour of Dubai's historic area bordering each side of the creek, and then broaden your exposure to the city, making sure you have time for the beach, shopping, and trips to Dubai's modern marvels. Those with a week will be able to develop a greater feeling for the city and to experience some of UAE life outside Dubai. I'll send you for a thrilling desert safari, encourage you to visit the cultural sites of Sharjah, and suggest a trip to the mountain village of Hatta. I've also provided special itineraries for families with children and those especially interested in Dubai's architecture.

NEIGHBORHOODS IN BRIEF

Bur Dubai On the western side of Dubai Creek lies Bur Dubai, which like Deira provides a window into the early days of the city. At the northern edge of Bur Dubai near Port Rashid, the Al Shindagha Tunnel connects Bur Dubai with Deira. Nearby, at the northern tip of the creek-side walkway are the Sheikh Saeed House and the Heritage and Diving Village. Walking south along the creek are the Dubai Museum and Bastakiya historic quarter. Visitors can catch a water taxi *(abra)* from the nearby Al Seef Road area across the creek to Deira. The upscale BurJuman Centre lies a couple blocks to the west, and next to it is Al Karama, a business and residential area known for shopping bargains. The beautiful Creekside Park lies between the creek's two bridges, Al Garhoud and Al Maktoum. One of the city's best walking areas, it includes waterfront pathways, a 30m-high (98-ft.) cable car, and a fun educational center for kids called Children's City. Wafi City is located just to the west of Creekside Park.

Deira Deira is Dubai's oldest and busiest neighborhood, filled with the traditional sights, sounds, and smells of the city. It's located on the east side of Dubai Creek and is connected to the western part of the city by two bridges: Garhoud Bridge and Al Maktoum Bridge. The Dubai Creek and Yacht Club lies next to the Garhoud Bridge and Deira City Center. However, most of the neighborhood's action takes place farther north, in a triangle between Maktoum Bridge (which connects to Bur Dubai), the Corniche (which runs along the coast), and Abu Baker al-Siddiq Road (which extends between Maktoum Bridge and the Corniche to the east). A number of leading hotels are located along Baniyas Road (such as the Hilton Dubai Creek and Sheraton Dubai Creek), which parallels the creek as it makes its way toward the Arabian Gulf. To the east near the Clock Tower Roundabout and Al Rigga Road are a number of more moderate hotels, restaurants, and shops, as well as unattractive apartment buildings and a whole lot of traffic. The Dubai International Airport is in the south of Deira.

The Deira wharfage area is located along the creek where Baniyas Road enters Al Ras, the area at the northwestern tip of Deira. Here you will see traditional dhows hauling their goods, and there are water taxis, called *abras,* ferrying people across the creek to Bur Dubai. This is the most interesting part of Deira. Al Ras is home to Dubai's famous street markets, including the Gold Souk, textile souk, Spice Souk, and fish souk. This area is very congested and therefore best explored on foot in the cooler hours of the day. The Heritage House and Al-Ahmadiya School, two of Dubai's most appealing historical attractions, are also located in Al Ras. Extending east is the Corniche Deira, where Al Khaleej Road leads to the bridge connecting the mainland to Palm Deira island and on past Hamriya Port to Mamzar Beach Park.

Jumeirah & New Dubai   Originally just a beach, Jumeirah today refers to the entire coastal area west of Dubai Creek toward Jebel Ali. Al Jumeirah Road, commonly called the "Beach Road," begins at the Jumeirah Mosque and extends west past waterfront resorts, shops, and restaurants. This is a terrific walking area by day and night, and tends to be filled with casually dressed Western expatriates. Throughout the area are some of the most extravagant and expensive villas

in Dubai. The Beach Road then passes the Jumeirah Beach Park as it makes it way toward the Jumeirah Beach Hotel, Burj al Arab, and Wild Wadi water park in the area called Umm Suqeim. At this point, the Beach Road merges with Al Sufouh Road, passing as it heads farther west by Madinat Jumeirah, Knowledge Village, and Internet City, and on to the Dubai Marina and Jumeirah Beach Residences. Some of Dubai's best beach resorts are nearby, such as the Ritz-Carlton, Hilton Dubai Jumeirah, Méridien Mina Seyahi, and One&Only Royal Mirage. Off the coast of this stretch of Jumeirah Beach lies the Palm Jumeirah island. Although the coastal roads are more picturesque, it's faster to reach this part of Jumeirah from the city center by taking Sheikh Zayed Road and exiting at Interchange 5.

In addition to the new sections of Jumeirah, New Dubai refers to the entire series of areas being developed from Dubailand to Dubai World Central. For a list of projects under construction, see p. 15.

Sheikh Zayed Road   Sheikh Zayed Road parallels the coast as it extends west from Za'abeel Park toward Abu Dhabi. Although it's also an inter-city highway, when referred to here, Sheikh Zayed Road is the modern business center of Dubai with gleaming skyscrapers lining the road from the Trade Center roundabout to the area past Interchange 1. The Dubai World Trade Center was the emirate's first high-rise when it was built in 1979 and everything around it was still sand. Since then, the area has transformed into a concrete jungle as increasingly modern, tall, and architecturally distinctive buildings have been constructed. The twin Emirates Towers housing a hotel and office space opened in 2000, followed in recent years by even grander hotels: the Dusit Dubai, Fairmont, and

Dubai's Neighborhoods

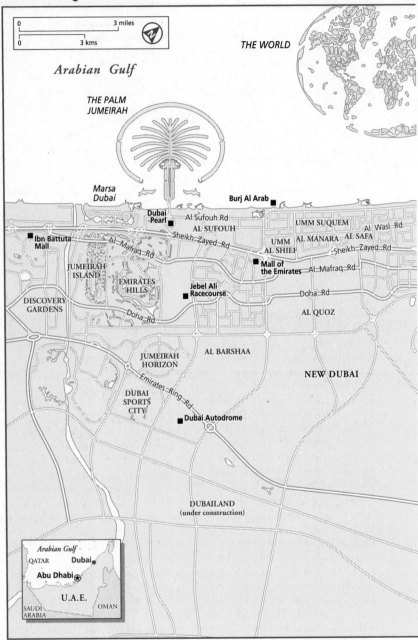

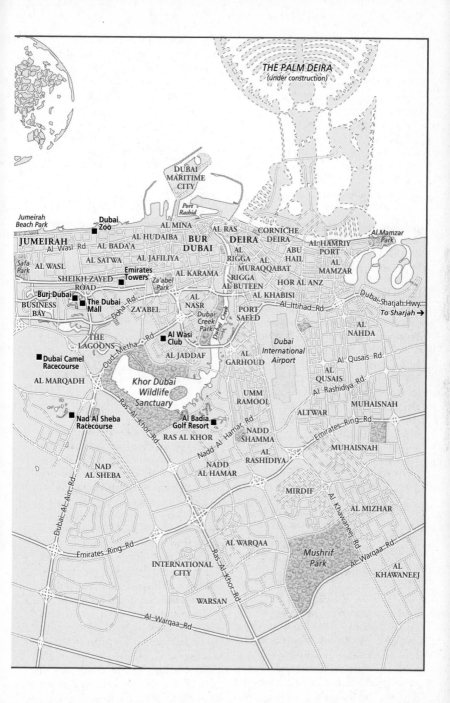

THE PALM DEIRA
(under construction)

DUBAI
MARITIME
CITY

Port
Rashid

Jumeirah
Beach Park

Dubai
Zoo

AL MINA

AL RAS

CORNICHE
DEIRA

Al.Mamzar
Park

JUMEIRAH

Al Wasl Rd.

AL HUDAIBA

BUR
DUBAI

DEIRA

AL HAMRIY
PORT

AL BADA'A

AL WASL

AL SATWA

AL JAFILIYA

AL
RIGGA

ABU
HAIL

AL
MURAQQABAT

AL
MAMZAR

Safa
Park

Emirates
Towers

AL KARAMA

RIGGA

HOR AL ANZ

SHEIKH ZAYED
ROAD

Za'abel
Park

AL BUTEEN

AL KHABISI

Burj Dubai

The Dubai
Mall

ZA'ABEL

AL
NASR

PORT
SAEED

Al-Ittihad-Rd.

Dubai-Sharjah-Hwy.

To Sharjah →

BUSINESS
BAY

Dubai
Creek
Park

AL
NAHDA

THE
LAGOONS

Al Wasi
Club

AL JADDAF

AL
GARHOUD

Dubai
International
Airport

AL
QUSAIS

Al-Qusais-Rd.

Dubai Camel
Racecourse

Khor Dubai
Wildlife
Sanctuary

AL MARQADH

Al-Rashidiya-Rd.

MUHAISNAH

UMM
RAMOOL

ALTWAR

Nad Al Sheba
Racecourse

Al Badia
Golf Resort

RAS AL KHOR

NADD
SHAMMA

Emirates-Ring-Rd.

MUHAISNAH

NAD
AL SHEBA

NADD
AL HAMAR

AL
RASHIDIYA

MIRDIF

AL MIZHAR

Emirates-Ring-Rd.

AL WARQAA

Mushrif
Park

AL
KHAWANEEJ

INTERNATIONAL
CITY

WARSAN

Al-Warqaa-Rd.

43

Shangri-La among them. In addition to hotels, the buildings lining Sheikh Zayed Road hold shopping centers, stores, art galleries, restaurants, cafes, and nightclubs, along with offices and luxury apartments.

Just to the west of Interchange 1, the Burj Dubai dominates the skyline as the world's tallest structure. It's surrounded by an area called Business Bay and Downtown Dubai, with hotels, restaurants, shops, office spaces, and entertainment projects still under construction at press time. As Sheikh Zayed Road continues its journey west, it passes the Mall of the Emirates and Ski Dubai at Interchange 4, with Dubai Internet City just beyond that, the Dubai Marina and Emirates Golf Club at Interchange 5, and finally Ibn Battuta Mall at Interchange 6 before entering Jebel Ali Village. From there, it's about an hour-and-a-half drive to Abu Dhabi.

1 Dubai in 3 Days

Day ❶: Cultural Tour

Begin your day in **Bur Dubai** with a morning walk through the historic area of **Bastakiya** 𝆑𝆑. If you're not staying close by, a taxi can drop you off here. Wander the meandering pathways surrounded by wind towers and traditional Arabian homes. Check in at the **Sheikh Mohammed Center for Cultural Understanding** 𝆑 (p. 101) to gather information about Emirati culture (the Center also arranges walking tours of the old quarter). You can then visit the Majlis Gallery, which was Dubai's first art gallery, and stop for a coffee at the Basta Art Café.

> **TAKE A BREAK**
> The cafe at the boutique **XVA** hotel and gallery in the center of Bastakiya is a perfect place to grab a light snack and a cold drink. This hidden spot offers creative salads, soups, and vegetarian sandwiches, as well as refreshing mint lemonade. ℭ 4/353-5383.

Just to the north you'll see the Al-Fahidi fort, the city's oldest surviving building. The **Dubai Museum** 𝆑𝆑 is here, offering the emirate's best opportunity to discover the history, culture, and traditions of Dubai. This key cultural museum can be visited in just a few hours.

Pass by the Grand Mosque and the Bur Dubai Souk, a bustling textile and clothing market in business since the 1830s.

>
> **TAKE A BREAK**
> There are several traditional Arabic restaurants of similar quality along the creek near the Bur Dubai Souk, where you can stop for a bite before you catch a water taxi to the other side.

Continue walking along the creek-side pathway toward the Al Shindagha Tunnel, before which you will find the **Sheikh Saeed House** 𝆑, the carefully restored courtyard home of Dubai's former ruler. It's a good example of the 19th-century architectural style of the Gulf coast, and includes an excellent collection of photographs from Dubai's pre-oil days.

Next to the Sheikh Saeed House and near the mouth of the creek, the **Heritage and Diving Village** 𝆑 showcases Dubai's maritime and pearl-diving traditions.

Just in front of the Bur Dubai souk along the creek, you'll find the *abra* (water taxi) station. The short boat ride across the creek will drop you off in the **dhow wharfage area of Deira,** just in front of Baniyas Road. Here you can watch the colorful dhows as they make their way back and forth along the creek to the Arabian Gulf. Take the pedestrian underpass to the left to the Grand Souk Deira, Dubai's oldest and busiest bazaar. Just behind the Grand Souk lies the Spice Souk.

From the Grand Souk, walk a short distance along Sikkat Al-Khaif Road to the heart of Al Ras, where you'll find the square with the **Heritage House** and, next to it, the **Al-Ahmadiya School**. The fully restored Heritage House is an excellent example of late-19th-century Arabian architecture and furnishings. Then visit the Al-Ahmadiya School, which sheds light on the history of education in Dubai. You will also see the Bin Lootah Mosque, dating from 1910, in front of the Al-Ahmadiya School.

Heading back on Sikkat Al-Khaif Road, and passing the **Grand Souk Deira** to your right, you will make your way to the **Gold Souk**, which is spread out to the left. The best time to visit is after 4pm, since most shops close during the heat of the afternoon. Nighttime is especially busy. Just beyond the Gold Souk lies the fragrant **Perfume Souk**.

Finish your day in Old Dubai with a **dinner dhow cruise**, an enchanting way to view the city at night while enjoying Arabic food and music. Many of the 2-hour dinner dhow cruises depart at 8:30pm from the Al-Boom Tourist Village in Deira, located near Garhoud Bridge between Creekside Park and Wonderland water park. There are also romantic late-night dhow trips that operate from 10:30pm to midnight. See p. 103.

Day ❷: Creek-Side Dubai

Having explored Dubai's historic area in depth on the first day, it's time on day 2 to broaden your exposure. Spend the morning discovering Dubai aboard a double-decker bus and creek tour before cooling off midday in one of Dubai's best shopping centers. As the afternoon heat fades, take a stroll through Dubai's best waterfront park. Then get ready for an unforgettable desert safari that will last into the night.

Start the day with an English-speaking tour of Dubai on one of the **Big Bus Company**'s open-air double-decker buses (ⓒ 4/324-4187; www.bigbus.co.uk), starting at Wafi City with hop-on hop-off privileges as you explore the city. A 1-hour guided creek tour is included in the price, so hop off at stop no. seven, and explore Dubai from the water on the Big Bus Arabian Dhow Creek Cruise (note that admission to the Dubai Museum and Sheikh Saeed House is also included in the price). If you'd prefer to skip the bus and just take a boat cruise, **Tour Dubai** (ⓒ 4/336-8407; www.tour-dubai.com) offers creek tours aboard a traditional dhow, with departures daily at 11:30am, 1:30, 3:30, and 5:30pm.

TAKE A BREAK

The Big Bus Company has returned you to Wafi City, and you're probably very hungry. You'll need some nourishment for the upcoming activities, and one of Wafi's best options is **Asha's**, serving outstanding Indian cuisine created by legendary Indian singer Asha Bhosle. ⓒ 4/324-4100. See p. 78.

Wafi City (p. 116) is one of the city's most exclusive malls, with hundreds of high-end stores, delectable cafes and restaurants, and fun places for families such as the Encounter Zone. Depending on your desire to shop, you could easily spend some hours here, especially when the midday outdoor temperatures make the mall's air-conditioning all the more alluring.

Once you break away from Wafi, take a short taxi ride to **Creekside Park** (p. 103), one of my favorite outdoor spots in Dubai. The beautiful park offers waterfront pathways leading to fishing piers, botanical gardens, restaurants, and an amphitheater. Ride a cable car as it makes its way over the creek. You could easily while away the afternoon here.

By 4pm, you'll be on the road to the expansive dunes of the Arabian Desert. Your **desert safari,** organized by a tour operator, begins with a thrilling ride over the dunes in a 4WD followed by a visit to a camel farm. You'll then continue with a sunset dinner at an Arabian campsite with live entertainment, including belly-dancing and henna artists. This quintessential Dubai experience lasts until about 9pm and is a wonderful adventure. See p. 104.

Day ❸: Sun & Snow

Visit Jumeirah's beautiful Islamic mosque, take a walk along the waterfront and go for a swim, and as the midday heat increases, make a run for the slopes at Ski Dubai. After skiing, you can do a bit of shopping in the fabulous Mall of the Emirates. Then, as the sun sets, make your way back to the coast for a carefully crafted cocktail at the Burj Al Arab followed by dinner and drinks at Madinat Jumeirah.

If you're here on a Saturday, Sunday, Tuesday, or Thursday, start your day with a tour of the beautiful **Jumeirah Mosque** ❦❦ (p. 101). This is the only mosque in Dubai open to non-Muslims, and it's breathtaking. Conservative attire is required, so if you're going to the beach after, be sure to bring a change of clothes.

After breakfast, take a walk along the **Jumeirah Beach Road** ❦❦, where you'll pass boutique shops, gourmet food stores, popular cafes and restaurants, and some extravagant villas. Dubai feels less crowded and assuredly beachy in this area. Mercato Mall is the most glamorous shopping center along this strip, but there are many smaller malls from which to choose.

You'll find the lovely public **Jumeirah Beach Park** ❦❦ a bit farther west off the Beach Road. If you're not already staying at a beach resort, this is my top pick for swimming and playing in the sand. See p. 103.

What could be more surreal than leaving the beach in the midday sun and substituting your bathing suit for a winter jacket? It's exactly what I recommend you do. Take the 15-minute drive to Mall of the Emirates where **Ski Dubai** ❦❦ (p. 105) is located, and they'll provide all your winter gear, included in the price of the ticket. You can ski or snowboard by the hour.

Dubai's number one après-ski activity is shopping. The largest mall outside North America (at least until Mall of Arabia opens, which will become the biggest in the world), **Mall of the Emirates** ❦❦❦ (p. 116) is a shopper's paradise. You'll find more than 400 stores and 65 restaurants here, as well as extensive entertainment options.

TAKE A BREAK
Jumeirah's most charming spot for breakfast is the casual **Lime Tree Cafe** ❦, set in a converted villa on Jumeirah Beach Road. Breakfast delights include hotcakes with blueberry sauce or toasted bagels with eggs. It's just a short walk from the mosque, and you can sit inside or out. ✆ 4/349-8498. See p. 91.

TAKE A BREAK
By now you've walked, swam, skied, and shopped, and you've had a blast but you're also exhausted. The solution is a sunset cocktail, prepared by a trained mixologist, at the **Skyview Bar** ❦❦ atop the Burj Al Arab. You must make a reservation in advance, and this is the best opportunity to visit the famous hotel short of spending an arm and a leg on a guest room. ✆ 4/301-7600. See p. 127.

Plan to spend your evening at **Madinat Jumeirah** ⭐⭐ (p. 112), the breathtaking Arabian complex adjacent to the sea. You can wander the fashionable souk, take a small boat along one of the many waterways, have dinner at one of the outstanding restaurants, and smoke *shisha* and enjoy a drink at one of the chic nightspots. There are 75 shops and galleries and more than 20 waterfront cafes, restaurants, and bars here.

2 Dubai in a Week (with Abu Dhabi & Sharjah)

Days ❶, ❷ & ❸
See days 1, 2, and 3 in "Dubai in 3 Days," above.

Day ❹: Beach Day
Camel racing takes place from late October to early April, with robotic jockeys now leading the speedy desert animals. If you wake up early enough, begin the day out at the Nad Al Sheba racing club, where the first race starts at 7:30am. See p. 106.

Following the race, make your way to the **beach.** If you're not staying at a beach resort or don't feel like paying for a private beach club, your best option is the **Jumeirah Beach Park** ⭐⭐ (p. 103). If you happen to be staying in Deira and would like a closer public beach, you can go to Mamzar Beach Park. The two best private beach clubs are at the Jumeirah Beach Hotel and Le Méridien Mina Seyahi, which allow non-hotel guests entrance for a fee. A less expensive option is at the Oasis Beach Hotel.

If you're not getting enough action at the beach, head to **Wild Wadi** ⭐⭐⭐ (p. 102). There's no better place to cool off than this exhilarating water park, one of the best I've ever visited. I know from personal experience that adults will have every bit as much fun here as kids, and there are 30 thrilling rides and attractions.

TAKE A BREAK
For a beachfront happy hour, head to **Barasti** ⭐⭐ at Le Méridien Mina Seyahi. If Jimmy Buffet were in Dubai, you can imagine this is where he'd hang out. The casual beach bar fills with a fun-loving Western crowd and has a different theme every night. ✆ 4/399-3333. See p. 127.

Day ❺: Shop 'til You Drop
Return to Deira to explore the age-old souks. You've walked through the Gold and Spice souks on day 1, but this is an opportunity to visit three more quintessential Dubai markets: the **Fish Souk** ⭐, **Perfume Souk** ⭐, and **Grand Souk Deira** ⭐⭐, all located within easy walking proximity in the Al Ras section of Deira (you can also return to the Gold and Spice souks, which are here as well). The best time to visit is during the cooler hours of the morning or at night. See p. 112.

Next, take time to explore the shops along **Jumeirah Beach Road** ⭐⭐. In addition to the Renaissance-style Mercato shopping center, there are a number of smaller malls popular with local residents, including Town Center (next to Mercato), Beach Center (near the Dubai zoo), Jumeirah Center (near the Jumeirah Mosque), Magrudy's Mall (also near the Jumeirah Mosque), and Palm Strip (across from the Jumeirah Mosque). Shops in these malls tend to have a relaxed beach feel and are not as crowded as some of the bigger shopping centers. See p. 112.

As for the big malls, you've already had a chance to visit Wafi City and Mall of the Emirates, two of the best Dubai offers. But there are a few other spectacular malls you should be aware of. In Deira, **BurJuman Centre** ⭐⭐ is especially popular for its high-street brands. **Deira City Centre** ⭐ is a perennial favorite, more accessible and less pretentious than BurJuman. On the other side of the city, **Ibn Battuta Mall** ⭐⭐ has shops categorized in six distinct shopping

Dubai (with Abu Dhabi & Sharjah) in 3 & 7 Days

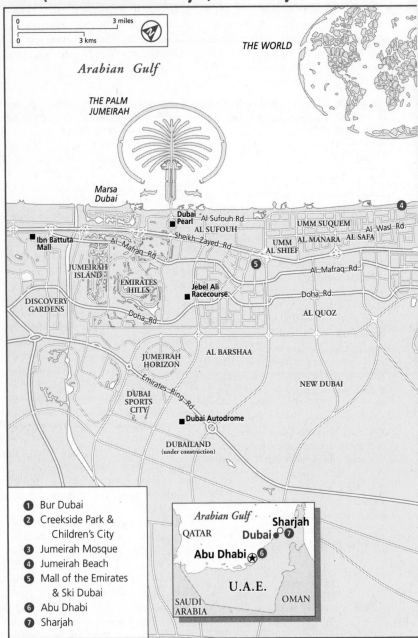

1 Bur Dubai
2 Creekside Park & Children's City
3 Jumeirah Mosque
4 Jumeirah Beach
5 Mall of the Emirates & Ski Dubai
6 Abu Dhabi
7 Sharjah

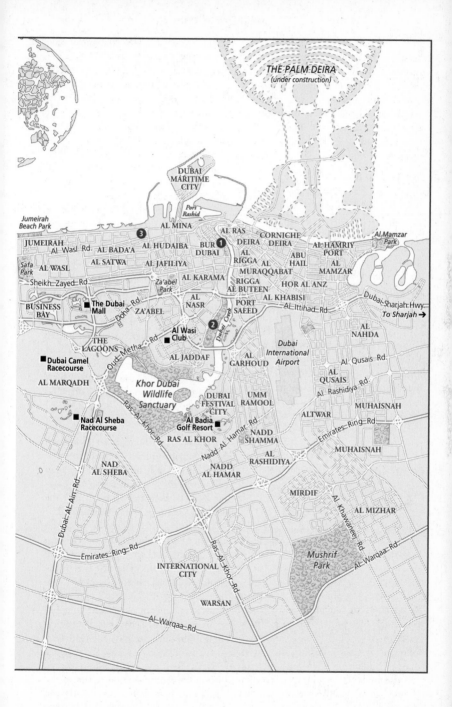

THE PALM DEIRA
(under construction)

Jumeirah
Beach Park

DUBAI
MARITIME
CITY

*Port
Rashid*

AL MINA

JUMEIRAH
AL Wasl Rd.   AL BADA'A   AL HUDAIBA   BUR ❶   AL RAS
DUBAI   DEIRA   CORNICHE DEIRA
Safa   AL WASL   AL SATWA   AL JAFILIYA   AL   AL HAMRIY
Park   RIGGA   ABU   PORT
Sheikh Zayed Rd.   AL MURAQQABAT   HAIL   AL
AL KARAMA   RIGGA   MAMZAR
Za'abel   AL BUTEEN   HOR AL ANZ
BUSINESS   The Dubai   Park   AL NASR   AL KHABISI
BAY   Mall   Doha Rd.   ZA'ABEL   PORT   AL-Ittihad Rd.   To Sharjah →
SAEED   Dubai-Sharjah Hwy.
THE   Al Wasi ❷   AL   AL
LAGOONS   Club   NAHDA
Dubai Camel   Oud Metha Rd.   AL JADDAF   AL   Dubai   AL Qusais Rd.
Racecourse   GARHOUD   International   AL
AL MARQADH   *Khor Dubai   Airport   QUSAIS
Wildlife   AL Rashidiya Rd.
Sanctuary*   DUBAI   UMM   ALTWAR   MUHAISNAH
Nad Al Sheba   FESTIVAL   RAMOOL
Racecourse   Al Badia   CITY   Emirates-Ring-Rd.
Golf Resort   NADD   MUHAISNAH
RAS AL KHOR   SHAMMA   AL
Nadd Al Hamar Rd.   RASHIDIYA
NAD   NADD   AL MIZHAR
AL SHEBA   AL HAMAR   MIRDIF
Ras-Al-Khor-Rd.   Al Khawaneej Rd.   AL-Warqaa-Rd.
Dubai–Al-Ain-Rd.   *Mushrif
Park*
Emirates-Ring-Rd.
INTERNATIONAL
CITY
WARSAN
AL-Warqaa-Rd.

zones. It's located about 20 minutes from the city center, on Sheikh Zayed Road near the Dubai Marina. Closer to center, my favorite shopping center is **Emirates Towers Boulevard** ✻✻✻, situated in the beautiful Emirates Towers complex. It's significantly smaller than Dubai's other malls and features some of the city's most exclusive boutique shops. See p. 113.

Day ⑥: Abu Dhabi

Allow about 2 hours to get to Abu Dhabi from Dubai. Begin your experience at **Heritage Village** ✻✻ in the city's Breakwater area. Here, you'll find Abu Dhabi as it originally was, before the city's unbelievable oil wealth transformed it from a simple Bedouin village to an enviable Arab capital. You'll get a good feel for traditional Emirati life and can take home a souvenir from a local craftsman. See p. 135.

If you want to visit Abu Dhabi's best shopping center, the **Marina Mall** ✻✻, it lies almost next door to Heritage Village. The modern center at the edge of the Breakwater offers designer shops, restaurants, cafes, and tons of entertainment options. These include a cinema, bowling alley, ice rink, and even a ski slope. See p. 140.

TAKE A BREAK
If it's sun you seek, the **Hiltonia Beach Club** ✻✻ is open to non-hotel guests and offers extensive facilities. In addition to an excellent beach with watersports activities, there's an outstanding health club and spa. ✆ 2/692-4368.

Next, you're off to the **Emirates Palace** ✻✻✻ to take in the most expensive hotel ever built. The magnificent resort sits on 1.3km (¾ mile) of beachfront and is truly a man-made marvel. The hotel no longer offers tours, but you can visit by booking a lunch reservation at one of the Palace's many gourmet restaurants. See p. 137.

Make your way now to the east side of the city taking the waterfront **Corniche** ✻✻. Stop along the way to walk on the landscaped greens and admire the city from the water's edge. Continue toward the **Dhow Harbor** ✻, where you can visit the Iranian souk, carpet souk, and fish and vegetable souks. Although they're not picturesque, they are authentic. Then take a stroll to the harbor and watch the traditional dhows return from sea at the end of the day. See p. 134.

A visit to Abu Dhabi is not complete without a stop at the **Grand Mosque** ✻✻✻ (p. 135), the third-largest mosque in the world. Free tours of the palatial mosque, decked out in marble, crystal, and gold, are available at 10am Sunday to Thursday.

Finish your day at the **Cultural Foundation** ✻✻, which lies on the grounds of the old fort. Many of the activities take place in the evenings, including literary and cultural events, photographic and other artistic exhibitions, concerts, theatrical performances, and festivals. Check the website (www.www.cultural.org.ae/e) for schedule information. See p. 134.

Day ⑦: Sharjah

Budget about an hour to get to Sharjah from Dubai, and remember not to travel there during rush hour, when the road connecting the two cities becomes a parking lot. The best time to go is after the morning commute or on the weekend.

Your first activity should be a walking tour of the emirate's historic neighborhood, called Heritage Square, which will take about 3 hours. The first stop is the **Souk Al Arash** ✻✻, where you can browse in one of the UAE's most traditional and authentic bazaars. Around 100 shops line covered alleyways, selling everything from antiques and jewelry to perfumes and Arabic souvenirs. See p. 143.

Next, cross the courtyard to the **Al Naboodah House** ✻, an excellent reconstruction of a 19th-century Arabian home, which today doubles as a heritage museum. Almost next door lies the **Islamic Museum** ✦✦✦, which illustrates the cultural history of Islam through an impressive collection of antiques, manuscripts, and artifacts. While in Heritage Square, you can also visit the peaceful **Al Midfaa House** and the austere **Sharjah Fort** (Al Hisn). See p. 143.

Your final stop in Heritage Square is the **Sharjah Art Museum** ✦✦, which is the largest art museum in the Arabian Gulf. It contains the Sharjah ruler's outstanding personal art collection and well as frequently changing exhibits. See p. 144.

>
> **TAKE A BREAK**
> Grab a drink and perhaps a snack at the **Arts Cafe,** located in front of the Sharjah Arts Museum in what's called the Arts Area. There are a number of galleries, workshops, and studios surrounding the cafe.

Now you're refreshed from your time at the Arts Cafe and are ready to continue your tour of this cultural capital. Make your way to the **Sharjah Archaeological Museum** ✦✦, not far from Heritage Square. This creative museum unveils the history of human progress across the Arabian Peninsula, including the emirate's earliest archaeological finds. See p. 144.

Before you finish your museum tour, there's one more you need to see. The **Sharjah Natural History Museum** ✦✦ highlights the emirate's unique ecology. There are five fascinating exhibition halls to explore. The site incorporates the Desert Park, a breeding center for animals native to the Arabian Peninsula, which children in particular love. See p. 144.

3 An Architecture Tour of Dubai

❶: Jumeirah Mosque ✦✦

Begin your architectural tour in Jumeirah by first visiting the **Jumeirah Mosque.** This beautiful example of modern Islamic architecture is open to non-Muslim visitors on Sunday and Thursday mornings (and sometimes more days) at 10am. See p. 101.

❷: Burj al Arab ✦✦ & Jumeirah Beach Hotel ✦✦✦

Continue your tour by traveling a few kilometers on the Jumeirah Beach Road to the **Burj al Arab** and **Jumeirah Beach Hotel,** two famous resorts located next to each other. From the shore, the sail-shape Burj Al Arab (built on a small man-made island) towers over the wave-shape Jumeirah Beach Hotel just in front, creating a marvelous architectural image over the sea. See p. 68 and 71.

❸: Madinat Jumeirah ✦✦

Within walking distance of the Burj Al Arab and Jumeirah Beach Hotel lies **Madinat Jumeirah,** the extravagant hotel and entertainment complex. Recently built, Madinat Jumeirah is an idyllic recreation of traditional Gulf architecture, designed to resemble an ancient Arabian citadel. Walk along the meandering pathways of the Souk Madinat Jumeirah, take a boat along one of the picturesque waterways, and view Madinat Jumeirah's two grand palace hotels and courtyard summer houses. See p. 112.

>
> **TAKE A BREAK**
> For lunch, select one of the lovely restaurants or cafes in the Souk Madinat Jumeirah. My favorite is the fun and casual **Noodle House.** ✆ 4/ 366-6730.

Dubai for Families & Architecture Buffs

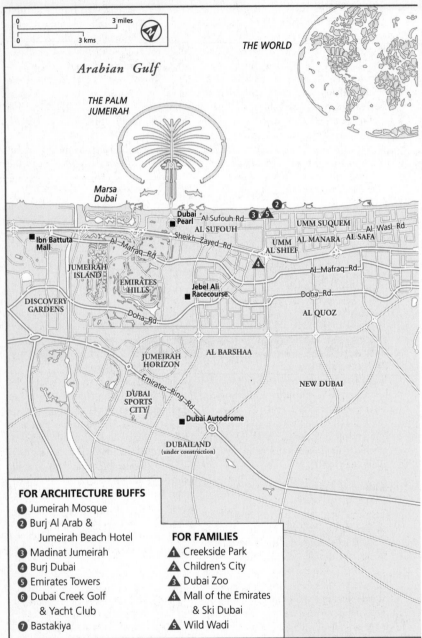

0   3 miles

0   3 kms

THE WORLD

Arabian Gulf

THE PALM
JUMEIRAH

Marsa
Dubai

Dubai
Pearl   Al Sufouh Rd.

AL SUFOUH

Ibn Battuta
Mall

Al-Mafraq-Rd.

Sheikh-Zayed-Rd.

UMM SUQUEM

Al Wasl Rd.

UMM
AL SHIEF

AL MANARA   AL SAFA

JUMEIRAH
ISLAND

EMIRATES
HILLS

Jebel Ali
Racecourse

Al-Mafraq-Rd.

DISCOVERY
GARDENS

Doha-Rd.

Doha-Rd.

AL QUOZ

JUMEIRAH
HORIZON

AL BARSHAA

Emirates-Ring-Rd.

NEW DUBAI

DUBAI
SPORTS
CITY

Dubai Autodrome

DUBAILAND
(under construction)

FOR ARCHITECTURE BUFFS

1. Jumeirah Mosque
2. Burj Al Arab &
   Jumeirah Beach Hotel
3. Madinat Jumeirah
4. Burj Dubai
5. Emirates Towers
6. Dubai Creek Golf
   & Yacht Club
7. Bastakiya

FOR FAMILIES

1. Creekside Park
2. Children's City
3. Dubai Zoo
4. Mall of the Emirates
   & Ski Dubai
5. Wild Wadi

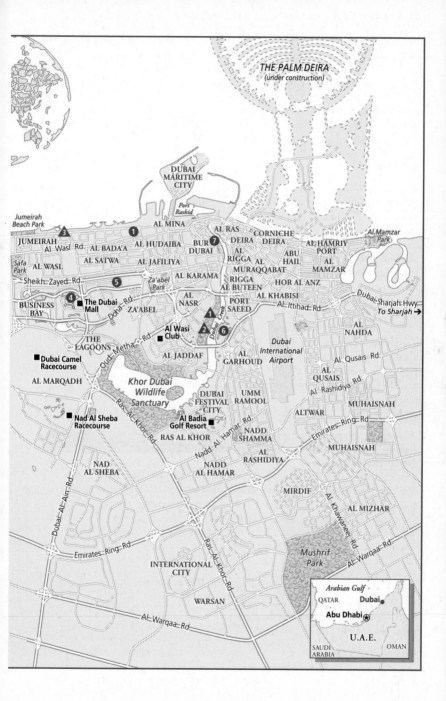

THE PALM DEIRA
(under construction)

Jumeirah
Beach Park

DUBAI
MARITIME
CITY

Port
Rashid

AL MINA

AL RAS
DEIRA

CORNICHE
DEIRA

Al Mamzar
Park

JUMEIRAH

Al Wasl Rd.

AL BADA'A

AL HUDAIBA

BUR
DUBAI

AL
RIGGA

ABU
HAIL

AL HAMRIY
PORT

Safa
Park

AL WASL

AL SATWA

AL JAFILIYA

AL
MURAQQABAT

AL
MAMZAR

Sheikh Zayed Rd.

AL KARAMA

RIGGA
AL BUTEEN

HOR AL ANZ

Za'abel
Park

AL KHABISI

Dubai-Sharjah Hwy

BUSINESS
BAY

The Dubai
Mall

Doha Rd.

AL
NASR

PORT
SAEED

AL-Ittihad-Rd.

To Sharjah →

ZA'ABEL

Al Wasi
Club

Dubai Creek

AL
NAHDA

THE
LAGOONS

Oud Metha Rd.

AL JADDAF

AL
GARHOUD

Dubai
International
Airport

AL
QUSAIS

Al Qusais Rd.

Dubai Camel
Racecourse

AL MARQADH

Khor Dubai
Wildlife
Sanctuary

DUBAI
FESTIVAL
CITY

UMM
RAMOOL

Al Rashidiya Rd.

ALTWAR

MUHAISNAH

Nad Al Sheba
Racecourse

Ras AL Khor Rd.

Al Badia
Golf Resort

RAS AL KHOR

Nadd Al Hamar Rd.

NADD
SHAMMA

Emirates-Ring-Rd.

MUHAISNAH

NAD
AL SHEBA

NADD
AL HAMAR

AL
RASHIDIYA

MIRDIF

Al Khawaneej-Rd.

AL MIZHAR

Dubai-Al-Ain-Rd.

Emirates-Ring-Rd.

Ras-AL-Khor-Rd.

INTERNATIONAL
CITY

Mushrif
Park

Al-Warqaa-Rd.

WARSAN

AL-Warqaa-Rd.

Arabian Gulf

QATAR

Dubai

Abu Dhabi

U.A.E.

SAUDI
ARABIA

OMAN

❹: Burj Dubai ❀❀❀

Now make your way back toward the city center on Sheikh Zayed Road. Just to the west of Interchange 1, the world's tallest building emerges from the sand. The **Burj Dubai** is predicted to have a final height of more than 800m (2,625 ft.), and is surrounded by a giant residential and business complex called Downtown Burj Dubai. See p. 14.

❺: Emirates Towers ❀❀❀

Continuing a bit farther on Sheikh Zayed Road, you will come to the twin **Emirates Towers.** At the time of their construction in 2000, they were taller than any buildings in Europe and the Middle East. Visit the incredible atrium lobby of the Emirates Towers hotel, and take a walk along the shopping Boulevard. See p. 113.

Just next to Emirates Towers on Sheikh Zayed Road stands the **World Trade Centre,** Dubai's first high-rise built in 1979. Take a look from here back along Sheikh Zayed Road, where skyscrapers today line both sides of the highway as far as the eye can see.

❻: Dubai Creek Golf & Yacht Club ❀

Next, cross the Dubai Creek at Garhoud Bridge to reach the **Dubai Creek Golf and Yacht Club.** The lush creek-side complex features a waterfront golf course, marina, and boardwalk. The distinctive clubhouse is a Dubai landmark, designed to resemble sailing dhow boats. See p. 105.

> **TAKE A BREAK**
> By now it's getting late in the day, and a beautiful spot for watching the sunset is the **Boardwalk,** situated on the waterfront of the Dubai Creek Golf and Yacht Club. Come for a drink, a snack, or even a full meal.

❼: Bastakiya ❀❀

Now that you're in Deira, finish your architecture tour with one more sight that you may not yet have visited: **Bastakiya.** This historical quarter represents Dubai in its pre-oil days, an idyllic Gulf neighborhood with traditional courtyard houses, wind towers, and mosques. See p. 100.

4 Dubai for Families

❶: Creekside Park ❀❀

Start the day at Creekside Park, a peaceful waterfront recreational area with playgrounds, picnic spots, and themed gardens. There's a minitrain that winds its way around the perimeter, and a cable car that rides over the shoreline at 30m (98 ft.) in the air. You can walk, jog, bicycle, or even rollerblade along a 2.5km (1.5-mile) pathway. Families often spread out blankets across the park's many open spaces, with some barbecuing on weekends. See p. 103.

❷: Children's City ❀❀

You'll find Children's City in Creekside Park. Bring the kids here to combine learning with fun. Children 2 to 15 will learn about the human body at the Discovery Space, explore the night skies in the 100-seat Planetarium, play with modern communication devices in the Computer Gallery, and discover the history of Dubai in the Way We Live. This is a wonderful place to meet children from all over the world who are living in and visiting Dubai. See p. 102.

❸: Dubai Zoo ❀

Although somewhat small and overcrowded, this old-fashioned zoo is a fun place for kids. There are about 200 species of mammals, including lions, tigers, bears, monkeys, giraffes, and deer, as well as exotic birds, reptiles, and fish. Be sure to check out the rare chimpanzee and Arabian wildcat. See p. 102.

❹: Mall of the Emirates & Ski Dubai ★★★

Mall of the Emirates is one of Dubai's best family destinations, and you could easily spend a day here. It includes **Ski Dubai,** where families can ski, snowboard, sled, or even throw snowballs. The **Magic Planet** offers a huge selection of rides and games, including a bowling alley and climbing wall for older kids as well as a supervised play area and day care for tinier tots. Mall of the Emirates also houses the **Cinestar Cinema** and the **Dubai Community Theater and Arts Center,** where children's shows are often performed. See p. 116 and 105.

TAKE A BREAK
It's time to take a break from the slopes, warm up, and fill your belly. **St. Moritz Cafe** is a casual restaurant that resembles a Swiss chalet and faces the snow-filled slopes of Ski Dubai through giant windows. The extensive menu has lots of options for kids. Mall of the Emirates. (✆ 4/409-4000.

❺: Wild Wadi ★★★

With 30 thrilling rides and attractions, Wild Wadi is one of Dubai's most fun destinations. In addition to rides for the big kids, it includes a family play area with games for small children. See p. 102.

5

Where to Stay

Dubai has one of the world's fastest-growing hotel scenes of any major city. If the emirate's plans to become a global tourism hub continue to take hold—and they probably will—Dubai is expected to expand from roughly six million annual visitors today to more than 15 million within a decade. There are already 40,000 hotel rooms in Dubai, with another 54 hotels set to open in 2008, but authorities envision the need to construct an additional 70,000 to 80,000 hotel rooms to meet this demand. This helps explain the construction cranes in almost every corner of the city, as well as on the imaginative Palm Islands. Dubai is a city literally reaching into the sky and across the sea.

Most of the hotels in this chapter are officially designated with four or five stars, which should not be confused with the zero- to three-star scale that we use. Many of the world's top name hotels are here, and some with multiple locations: Ritz-Carlton, Marriott, Raffles, Hyatt, Hilton, Fairmont, Sheraton, Sofitel, and One&Only, to name a few. The Jumeirah Group, overseen by Dubai's royal family, boasts some of Dubai's best-known resorts and hotels. These include the iconic Burj al Arab, which is so big it almost eclipses the horizon, the Jumeirah Beach Hotel, Emirates Towers, and the Arabian palace hotels inside Madinat Jumeirah. Jumeirah Group also owns the desert oasis resort, Bab Al Shams, whose only real competition is Al Maha Desert Resort & Spa. A visit to either is like a trip to heaven.

As if the so-called "seven star" Burj al Arab were not already sufficiently over-the-top, Dubai is building the world's largest hotel—Asia-Asia—which, with 6,500 rooms, will substantially surpass the current room record holder MGM Las Vegas. Asia-Asia will be the centerpiece of a future resort called Bawadi, a long luxury strip with 31 hotels resembling Egyptian palaces, Hollywood, the U.K. Parliament, and apparently even the moon. These hotels will begin to open in 2010. Perhaps one day Las Vegas will be looking to Dubai for inspiration, rather than the other way around.

Most all of Dubai's entertainment revolves around the hotel scene. Because hotels are uniquely permitted to hold liquor licenses, the majority of the city's top restaurants and virtually all bars and nightclubs lie in hotels. The action is non-stop, except during Ramadan, when all Muslims are required to fast by day and non-Muslims are asked to be respectful of the holy month. Live music and dancing are not allowed during this period, so many bars and most clubs shut down temporarily. Eating during the day and drinking often still takes place in hotels during Ramadan, but discreetly. Year-round, visitors to Dubai are technically not allowed to drink outside the hotel they are visiting unless they get a liquor permit.

The most extravagant, and expensive, hotels in Dubai are the international resorts lining Jumeirah Beach, which stretches for miles along the Gulf. The beaches here are beautiful—soft golden sand fronts a blue-green sea, with water as warm as the Caribbean. These world-class resorts offer amenities equal to the best establishments in the world. Most of them have spas, health clubs, sports activities, and beach centers with extensive watersports, as well as wide-ranging dining and entertainment options. They are the reason one magazine characterized Dubai as "the new Ibiza." And, just off the Palm Jumeirah island, the famous *Queen Elizabeth 2* ocean liner, purchased for $100 million by a Dubai-based company in early 2008, will open as a hotel with entertainment and dining attractions in 2009.

The hotels lining Sheikh Zayed Road are also very impressive. To lure travelers and ensure that Dubai is internationally recognized as the region's tourist capital, the sleek accommodations lining Dubai's main thoroughfare compete for design, luxury, service, and amenities. Dubai's twin towers, known as Emirates Towers, first set the stage for the road's surrounding architectural splendor, and today the hotels and other high-rises spanning the skyline form an urban desert wonder. Business travelers tend to stay on Sheikh Zayed Road, but these hotels also have extensive services for visitors who are on holiday, and they lie just minutes away from Jumeirah Beach and the best sights of old Dubai.

The old town consists of Deira and Bur Dubai. It's not as glitzy as Jumeirah Beach or Sheikh Zayed Road, but it has much more local flavor. The best hotels here overlook Dubai Creek, but they're also the most expensive in the area. For travelers seeking more moderate accommodations, Deira and Bur Dubai offer the city's least expensive options. We've selected the best of them in this chapter,

especially those that lie within easy walking distance of key cultural sights. Be cautious when choosing other hotels in the area—some are used for prostitution and are simply not recommended.

Just as the guests to Dubai's hotels seem to come from every corner of the globe, so too does the staff. Service has improved markedly, but limited English-speaking abilities and lack of familiarity with Western expectations among some staffs occasionally means that service isn't quite up to par with other tourist hubs. This is more the case with inexpensive hotels than with the expensive, international ones. As you might expect, you'll find a significant difference between the attention you'll receive at a five-star hotel and at one more modest in quality and price.

Dubai hotels are expensive and unfortunately getting more so, especially for U.S. travelers who face falling dollar value in currency exchanges. Hotel prices tend to drop 30% to 40% in summer (late June to Aug), but Dubai is so hot then that you may feel like you should be the one paid to stay during those months. There are occasionally discounts around some of the festival periods, as well. Europeans and other travelers are likely to find the prices a little more manageable, but still high. I strongly suggest you check Internet promotional rates before booking. Most hotels will quote rates in dirhams but can easily convert that to dollars, pounds, or euros. Foreign credit cards are widely accepted. All rates are subject to a 10% municipality fee and 10% service charge.

As of January 15, 2008, smoking is regulated in all public places in Dubai and only allowed in designated areas and rooms.

1 Deira & Bur Dubai

VERY EXPENSIVE

Park Hyatt ★★ The understated Moorish design and inspiring landscape of the Park Hyatt make this a peaceful oasis in the heart of the city. Located within the grounds of the Dubai Creek Golf and Yacht Club, the low-rise waterfront hotel offers guests special golf privileges, access to private charter yachts, and entry to the exclusive day spa. All of the richly appointed guest rooms have flatscreen TVs, large bathrooms with separate deep-soaking tubs and rain showers, and terraces with views of the creek. Eight concept spa rooms feature in-room massage tables, beauty treatment chairs, and steam rooms. In addition to the hotel's fine-dining restaurants, including **Café Arabesque** (p. 78) offering specialties from the Levant and **Traiteur** (p. 76) serving sophisticated European cuisine, the Park Hyatt Terrace Lounge boasts one of Dubai's best sunset-viewing spots, with the creek directly in front and the city skyline in the background. This is Dubai's most beautiful hotel situated in the city center, but the service on occasion falls short of the hotel's five-star status.

Dubai Creek Golf and Yacht Club, P.O. Box 2822, Dubai. ✆ **4/602-1234.** Fax 4/602-1235. www.dubai.park. hyatt.com. 225 units. AED 2,550 ($695/£352) and up double. AE, DC, MC, V. **Amenities:** 4 restaurants; terrace lounge; pastry shop; large outdoor pool; spa; fitness center; 18-hole golf course and floodlit driving range; private yacht charters available; multilingual concierge; airport limousine service; business center; laundry service; dry cleaning; currency exchange. *In room:* A/C, TV, DVD, CD, MP3 player, high-speed Internet, minibar, hair dryer, safe.

EXPENSIVE

Grand Hyatt Dubai 🎯🎯 *(Kids)*   This city resort and conference center towering over Dubai Creek sits on 15 hectares (37 acres) of landscaped gardens. The extraordinary foliage-filled lobby is designed as though underwater, and you'll see the bottom of a giant dhow if you look up to the ceiling. Outside, the lush landscape includes artificial lakes, fountains, and tropical birds roaming the gardens. The hotel's 674 rooms and suites are generously appointed with quality fabrics and soft natural tones, and offer marble bathrooms with separate showers and tubs. Guests staying in the Grand Club enjoy airport transfers, complimentary breakfast, and evening cocktails. This is a great place for those looking to keep in shape, with an extensive spa, tennis center with professional instructors, squash courts, jogging track, and sprawling outdoor and indoor pools. Most of the restaurants, including the Singaporean **Peppercrab** (p. 78), are located inside the stunning atrium lobby and offer open kitchens and alfresco dining. There's also a kids' club with daytime activities for children up to 12.

Al Qutaeyat Rd., P.O. Box 7978, Dubai. ✆ **4/317-1234.** Fax 4/317-1235. www.dubai.grand.hyatt.com. 674 units. AED 2,250 ($613/£310) and up double. AE, DC, MC, V. **Amenities:** 8 restaurants; cafe; 2 bars; disco; 3 outdoor pools (including kids' pool) and 1 indoor lap pool; spa w/treatment rooms, relaxation area, and 24-hr. fitness center; 2 squash courts; tennis center w/4 courts; jogging track; kids' club; concierge; car rental; business center; shops; babysitting; laundry service; dry cleaning; executive floors. *In room:* A/C, TV, high-speed Internet, minibar, hair dryer, safe.

Hilton Dubai Creek 🎯🎯   Not what you'd expect from a Hilton—that's the best way to describe the minimalist styling of this creek-side establishment, designed in steel and glass by renowned architect Carlos Ott. Public spaces display beechwood and soft leather-upholstered furniture, rich wool carpets, and extensive use of chrome and glass. The sleek guest rooms are ultra-modern but may lack a sense of warmth for some, decorated in neutral tones with floor-to-ceiling windows and generous use of black and gray marble. It's hard not to love the luxurious bathrooms, offering a separate shower and sunken bathtub, glass-top sink, and amenities by Crabtree & Evelyn. A "bathmaster" will even come draw you a themed bath upon request. All of the rooms have views of the creek, and the best are the "panorama rooms" with excellent vistas and private Jacuzzis. Although popular with business travelers, this hotel is also a strategic location for tourists exploring Dubai's old town and the Gold Souk. One of the city's top restaurants, run by acclaimed chef Gordon Ramsay (of TV's *Hell's Kitchen* fame), **Verre** (p. 76), is here, as is the less expensive **Glasshouse** (p. 79).

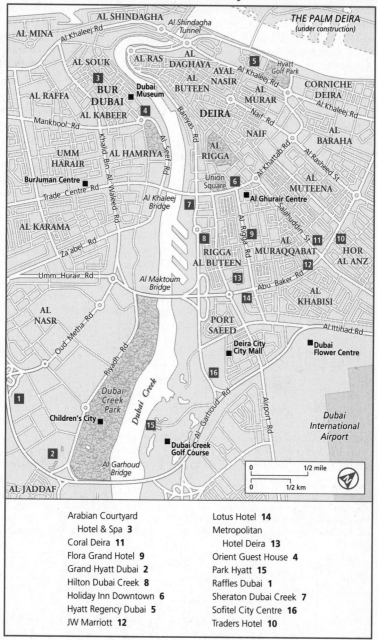

Where to Stay in Deira & Bur Dubai

Arabian Courtyard
  Hotel & Spa **3**
Coral Deira **11**
Flora Grand Hotel **9**
Grand Hyatt Dubai **2**
Hilton Dubai Creek **8**
Holiday Inn Downtown **6**
Hyatt Regency Dubai **5**
JW Marriott **12**

Lotus Hotel **14**
Metropolitan
  Hotel Deira **13**
Orient Guest House **4**
Park Hyatt **15**
Raffles Dubai **1**
Sheraton Dubai Creek **7**
Sofitel City Centre **16**
Traders Hotel **10**

Hotel guests have access to the Hilton Jumeirah's beach club, located about 25 minutes away.

Benyas Rd., P.O. Box 33398, Dubai. ⓒ **4/227-1111.** Fax 4/227-1112. www1.hilton.com. 154 units. AED 1,550 ($422/£214) and up double. AE, DC, MC, V. **Amenities:** 2 restaurants; 2 bars; rooftop pool; spa; fitness center; transfer to beach club; concierge; car rental; business center; salon; laundry service; dry cleaning; executive level rooms. *In room:* A/C, interactive TV w/Internet, DVD upon request, high-speed Internet, minibar, safe.

Hyatt Regency Dubai ⓐ   Polished marble floors dotted with potted palm trees and contemporary furniture fill the lobby of the completely refurbished Hyatt Regency. Guest rooms are designed with hardwoods, marble, and earth tones, and bathrooms offer glass mosaic accents. The self-contained hotel has its own shops, men's and women's hairdressers, and banking facilities, among many other services. There's a 9-hole pitch-and-put golf course, a fitness club, and even an ice-skating rink. The outstanding **Shahrzad** restaurant (p. 81), serving traditional Persian food, is located here, along with the revolving Al Dawaar international restaurant. There are Japanese and Italian options, as well, and a karaoke bar and disco. Service throughout the hotel is professional, if not entirely personalized. Guests can walk from here to the Gold Souk. Special packages are typically available online.

Al Khaleej Rd., P.O. Box 5588, Dubai. ⓒ **4/209-1234.** Fax 4/209-1235. www.dubai.regency.hyatt.com. 414 units. AED 1,500 ($409/£207) and up double. AE, DC, MC, V. **Amenities:** 5 restaurants; 5 bars; outdoor pool; Club Olympus health club; tennis courts; squash courts; ice-skating rink; concierge; car rental; business center; ATM; shops; babysitting; laundry service; dry cleaning. *In room:* A/C, TV, high-speed Internet, minibar, safe.

JW Marriott ⓐ *(Kids*   This is one of Dubai's largest hotels in the city center, and the only reason not to stay here—besides perhaps preferring a less expensive option—is if you prefer more local flavor. This family-friendly JW Marriott caters to business travelers and is similar to upscale JW Marriott hotels found elsewhere. Spacious guest rooms have elegant furnishings, including plush sitting areas and beds with down comforters and custom duvets. Luxurious bathrooms include robes and separate showers and tubs. East-facing rooms look out to the city, while others have a view of the hotel's town square (an indoor, parklike setting). Griffins Health Club offers massages, a steam room and plunge pools, a fitness center with on-hand trainers, and a squash court. The diversity of dining options here is great: JW Steakhouse serves some of the best steaks in town, and the casual Italian restaurant, Cucina, is a nice change of pace. For something with a Middle Eastern feel, head to the pool for *shisha* under the stars and a nice view of the city. Service here is outstanding.

Abu Baker Al Siddique Rd. (next to Hamarain Shopping Center), P.O. Box 16590, Dubai. ⓒ **4/262-4444.** Fax 4/262-6264. www.marriott.com. 351 units. AED 2,450 ($668/£338) and up double. AE, DC, MC, V. **Amenities:** 10 restaurants and bars; rooftop pool; fitness center; spa; Jacuzzi; squash court; sauna and steam room; game room; concierge; business center; ATM; babysitting; laundry service; dry cleaning; executive floors. *In room:* A/C, TV, highspeed Internet, minibar, hair dryer, iron, safe.

Raffles Dubai ⓐ   This pyramid-shape hotel in Wafi City is one of the newest properties in Dubai, and merges Asian style (hanging lanterns, a large water feature) with an Egyptian aesthetic (hieroglyphic-carved columns). Rooms are on the larger scale, with the smallest (Grand State rooms) covering more than 70 sq. m (753 sq. ft.), each with a private balcony with a view of the city skyline. Rooms have a residential feel, with lots of mirrors and closet space, and extras such as an espresso machine, free Wi-Fi, a dressing room, a flatscreen TV, and an iPod docking station; suites come with a Jacuzzi and bathroom TV, too. Raffles Inc suites are catered to business travelers and include access to a private lounge.

Dining options range from the all-day international and Arabic restaurant Azure to **Fire & Ice,** the hotel's signature restaurant that focuses on meat, seafood, and wine pairings. After-hours, head to the Balinese-inspired Crossroads Cocktail Bar (if the weather's nice, you can step out to the garden and lounge under a gazebo), which opens to the hotel's 1-hectare (2½-acre) botanical garden, or the New Asia Bar & Club/China Moon Champagne Bar, located at the top of the pyramid, where you can get creative cocktails, quality cigars, and a great view of the city. There's also a library, which carries more than 15,000 books, and the Amrita Spa.

Though the hotel is adjoined to the **Wafi City** (p. 116), the area seems a bit quiet at night, and catching a cab can require a bit of a wait.

Sheikh Rashid Rd., Wafi City. ✆ 4/324-8888. Fax 4/324-6000. www.dubai.raffles.com. 248 units. AED 1,750 ($477/£241) and up double. AE, DISC, MC, V. Basement parking. **Amenities:** 8 restaurants; 3 bars; pool; gym; spa; concierge; car/limo transfer; business center; Wi-Fi; salon; 24-hr. room service; babysitting; same-day laundry and valet; executive-level rooms; nonsmoking rooms; 24-hr. on-call doctor; library. *In room:* A/C, satellite TV, Wi-Fi, iPod docking station, minibar, espresso machine, safe, personal butler service (Grand State rooms).

Sheraton Dubai Creek ✿   This Sheraton overlooks Dubai Creek and is an excellent choice for travelers wanting to be based near Dubai's older neighborhoods. Guests can walk from here to the Gold and Spice souks, and the tourism office lies just next door. The hotel is more appealing on the inside than on the outside, so don't judge it by the somewhat cold exterior. The atrium lobby succeeds in creating a sense of serenity, and the staff is particularly good for such a large hotel. Rooms enjoy city or creek views, Japanese-style furnishings with soft coloring, and "sweet sleeper beds," which Sheraton says it guarantees for comfort and sound sleep. Executive "Tower" rooms have private butler service. The gym and pool are small, but the restaurants are excellent, including Japanese, Italian, Indian, and international options. The hotel offers sit-down check-in, a nice personal touch.

Baniyas St., P.O. Box 4250, Dubai. ✆ 4/228-1111. Fax 4/221-3468. www.sheraton.com/dubai. 414 units. AED 1,650 ($450/£228) and up double. AE, DC, MC, V. **Amenities:** 5 restaurants; 2 bars; outdoor pool; kids' pool; lighted tennis court; health club w/sauna, steam room, and massage treatments; fitness center; concierge; business center; laundry service; dry cleaning; executive floors. *In room:* A/C, TV, high-speed Internet, minibar, safe.

Sofitel City Centre   This reputable French chain hotel lies across the street from the Dubai Creek Golf and Yacht Club and is attached to the Deira City Centre shopping complex, which has 250 shops, a bowling alley, and cinema. Although not Dubai's newest mall, City Centre remains one of the most popular. The Sofitel is modest in design, offering quality guest rooms with European touches. There's a first-rate French restaurant, as well as a lively English pub and a stylish martini lounge. Le Café offers homemade chocolates and pastries. The clientele here tends to be European, especially French. Guests have access to a free airport shuttle. The Sofitel is a bit overpriced for what you get, but check the Internet for occasional special rates.

Deira City Center, P.O. Box 61871, Dubai. ✆ 4/294-1222. Fax 4/295-4444. www.sofitel.com. 318 units. AED 2,000 ($545/£276) and up double. AE, DC, MC, V. **Amenities:** 2 restaurants; cafe; 3 bars; outdoor pool; fitness center; concierge; business center; laundry service; dry cleaning. *In room:* A/C, TV, high-speed Internet, minibar, safe.

MODERATE

Arabian Courtyard Hotel & Spa ✿✿   Located across the street from the Dubai Museum, this is one of the city's best value four-star hotels. The decor is distinctly Arabian, and you'll feel more in the Middle East here than at many of Dubai's ultra-modern resorts. Stunning chandeliers hang from the ceiling of the nine-story atrium lobby, which is decorated with white marble, dark wood, and stone. Despite its traditional touches, the Arabian Courtyard is full of modern conveniences, such as a full-service spa, fitness center, and pool. Cozy rooms offer either one queen-size or two twin beds, small marble bathrooms with robes, dark wood furnishings, and prints of idyllic Arabian scenes. Guests receive a complimentary fruit basket and 10-minute massage in the spa. The staff goes out of its way to be helpful.

Al Fahid St. (opposite Dubai Museum), P.O. Box 46500, Dubai. (✆ **4/351-9111.** Fax 4/351-7744. www.arabiancourt yard.com. 173 units. AED 750 ($204/£103) double. AE, DC, MC, V. **Amenities:** 4 restaurants; bar; small outdoor pool; spa; fitness center; business center; tour desk; car rental; gift shop; salon; babysitting; laundry service; dry cleaning; executive level rooms. *In room:* A/C, TV, high-speed Internet, minibar, coffeemaker, hair dryer, iron, safe.

Coral Deira

One of the city's least expensive five-star hotels, the Coral Deira is located near the busy Clock Tower roundabout. Themed guest rooms have light wood furnishings, simple tile bathrooms, and nice touches such as satellite TV and tea/coffeemakers. Guests receive complimentary access to the beach facilities at the sister Coral Beach Resort in Sharjah (p. 145), although that's about 30 minutes away. The hotel's signature restaurant offers theme nights focusing on different world cuisines. The friendly staff will help make arrangements for city tours, desert safaris, and dhow cruises. The Coral Deira is less expensive than other five-star hotels because of its location and no-alcohol policy, and guests tend to be more conservative here than at some other Dubai hotels.

Al Muraqabbat St. (at Abu Baker St.), P.O. Box 82999, Dubai. (✆ **4/224-8587.** Fax 4/221-7033. www.coral-international. com. 140 units. AED 1,000 ($272/£138) double. AE, DC, MC, V. **Amenities:** 3 restaurants; rooftop pool; spa; fitness center; tour desk; business center; gift shop; women's salon; babysitting; laundry service; dry cleaning; executive level rooms. *In room:* A/C, TV, high-speed Internet, minibar, coffeemaker, hair dryer, safe.

Flora Grand Hotel

A comfortable midrange hotel in the heart of Deira, the Flora Grand offers a notable array of amenities including a rooftop pool, full-service spa and health club, and terrace restaurant. Glass elevators leading to the rooms shoot up the atrium lobby, tropically decorated with palm trees and a bubbling rock fountain. Guest rooms are comfortable but unremarkable, and include standards and deluxe and royal suites. The Flora Grand Spa offers massages ranging from Swedish and Balinese to Indian and hot stone, in addition to "body coffee" treatments meant to invigorate and detoxify the body. The hotel is often used by airline crews.

Al Rigga Rd., P.O. Box 120328, Dubai. (✆ **4/223-3344.** Fax 4/222-2880. www.florahospitality.com. 200 units. AED 1,000 ($272/£138) double. AE, MC, V. **Amenities:** 3 restaurants; coffee shop; outdoor pool; spa; fitness center; sauna and steam room; travel desk; car rental; concierge; business center; gift shop; salon; babysitting; laundry service. *In room:* A/C, TV, minibar, safe.

Holiday Inn Downtown ⊛

Expect friendly service and a comfortable room at this downtown Holiday Inn, which provides free transportation to the public beach as well as airport transfers. Guest rooms have one king-size or two twin beds, and are decorated in a simple classic style with pinstripe bedspreads and generic artwork. Some are quite dark, unfortunately. There's a small rooftop pool, fitness center, and bistro, as well as a lobby cafe and bar that offers *shisha* at night. The friendly tour desk will assist you with your Dubai itinerary. Kids eat free in the hotel's restaurants. There's nothing particularly unique about staying at the Holiday Inn, but it's a good, reputable hotel.

Al Rigga St., Dubai. (✆ **4/228-8889.** Fax 4/228-0033. www.ichotelsgroup.com. 140 units. AED 1,100 ($300/£152) and up double. AE, DC, MC, V. **Amenities:** 2 restaurants; 2 bars; rooftop pool; sauna; steam room; fitness center; tour desk; business center; salon; babysitting; laundry service; dry cleaning; executive level rooms. *In room:* A/C, TV, high-speed Internet, minibar, hair dryer, safe.

Lotus Hotel   Lotus Hotel is one of the best moderately priced options in the city—a good choice for budget-minded travelers wishing to explore Dubai's old city. The modern guest rooms are perfectly comfortable but on the small side, with satellite TVs and high-speed Internet access. The small marble lobby leads to a 24-hour international restaurant and bar, and there's a second restaurant serving Indian cuisine. Leisure activities include a rooftop pool, gymnasium, and Jacuzzi, as well as complimentary transfer to the beach. Service here is generally friendly and efficient.

Rigga Rd., P.O. Box 63833, Dubai. ✆ 4/227-8888. Fax 4/228-0840. www.lotus-hospitality.com. 102 units. AED 825 ($225/£114) double. AE, DC, MC, V. **Amenities:** 2 restaurants, lounge; outdoor pool; Jacuzzi; complimentary transport to beach; business services; babysitting; laundry service. *In room:* A/C, TV, high-speed Internet, minibar, hair dryer, safe.

Metropolitan Hotel Deira   A reasonable choice for travelers looking for a moderately priced option in Dubai, the Metropolitan Hotel lies near a range of good-value neighborhood restaurants and bars. Rooms are comfortable but a bit dated in decor, and service is reliable if unmemorable. Superior rooms feature a king-size or two queen-size beds as well as two easy chairs; deluxe rooms add to that a complimentary bottle of wine, mineral water, and tea or coffee in the lounge. The hotel is best known for its traditional Irish pub, Dublin Arms, which serves Guinness by the pint and has billiards and a big-screen TV. The comfortable hotel is decorated in classic English style and tends to fill with fun-loving British travelers. Free transfers to the beach and Deira City Centre are offered. There's also a small rooftop pool and sun deck.

Al Maktoum Rd. (next to Clock Tower roundabout), P.O. Box 33214, Dubai. ✆ 4/295-9171. Fax 4/295-9091. www.habtoorhotels.com. 135 units. AED 600 ($163/£83) and up double. AE, DC, MC, V. **Amenities:** 2 restaurants; 2 bars; small outdoor pool and sun deck; fitness center; sauna; business services; salon; laundry service. *In room:* A/C, TV, minibar, hair dryer, safe.

Orient Guest House ★★ *(Finds*   Located at the entrance to the Bastakiya Heritage area, this boutique hotel in a restored two-story villa opened in 2007. Each of the 10 intimate guest rooms is designed in a traditional Arabian style, most with wood-beam ceilings, four-post queen-size beds, rustic furnishings, and small tile bathrooms. Mumtaz rooms are slightly larger than the Heritage rooms, offering separate seating areas and larger bathrooms. Twenty-four-hour butler service ensures that guests receive individual attention, including fresh fruit daily. Continental or Arabian breakfast is served in the center courtyard, and tea and coffee are available anytime. The lobby has a small gift shop selling candleholders and some antiques. Guests have access to the inn's traditional *majlis* (traditional Arabian meeting room), as well as to facilities (including the spa) at the nearby Arabian Courtyard hotel.

Al Fahidi St., Bastakiya Heritage area, P.O. Box 46500, Dubai. ✆ 4/351-9111. Fax 4/351-7744. www.orientguest house.com. 10 units. AED 900 ($245/£124) and up double. AE, MC, V. **Amenities:** Access to facilities at the Arabian Courtyard Hotel & Spa (above). *In room:* A/C, high-speed Internet, cellphone, hair dryer, safe.

INEXPENSIVE

Traders Hotel   When your sister is the Shangri-La (p. 66), there's bound to be some envy, but Traders, the company's four-star property, has similar style and service at a lower price. Rooms are decorated in the modern aesthetic that's associated with the Shangri-La brand, but they lack the luxurious touches and the space that you'll get in a five-star property. Rooms have either a view of the city or the courtyard; I prefer the city view. Standard (Superior) rooms have either a shower or a bathtub/shower combo; the rooms on the sixth floor have separate bathrooms and showers. Deluxe rooms have extra space and a larger sitting area.

The hotel is across the street from the Hamarain Shopping Centre and a 10-minute walk to the Reef Mall. The Junction serves international and local cuisine, while the Chameleon Bar hosts a live band and a magician on Thursday and Friday nights.

Corner of Abu Baker al Siddique and Salah Al Din roads. © 4/265-9888. Fax 4/265-9777. www.shangri-la.com. 250 units. AED 420 ($114/£60) and up double. Basement parking. AE, DC, MC, V. **Amenities:** 2 restaurants; bar; indoor pool; gym; Jacuzzi; sauna and steam rooms; concierge; limo and car-rental desk; 24-hr. room service; massage; same-day laundry and valet service; executive-level rooms; Wi-Fi; free entrance and transfers to beach club and City Centre mall. *In room:* A/C, TV, fax/printer (in suites), dataport, Internet, minibar, fridge, coffeemaker, hair dryer, iron, safe.

2 Sheikh Zayed Road

VERY EXPENSIVE

Dusit Dubai ⊛⊛   This outstanding Thai hotel is one of Dubai's best, offering sumptuous accommodations and refined service. The blue-glass arched building is easily discernible toward the end of Sheikh Zayed Road, featuring a stunning glass-enclosed atrium lobby bathed in shades of gold and brown. Guest rooms have rich Thai decor and inviting bathrooms with vanity sets and luxurious amenities; many offer impressive views of the Dubai skyline, including the new Burj Dubai. The traditionally dressed staff extends the same level of warm, gracious attention that you would find in the best accommodations in Thailand. The Dusit's signature restaurant, **Benjarong** (p. 85), serves exquisite Royal Thai cuisine. Before or after dinner, consider celebrating with some bubbly at the Champagne Lounge next door. Guests staying in Dusit Club or Grand rooms receive complimentary breakfast, afternoon tea, all-day non-alcoholic drinks, butler service, pressing and laundry services, and limousine airport transfers.

Sheikh Zayed Rd., P.O. Box 23335, Dubai. © 4/343-3333. Fax 4/343-4222. www.dubai.dusit.com. 321 units. AED 2,000 ($545/£276) and up double. AE, DC, MC, V. **Amenities:** 3 restaurants; 3 bars; rooftop pool; fitness center; concierge; business center; shopping arcade; laundry service; dry cleaning; executive level rooms. *In room:* A/C, TV, high-speed Internet, minibar, coffeemaker, safe.

Emirates Towers ⊛⊛⊛   One of a pair of silver high-rises that for a decade were the tallest in Dubai, the iconic Emirates Towers is among the world's top business hotels. High-speed elevators dash up and down the 56-floor building with its buzzing atrium lobby and reflective glass windows, and those who travel to the top will find **Vu's** restaurant and bar (p. 84), which has an unbeatable view of the city. Most of the spacious guest rooms also offer stunning views, and while their decor is not as fashionable as when the hotel opened in 2000, the rooms still offer high-tech luxury. A dedicated women's floor features an all-female staff, amenities tailored for women travelers, and yoga mats and instruction videos. Executive-level rooms have flatscreen TVs, DVD players, and CD and iPod interfaces. The top male spa (p. 120) in the region lies in the hotel, wonderful for de-stressing and rejuvenating after a long trip. The hotel staff is outstanding, treating all guests like VIPs (of which there are many). Emirates Towers connects to the Boulevard shopping arcade, with luxury shops and some of the city's top restaurants and bars. Guests staying here have free access to Wild Wadi water park, and can easily arrange to visit other Jumeirah Group hotels.

Sheikh Zayed Road, P.O. Box 72127, Dubai. © 4/330-0000. Fax 4/330-3030. www.jumeirahemiratestowers.com. 400 units. AED 2,000 ($545/£276) and up double. AE, DC, MC, V. **Amenities:** 15 restaurants, lounges, and bars; outdoor pool; 2 health clubs including Male Spa; concierge; business center; shopping center; laundry service; dry cleaning; executive level rooms; women's floor. *In room:* A/C, TV, high-speed Internet, minibar, safe.

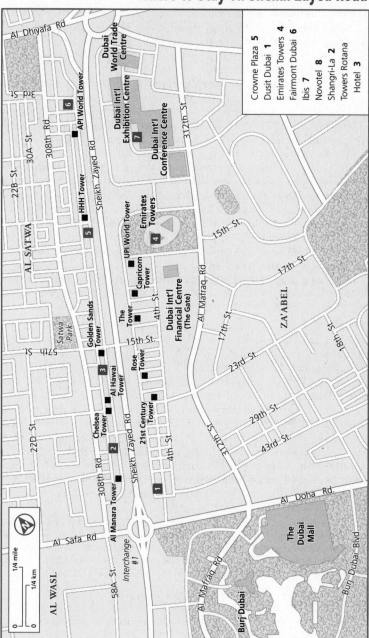

Where to Stay on Sheikh Zayed Road

Crowne Plaza **5**
Dusit Dubai **1**
Emirates Towers **4**
Fairmont Dubai **6**
Ibis **7**
Novotel **8**
Shangri-La **2**
Towers Rotana
Hotel **3**

Al Dhiyafa Rd.

Dubai World Trade Centre

API World Tower

Dubai Int'l Exhibition Centre

Dubai Int'l Conference Centre

3rd St.

30A St.

308th Rd.

22B St.

HHH Tower

Sheikh Zayed Rd.

AL SATWA

UPI World Tower

Emirates Towers

15th St.

17th St.

ZA'ABEL

57th St.

Satwa Park

Golden Sands Tower

Capricorn Tower

The Tower

15th St.

Al Mafraq Rd.

17th St.

17th St.

18th St.

22D St.

Rose Tower

Al Hawai Tower

Chelsea Tower

Dubai Int'l Financial Centre (The Gate)

23rd St.

29th St.

43rd St.

312th St.

Sheikh Zayed Rd.

21st Century Tower

4th St.

4th St.

Al Doha Rd.

58A St.

Al Manara Tower

308th Rd.

Al Safa Rd.

Interchange #1

The Dubai Mall

AL WASL

1/4 mile
1/4 km

Burj Dubai

Al Mafraq Rd.

Al Mafraq Rd.

Burj Dubai Blvd.

Fairmont Dubai ✸✸✸   The Fairmont is popular with business travelers, who can access the convention center across the street without having to walk outside. The 33rd floor houses dedicated meeting space and a dining area. The hotel's interior takes a cue from the nearby Gulf, with wave-inspired decor, a large lobby fountain, and a blue, green, and silver color palette.

Rooms are elegantly appointed with granite floors (the cool touch is welcome during those fiery summers), chaise longues, a neutral but rich color palette, and business amenities such as a writing desk and high-speed Internet; all rooms have panoramic views of the city, and 24-hour technology help and Blackberry checkout are available. Gold rooms, on the 30th and 32nd floors, offer extras such as airport transfers, 24-hour butler service, free Internet, and access to the Gold lounge.

The hotel's 10 dining and entertainment venues include the **Exchange Grill** (p. 84) steakhouse (voted best steakhouse by *Time Out* Dubai) and the multinational **Spectrum on One** (p. 84) signature restaurant. The **Cin Cin** (p. 129) champagne and cocktail lounge is super chic with black and white decor, creative wine displays, and intimate seating areas; the hotel's Cigar Bar is next door. The **Willow Stream spa** (p. 120) and health club offers separate male and female spas, a gym, two outdoor terrace pools, an aerobics studio, and a juice bar; there's an art gallery on the same floor.

Sheikh Zayed Rd., P.O. Box 97555, Dubai. ✆ **4/332-5555**. Fax 4/332-4555. www.fairmont.com. 394 units. AED 2,700 ($736/£372) and up double. AE, DC, MC, V. **Amenities:** 5 restaurants; 5 bars; 2 outdoor pools; separate male and female spa; fitness center; aerobics studio; sauna; concierge; business center; salon; laundry service; dry cleaning; executive floors. *In room:* A/C, TV, high-speed Internet, minibar, safe.

Kempinski ✸ *(Kids)*   With a select number of ski chalets attached to the indoor snow park in the middle of one of the world's hottest deserts, the alpine-themed Kempinski achieves a level of unmatched creativity. For people wishing to ski and shop (and who doesn't want this when in the desert?), there's no better location: The hotel connects to Ski Dubai and Mall of the Emirates, the largest shopping center outside North America. It even offers personal shopping butler service. Tastefully designed rooms and suites, including the innovative "ski chalets" overlooking the man-made ski slope, feature large flatscreen plasma TVs, DVD and multimedia players, dining areas with service pantries, and white marble bathrooms with separate showers and wide tubs. The extensive spa focuses on beauty, wellness, and healing treatments, and there's a "vitamins bar" alongside the fully-equipped fitness center. The family-friendly hotel offers "Kidcierge," a club with special attention and amenities for children. The Kempinski is a bit removed from Dubai's other sights, and you'll need to take a taxi to all destinations outside Mall of the Emirates.

Al Barsha, Sheikh Zayed Rd. (at Mall of the Emirates), P.O. Box 120679, Dubai. ✆ **4/341-0000**. Fax 4/341-4500. www.kempinski-dubai.com. 393 units. AED 1,920 ($523/£265) and up double. AE, DC, MC, V. **Amenities:** 3 restaurants; 3 bars; outdoor pool; lighted tennis court; spa; fitness center; concierge; business center; salon; shopping center; babysitting; laundry service; dry cleaning; shopping butler; indoor snow park. *In room:* A/C, TV, DVD, high-speed Internet, minibar, coffeemaker, safe.

Shangri-La ✸✸✸   The beautiful Shangri-La, which reaches 43 stories into the Dubai skyline, is a favorite of business elites and visiting celebrities. Earth tones and soft curves define the chic guest rooms, which have city or sea views (you can see the World islands), original artwork, a full-size writing desk, lots of closet space, and luxurious bathrooms with deep soaking tubs, rainforest showers, more than ample counter space, and Aigner bath amenities. Guests staying in rooms and suites in the executive Horizon Club enjoy a private club lounge, buffet breakfast, complimentary beverages, purser service, exclusive health club, sun deck, and infinity pool. Whether or not you're staying on an executive floor, the sharply dressed hotel staff provides gracious and personalized service—among the best service you will find at any Dubai hotel. The hotel's fourth floor is dedicated to health and fitness, with an outdoor pool, wonderful spa and fitness center, and tennis court. Among the superb restaurants are international, seafood, Vietnamese, and Moroccan selections, as well as the signature Cantonese restaurant, Shang Palace. When weather permits, the pool hosts ikandy Ultra Lounge from 6pm onward, where you can enjoy cocktails, *shisha,* and music under the stars. The Shangri-La's only drawback is the price, but promotional rates are often available on line.

Sheikh Zayed Rd., P.O. Box 75880, Dubai. ℂ **866/565-5050** in the U.S., or 4/343-8888. Fax 4/343-8886. www.shangri-la.com. 393 units. AED 2,400 ($654/£331) and up double. AE, DC, MC, V. **Amenities:** 5 restaurants; 2 bars; outdoor pool; tennis court; squash court; spa; fitness center; concierge; business center; salon; laundry service; dry cleaning; executive floors. *In room:* A/C, TV, high-speed Internet, minibar, coffeemaker, safe.

EXPENSIVE

Crowne Plaza   As with other hotels along Sheikh Zayed Road, the enormous Crowne Plaza caters to business travelers but is also friendly to holidaygoers. It connects to a shopping center and offers complimentary transfer and entrance to a beach club. The health club includes Nautilus equipment and an aerobics studio, sauna, massage rooms, and two squash courts. Among the numerous dining options are the **Western Steakhouse** (p. 85), festive Polynesian restaurant **Trader Vic's** (p. 85), and **Wagamama** (p. 86) noodle house. There are excellent nightlife options here, as well, including an English-style pub, piano bar with live jazz and blues, and Zinc dance club. Guest rooms range from standard to suites and apartments, and are comfortable if lacking in any particularly memorable character.

Sheikh Zayed Rd., P.O. Box 23215, Dubai. ℂ **4/331-1111.** Fax 4/331-5555. www.crowneplaza.com. 560 units. AED 1,700 ($463/£234) and up double. AE, DC, MC, V. **Amenities:** 12 restaurants and bars; outdoor pool; health club; business center; shopping center; laundry service; dry cleaning; executive floors. *In room:* A/C, TV, high-speed Internet, minibar, coffeemaker, hair dryer, safe.

MODERATE

Towers Rotana Hotel ⓡ   Filling a gleaming skyscraper along the busiest part of Sheikh Zayed Road, the Towers Rotana is principally a business hotel but with tourist-friendly amenities. The inviting health club includes a large rooftop pool, well-equipped fitness center, sauna, steam room, and massage services. The Rotana also houses an excellent international restaurant called Teatro and the popular Long's Bar, which packs most nights with expatriates looking for a good time. Guest rooms are modern but without any special character, and two- and three-bedroom rooms are available for longer stays. Service throughout the hotel is generally friendly and responsive.

Sheikh Zayed Rd., P.O. Box 30430, Dubai. ℂ **4/343-8000.** Fax 4/343-5111. www.rotana.com. 360 units. AED 1,100 ($299/£153) and up double. AE, DC, MC, V. **Amenities:** 3 restaurant; 2 bars; outdoor pool; sauna; steam room; fitness center; car rental; business center; bookstore; salon; babysitting; massage; laundry service; dry cleaning; executive floors. *In room:* A/C, TV, high-speed Internet, minibar, coffeemaker, hair dryer, safe.

INEXPENSIVE

Ibis ⓥⓐⓛⓤⓔ   You can't accuse the Ibis of going overboard on luxury. On the contrary, it offers virtually none. Designed primarily for business travelers, this reliable French chain hotel nevertheless provides comfort, convenience, and value, although service is somewhat limited. Tucked inside the World Trade Centre complex, it's also a smart choice for budget-minded travelers who want to be close to the action but not pay exorbitant hotel rates. Rooms are small but adequate for a good night's rest, with forceful air conditioners and soundproof windows. The small tile bathrooms have showers only. You'll find French and Italian restaurants in the lobby, as well as a wine bar with selections from Italy and the New World. Keep in mind that you won't be able to walk anywhere interesting from here, but the beach, Dubai Creek, and major entertainment destinations are all minutes away by taxi.

World Trade Centre, Sheikh Zayed Rd., P.O. Box 9544, Dubai. © 4/332-4444. Fax 4/331-1220. www.ibishotel.com. 210 units. AED 425 ($116/£59) double. AE, DC, MC, V. Free parking. **Amenities:** 2 restaurants; wine bar; business center; laundry service; dry cleaning; Wi-Fi in lobby. *In room:* A/C, TV.

Novotel ★★ (*Value* Simple yet stylish, this is one of the city's best inexpensive choices. The French-chain hotel lies next to the World Trade Centre, just off Sheikh Zayed Road, and by offering a touch of luxury is a notch above many other Novotel branches. Bright guest rooms are decorated with blonde wood furnishings, a queen-size bed, sofa, table, and chair; the tile bathrooms are on the small side. Guests can take a plunge in the large outdoor pool or prove their physical agility in the well-equipped fitness center. Massages are offered for the lazy, like me. The breakfast buffet here is better and less expensive than those of many Dubai hotels. Service throughout the contemporary-designed Novotel is friendly and impressively efficient.

2nd Zaabeel Rd., P.O. Box 9622, Dubai. © 4/318-7000. Fax 4/318-7100. www.novotel.com. 412 units. AED 600 ($163/£83) and up double. AE, MC, V. **Amenities:** 2 restaurants; bar; outdoor pool; health club; concierge; business center; laundry service; dry cleaning. *In room:* A/C, TV, minibar, hair dryer, safe.

3 Jumeirah & New Dubai

VERY EXPENSIVE

Al Qasr ★★ Also known as the Palace Hotel, Al Qasr is the more formal of Madinat Jumeirah's two grand Arabian-style resorts. Eighteen gold, sculpted horses lead the way along a tree-lined path to the majestic entrance, and the interior is an opulent celebration of Dubai's fabulous wealth. The extraordinarily expensive hotel sits on its own island within the sprawling Madinat Jumeirah complex, and is surrounded by waterways, lush gardens, and the re-creation of ancient Gulf architecture. Spacious guest rooms feature antique-style Arabian furnishings and decorations, luxurious bathrooms with large tubs and rain showers, and sumptuous seating areas. A variety of suites are also available, and about half the rooms face the sea. The resort is connected by water taxi to all areas of Madinat Jumeirah, and there's a private beach offering water activities. Adults will appreciate Talise Spa with techniques ranging from Chinese medicine to Thai and Balinese massage, while children will love Sinbad's Kids Club and Adventure Playground. You will never get bored here.

Madinat Jumeirah, P.O. Box 75157, Dubai. © 4/366-8888. Fax 4/366-7788. www.madinatjumeirah.com. 292 units. AED 4,100 ($1,117/£566) and up double. AE, DC, MC, V. **Amenities:** 4 restaurants; 4 bars; outdoor pool; private beach w/watersports; 5 lighted tennis courts; spa; fitness center; kids' club; concierge; business center; Souk Madinat w/dozens of shops, restaurants, and bars; laundry service; dry cleaning; executive level rooms. *In room:* A/C, TV, high-speed Internet, minibar, coffeemaker, hair dryer, iron, safe.

Burj al Arab ★★ You're likely to have heard of the Burj Al Arab (the "Arabian Tower") long before arriving in Dubai. The so-called seven-star landmark hotel resembles a giant sail rising over the Gulf, with changing colors visible for miles at night. Las Vegas couldn't have done it better: The Burj is among the world's tallest

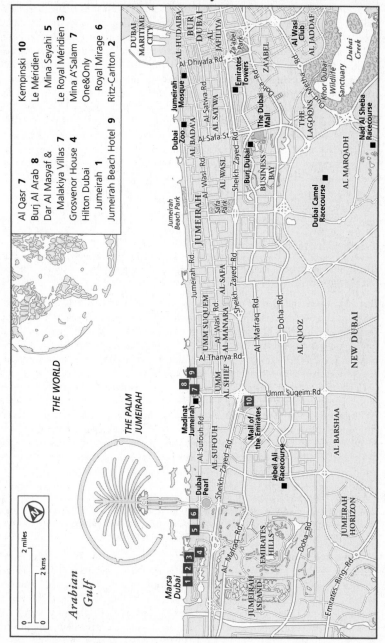

Where to Stay in Jumeirah & New Dubai

Al Qasr **7**
Burj Al Arab **8**
Dar Al Masyaf &
  Malakiya Villas **7**
Grosvenor House **4**
Hilton Dubai
  Jumeirah **1**
Jumeirah Beach Hotel **9**

Kempinski **10**
Le Méridien
  Mina Seyahi **5**
Le Royal Méridien **3**
Mina A'Salam **7**
One&Only
  Royal Mirage **6**
Ritz-Carlton **2**

(at 321m/1,053 ft.) and most expensive hotels, certainly in first place for sheer over-the-top appeal. Guests—a combination of celebrities and people who have landed on more money than they know what to do with—are greeted at the airport with a Rolls Royce and bouquet of roses, followed upon arrival at the hotel with a personalized waterfall and fire spectacle. En-suite check-in and round-the-clock butler service ensure you'll be expertly attended to throughout your stay. Each of the stunning suites has two floors, and includes a kitchen and private bar, state-of-the-art entertainment system with 42-inch plasma TV, floor-to-ceiling windows overlooking the sea, and bathroom with separate shower and Jacuzzi tub with a decadent bath menu. A "pillow menu" lets you choose from 13 pillows and quilts to make for a decadent night's sleep. Public spaces boast more marble and gold than some entire countries possess, and the Burj is known to push the gaudy envelope. The spa, beach club, gourmet restaurants, and highly attentive service make it a self-contained vacation oasis. Is it all worth it? That depends entirely on your relationship to money. If you thought Al Qasr was expensive, check out the rates here.

Jumeirah Beach, P.O. Box 74147, Dubai. © **4/301-7777**. Fax 4/301-7000. www.burj-al-arab.com. 202 units. AED 5,600 ($1,525/£772) and up suite. AE, DC, MC, V. **Amenities:** 5 restaurants; 3 bars; 2 outdoor pools; 2 indoor pools; private beach; spa and health club w/separate ladies' and men's sauna, steam room, and Jacuzzi; fitness center; yoga and aerobics classes; unlimited access to Wild Wadi water park; Rolls Royce chauffeur shopping experience; luxury airport transfer; private check-in and butler service. *In room:* A/C, TV, DVD, laptop, high-speed Internet, private bar, safe, pillow menu.

Dar Al Masyaf and Malakiya Villas ⭐⭐⭐   The best of Madinat Jumeirah's many types of accommodations, **Dar Al Masyaf** features exquisitely designed rooms and suites grouped within 29 summer courtyard houses. These Arabian- and Gulf-style houses are only reachable by waterway or garden paths, and each has its own idyllic outdoor pool. The enormous rooms and suites feature traditional Arabian furniture, large marble bathrooms, wide terraces or balconies, and private butler service. Travelers looking for even greater exclusivity may want to book one of the seven **Malakiya Villas.** These expensive villas, also along the waterways, are fit for royalty (and often accommodate royalty). They have separate living, bedroom, and kitchen areas, lavish furnishings, individual courtyards and pools, and private check-in and butler service. Guests staying in any of these rich accommodations have full access to all the facilities of the Madinat Jumeirah complex, including the private beach, luxury spa, modern day souk, and varied restaurants and bars. Service is outstanding.

Madinat Jumeirah, P.O. Box 75157, Dubai. © **4/366-8888**. Fax 4/366-7788. www.madinatjumeirah.com. 283 units. AED 4,250 ($1,158/£586) and up double. AE, DC, MC, V. **Amenities:** 2 restaurants; semi-private outdoor pools in Dar Al Masyaf, private pools in Malakiya Villas; private beach w/watersports; 5 lighted tennis courts; spa; fitness center; kids' club; concierge; Souk Madinat w/dozens of shops, restaurants, and bars; laundry service; dry cleaning. *In room:* A/C, TV, high-speed Internet, minibar (kitchen in Malakiya Villas), hair dryer, iron, safe.

Grosvenor House ⭐⭐⭐   The Grosvenor House is what the British like to call "posh," with an impeccable staff to match the illustrious clientele. The sleek hotel interior blends Arabian touches with an ultra-contemporary design, and is among Dubai's most stylish. Half of the guest rooms and suites face the sea, and all include plasma TVs, DVD and CD on demand, and butler service. Larger apartment suites are available, as well. The Retreat Health & Spa takes up an entire floor, offering the latest spa treatments, a hair and nail salon, hydro-pools, and sauna, steam, and Jacuzzi baths. Among the hotel's world-class restaurants and bars are the beautiful Turkish restaurant **Ottomans** (p. 90), award-winning British restaurant **Mezzanine** (p. 87),

44th floor **Bar 44** (p. 127), and world-famous **Buddha Bar** (p. 126). The towering Grosvenor House overlooks the new Dubai Marina, but is not right on the beach. Guests have access to the beach and pool facilities at the sister Le Royal Méridien resort (p. 72).

Jumeirah Beach, P.O. Box 118500, Dubai. ✆ 4/399-8888. Fax 4/399-8444. www.grosvenorhouse-dubai.com. 422 units. AED 1,650 ($450/£228) and up double. AE, DC, MC, V. **Amenities:** 12 restaurants and bars; terrace pool; spa; fitness center; access to beach resort; car rental; concierge; business center; shopping arcade; salon; laundry service; dry cleaning; executive floors; medical clinic; shuttle service to various malls. *In room:* A/C, TV, high-speed Internet, minibar, safe.

Hilton Dubai Jumeirah 🎭🎭 *Kids*   This Hilton (not to be confused with the Hilton Dubai Creek) enjoys one of the best beachfront locations in Dubai, and takes advantage of it with a beautiful pool and beach club offering watersports such as sailing, water-skiing, parasailing, windsurfing, and snorkeling. Landscaped gardens add to the picturesque setting. Colorful guest rooms have entertainment centers with satellite TVs and wireless keyboards for Internet access, balconies with full or partial sea views, marble bathrooms, and amenities including robes, mineral water, and magazines. There's also a terrific spa with separate ladies' and men's saunas and steam rooms, and services ranging from facials to Balinese-inspired body treatments. Fashion-conscious expatriates consider the modern Italian **Bice** (p. 88) bistro to be one of the hottest restaurants in town, and the Hilton also houses a popular South American restaurant, sports bar, and Cuban bar serving tapas and Cuban cigars. The family-friendly resort has a playground and special activities for kids, as well.

Jumeirah Beach, P.O. Box 2431, Dubai. ✆ 4/399-1111. Fax 4/399-1112. www.hilton.com. 389 units. AED 1,650 ($450/£228) and up double. AE, DC, MC, V. **Amenities:** 5 restaurants; 4 bars; outdoor pool; beach club w/watersports; spa; fitness center; kid's club; concierge; tour desk; business center; babysitting; laundry service; dry cleaning; executive level rooms. *In room:* A/C, TV, high-speed Internet, minibar, hair dryer, iron, safe.

Jumeirah Beach Hotel 🎭🎭🎭 *Kids*   For those looking for the ultimate Dubai beach vacation, there's no better option than the Jumeirah Beach Hotel. The resort is enormous and lacks any sort of intimate feel, but service is overall top-notch and there's more to do here than you can imagine. The stunning wave-shape hotel includes 598 oceanfront rooms and suites, and 19 Arabian-style beachside villas. Even the simplest rooms are spacious, with seating areas, walk-in showers, and colorful beach decor. The exclusive villas feature Bedouin-style furnishings, luxurious bathrooms with Jacuzzis, and private gardens with plunge pools. Once you've checked in, there's really no need to go anywhere else. You'll find the outdoor pool area and beach club Dubai's most extensive, with sailing, kayaking, snorkeling, and windsurfing all possible. There's an on-site dive center, and yacht charters and deep-sea fishing are available. The enormous health club includes a spa, high-tech fitness center, aerobics classes, and tennis and squash courts. Sinbad's Kids Club provides daylong activities and evening programs, and guests have unlimited access to Wild Wadi water park next door. There are more restaurants and bars here than at any other Dubai hotel. This place is sheer fun.

Jumeirah Beach, P.O. Box 11416, Dubai. ✆ 4/348-0000. Fax 4/301-6800. www.jumeirahbeachhotel.com. 617 units. AED 2,400 ($654/£331) and up double. AE, DC, MC, V. **Amenities:** 23 restaurants, cafes, and bars; 4 outdoor pools; 6 lighted tennis courts; squash courts; spa and health club w/fitness classes; beach club w/watersports; dive center; mini golf driving range; kids' club; shopping arcade; salon; babysitting; laundry service; dry cleaning; access to Wild Wadi water park. *In room:* A/C, TV, high-speed Internet, minibar, hair dryer, safe.

Le Méridien Mina Seyahi 🎭🎭 *Kids*   This family-friendly beach resort boasts outstanding recreational facilities and is a personal favorite. The beach club offers sailing, water-skiing, windsurfing, banana boat rides, and daylong beach games. Guests can arrange deep-sea fishing and sailing courses at the adjacent marina, as well as visits to an exclusive polo club. The fitness center and tennis club are among the city's best, and Clarins Spa provides massages, facials, manicures, and body treatments. Emirates Golf Course and Montgomery Golf Course are located just opposite the hotel. In other words, this resort is all about having a good time. A beachfront bar called Barasti hosts one of the most popular happy hours in town. Restaurants include Italian, international, and seafood options. As for the guest rooms, try to get one with a sea view. Guests staying in the Royal Club receive complimentary airport transfers, continental breakfast, evening cocktails, and upgraded amenities.

Jumeirah Beach, P.O. Box 24883, Dubai. ℂ 4/399-3333. Fax 4/399-3000. www.lemeridien.com/minaseyahi. 211 units. AED 2,075 ($565/£286) and up double. AE, DC, MC, V. **Amenities:** 8 restaurants and bars; 5 outdoor pools, including 2 kids' pools; 4 lighted tennis courts; spa; fitness center and aerobics studio; sailing; kids' club; concierge; business center; laundry service; dry cleaning. *In room:* A/C, TV, high-speed Internet, minibar, safe.

Le Royal Méridien ☘ (Kids)

Le Royal Méridien may have lost some of its splendor to newer rivals, but it remains one of Jumeirah's most extensive beach resort hotels. All of the guest rooms are elegantly appointed with sea-view balconies, and rooms in the Tower building offer private butler service. Sports and leisure activities abound, including tennis, squash, water-skiing, windsurfing, sailing, and kayaking, as well as access to golf, scuba diving, and deep-sea fishing. Tanning by the idyllic outdoor pool may be as active as you're looking to get, but there are also daily recreational activities such as yoga, beach volleyball, French boules, and squash social nights. An extensive list of spa services beckons, including massages in private gazebos scattered about the gardens. For kids, the Penguin Club organizes programs throughout the day with games, arts and crafts, and loads of playtime. Fifteen restaurants and bars are housed in the resort. The public areas require guests to wear modest dress in respect of the local culture.

Jumeirah Beach, P.O. Box 24970, Dubai. ℂ 4/399-5555. Fax 4/399-5999. www.leroyalmeridien-dubai.com. 500 units. AED 1,800 ($490/£248) and up double. AE, DC, MC, V. **Amenities:** 10 restaurants, 5 bars; 3 outdoor pools; beach club w/watersports; four lighted tennis courts; spa; fitness center; kids' club; concierge; business center; shopping arcade; separate salons for women and men; babysitting; laundry service; dry cleaning; shuttle service to various malls; medical clinic. *In room:* A/C, TV, high-speed Internet, minibar, safe.

Mina A'Salam ☘☘

This is one of the Jumeirah Group's newest and most grandiose hotels, a romantic retreat showcasing Arabian design and hospitality. Mina A'Salam, which means "harbor of peace," is connected by waterways to all areas of the magnificent Madinat Jumeirah complex, with its modern-day souk, spa, theater, private beach, and 45 restaurants, cafes, and bars. Guests are pampered in the treatment-rich Talise Spa, and share access to the extensive Quay health club. It's an easy walk from here to the famous Jumeirah Beach Hotel and Burj al Arab along a boardwalk, as well as to Wild Wadi water park. Although less formal than Al Qasr, Mina A'Salam is luxurious in its own right, and guests are assured highly attentive service and oceanview rooms with traditional dark-wood furnishings and locally inspired designs.

Madinat Jumeirah, P.O. Box 75157, Dubai. ℂ 4/366-8888. Fax 4/366-7788. www.madinatjumeirah.com. 292 units. AED 3,900 ($1,063/£538) and up double. AE, DC, MC, V. **Amenities:** 4 restaurants; 5 bars; outdoor pool; health club w/indoor pool; private beach w/watersports; 5 lighted tennis courts; spa; fitness center; kids' club; concierge; business center; Souk Madinat w/dozens of shops, restaurants, and bars; laundry service; dry cleaning; executive level rooms. *In room:* A/C, TV, high-speed Internet, minibar, coffeemaker, hair dryer, iron, safe.

One&Only Royal Mirage ★★★   The exquisite One&Only Royal Mirage shines like an Arabian jewel across a kilometer-long stretch of Jumeirah Beach. No other Dubai hotel so tastefully combines the region's heritage with beachfront appeal. Set amid 24 hectares (60 acres) of flowering gardens and fountain-filled waterways, the resort comprises three sections, including the Palace, Arabian Court, and Residence and Spa. Spacious guest rooms blend soft earth colors with Arabian touches and feature carved archways, custom-made furnishings, luxurious bathrooms, and garden patios or sea-view balconies. As enticing as the rooms are, you'll want to be outside as much as possible. Palm trees on their own tiny islands dot the sparkling pools, and the beach in front is one of Dubai's loveliest. At night, candles and lamps transform the landscape into a magical oasis. The resort's Health and Beauty Institute offers Givenchy spa and Oriental Hamman treatments (soothing steam baths steeped in Arab tradition). Outstanding restaurants such as the Moroccan **Tagine** (p. 91) and waterfront **Beach Bar & Grill** (p. 88) mean you can enjoy world-class meals just steps from your room.

Jumeirah Beach, P.O. Box 37252, Dubai. ℂ 4/399-9999. Fax 4/399-9998. www.oneandonlyroyalmirage.com. 425 units. AED 2,200 ($599/£303) and up double. AE, DC, MC, V. **Amenities:** 8 restaurants and bars; 4 sprawling outdoor pools; beach club w/watersports; spa; fitness center; concierge; business center; laundry service; dry cleaning. *In room:* A/C, TV, high-speed Internet, minibar, safe.

Ritz-Carlton Dubai ★★ *Kids*   The marina area around the Ritz-Carlton is dotted with towering skyscrapers, but this six-story resort has nothing to worry about when it comes to its gorgeous view—it's got a front row seat right on the beach. All rooms take advantage of this, with balconies that overlook the Gulf and/or the resort's pool and garden area. Rooms are a mix of classic European and Arabic design, with large sitting areas and some of the most comfortable beds I've ever slept on (you literally melt into the mattress).

A Club Level room gains you access to a private lounge (where there's food and drinks throughout the day and free Wi-Fi) and a special concierge. The Ritz-Carlton Spa offers "rituals" using Carita Paris products in a Balinese-inspired space (try the Degrees hot stone massage). The Lobby Lounge is popular for its afternoon tea, and the outdoor Amaseena serves a traditional Lebanese menu buffet-style in Bedouin tents with live music, a belly dancer, and 109 different flavors of *shisha*. The hotel's signature **La Baie** (p. 87) offers seafood with a strong Asian influence. Kids have access to their own play area, pool, and activities. Service here is superb.

P.O. Box 26525, Dubai. ℂ 4/399-4000. Fax 4/399-4001. www.ritzcarlton.com. 138 units. AED 1,400 ($381/£193) and up double. AE, DC, MC, V. **Amenities:** 5 restaurants; bar; 3 pools; private beach; 4 floodlit tennis courts; 2 squash courts; miniature golf course; 2 golf courses (5 min. away); gym; spa w/ ladies-only rooms; children's program; concierge; 2 salons (men's and women's); 24-hr. room service; laundry; technology butler, Internet. *In room:* A/C, TV, dataport, Internet, honor bar, hair dryer, iron, safe.

4 Outside Dubai

Al Maha Desert Resort & Spa ★★★   Located 45 minutes outside Dubai on its own 225-sq. km (87-sq. mile) nature reserve, this exclusive desert resort combines luxury with eco-tourism. Al Maha is designed to resemble a Bedouin encampment set against the backdrop of the Hajar Mountains, with detached suites interspersed around the idyllic resort. Each suite offers handcrafted furnishings and antiques, a spacious bathroom with Bulgari amenities, and a private temperature-controlled plunge pool. On-site activities include falconry, camel treks, horse riding, archery, desert drives, and guided nature walks. Off-site activities include mountain safaris, and excursions to Hatta or Al Ain. Oryx (Arabian Desert antelope), gazelles, camels, and other exotic wildlife make up the sanctuary's unique flora and fauna. Al Maha's "Timeless Spa" sits amid lush gardens and the main pool area, and offers relaxing massages and other body treatments as well as a sauna, steam room, and Jacuzzi. Guests can dine in the acclaimed Al Diwaan restaurant or in the privacy of their own veranda. The staff to guest ratio is 3:1, ensuring highly personalized service. The resort never feels crowded, and this is truly a place to escape.

65km (40 miles) from Dubai. From Dubai, take exit 51 or 56 off Sheikh Zayed Rd. Follow the signs to Al Ain on to the E66 and continue to Al Maha. ℂ 4/303-4222. Fax 4/343-9696. www.al-maha.com. 42 units. AED 4,040 ($1,100/£563) and up double. Prices include activities and full board. AE, DC, MC, V. **Amenities:** Restaurant; lounge; outdoor pool; spa w/sauna, steam room, and Jacuzzi; fitness center; concierge; falconry; horse riding; camel treks; archery; desert drives; nature walks; off-site excursions. *In room:* A/C, TV, DVD, dataport, minibar, coffeemaker, safe.

Bab Al Shams ✩✩✩ *Finds*   Relaxation defines this enchanted desert resort, located roughly 45 minutes outside Dubai near Endurance City. It was built in the style of an Arabian fort, with quiet pathways, gardens, and courtyards spread throughout the property. The brilliant use of water, from the sparkling pools to the trickling garden fountains, creates the illusion of a natural desert oasis. The resort maintains a sense of privacy even when full, and manages to be family friendly while also preserving its exclusive quality. Service here is gentle and personalized, exuding Arabic warmth. Romantic guest rooms range from "deluxe" to larger suites with private sitting rooms, and all have richly appointed bathrooms with deep soaking tubs. Although you may choose to do little more than relax by the pool during your stay, the list of activities goes beyond anything you're likely to see elsewhere, with spa services, desert safaris, horseback riding, volleyball, archery, bicycle rental, falcon shows, and an extensive kids' club, to name a few. **Al Hadheerah** is the resort's open-air restaurant (p. 92) serving traditional Arabic cuisine as part of an evening show in the desert. Note that it's usually 41°F (5°C) cooler here than inside the city, making for a welcome summer getaway.

45 min. from Dubai, close to Endurance City, P.O. Box 8168, Dubai. ℂ **4/832-6699.** Fax 4/832-6698. www.jumeirah babalshams.com. 115 units. AED 1,700 ($463/£234) and up double. AE, DC, MC, V. **Amenities:** 4 restaurants; 4 bars; 3 outdoor pools; Satori Spa w/outdoor and indoor treatment rooms; fitness center; kids' club; horse riding; camel rides and safari; table tennis; golf putting; volleyball; archery. *In room:* A/C, TV, DVD player, minibar, coffeemaker, safe.

6

Where to Dine

Dubai has come a long way in the last few years, when the breadth and quality of its restaurants remained limited. The city's relentless growth has brought an explosion of restaurants of seemingly every cuisine type, ranging from European, Asian, and American to Latin, Middle Eastern, and African. With the expanded variety has come improved quality—so much so that Dubai is now able to attract the likes of award-winning chefs Gordon Ramsay and Gary Rhodes. Ironically, it's difficult to find good Emirati cooking in Dubai, in large part because local food is bland when compared with that of, say, Lebanese or Moroccan. Don't despair—if you're looking for quality Arabic food, Dubai's Lebanese and Moroccan restaurants are world-class.

Just as the diners at Dubai's restaurants seem to come from every corner of the globe, so too does the staff. Service has improved markedly, but the limited English ability and lack of familiarity with Western tastes among some waitstaffs means that service isn't quite up to par with London or New York yet. Nevertheless, you can almost always get by with English, and most every restaurant offers an English menu. As you might expect, you'll find a significant difference between the attention you receive at a five-star restaurant and a hole-in-the-wall establishment. But the latter are quickly disappearing, as Dubai positions itself as a regional hub and major world city.

Lunch is generally served between noon and 3pm and dinner between 7pm and midnight. Emiratis often dine around 9pm, and restaurants are seldom crowded before then. You can usually find breakfast at more casual establishments. Most restaurants are open 7 days a week, although many serve only brunch on Friday, which is a weekend tradition here.

The city's top restaurants lie inside hotels, for the simple reason that they're by and large the only establishments that receive liquor licenses (public drinking is only allowed in hotel restaurants, bars, and clubs). You should always make a reservation for dining at hotel restaurants. Smart casual is the dress code for five-star establishments, and beachwear is only appropriate at casual Western-oriented venues in Jumeirah beach. Note that during the fasting month of Ramadan, most restaurants (with the exception of those in some international hotels) do not open until after sundown. There is also no live music or dancing during this period.

Prices in Dubai have been rising rapidly in the past few years. The most expensive international restaurants are found in the five-star hotels spanning Jumeirah beach. As you might expect, the seafood is particularly good in this area. Less expensive, but still delicious, Arabic and South Asian restaurants dot the traditional neighborhoods of Deira and Bur Dubai. You will find a wide selection of moderately priced restaurants along Sheikh Zayed Road, where the city's key business hotels stretch high into the sky. I have divided restaurants into the following categories: Very Expensive (main courses AED 184/$50/£25 and up), Expensive (AED 110/$30/£15 and up), Moderate (AED 55/$15/£7.60 and up), and Inexpensive (less than AED 55/$15/£7.60). When you receive your bill, check to see if the tip has already been included. If not, 10% is the rule of thumb.

1 Deira & Bur Dubai

VERY EXPENSIVE

JW Steakhouse ★★ STEAKHOUSE   JW Marriott hotels around the world are known for their first-rate steakhouses, and this one is no exception. Bragging that the steaks "cut like butter," the chefs here prepare thick, juicy cuts of high quality American, Australian, and Wagyu beef aged just right and bursting with flavor. The JW Trio allows you to sample Tasmanian, Wagyu, and American filets, each served in 4-ounce portions. Grilled lamb or veal chops are also available. The steaks are accompanied by delectable sauces, but otherwise everything is served a la carte. My favorite side dishes are garlic mashed potatoes or steak fries, sautéed mushroom caps, and creamed spinach or green asparagus with hollandaise sauce. The restaurant offers excellent seafood selections as well, including Maine lobsters fresh from the tank. There are two vegetarian options on the menu. Come to the JW Steakhouse for a special occasion: The atmosphere is typical of a New York–style steakhouse, with dark woods, white linen tables, green leather chairs, and dim lighting. For many local residents, this steakhouse is the best in Dubai, and it includes an excellent international wine list. Service is top-notch.

JW Marriott Dubai. © 4/607-7977. www.marriottdiningatjw.ae. Reservations required. Main courses AED 150–AED 300 ($41–$82/£21–£42). AE, MC, V. Daily noon–11:30pm.

Traiteur ★★ MODERN EUROPEAN   With an exquisite stainless-steel open kitchen and beautifully understated dining room, Traiteur is one of the city's most stylish restaurants. At night, the candlelit tables sparkle like fireflies inside and outside, where an intimate terrace overlooks the Dubai Creek. The ambitious menu is balanced between steak and seafood. Among these, the prime beef tenderloin from Nebraska, the organic and very tender milk-fed veal chop from Austria, and the char-grilled blue fin tuna from Malta are excellent. Some of the more complicated dishes try to accomplish too much—in this case, simpler is better. A private wine cellar houses separate chambers for the French, Italian, and vintage selections, creating a varied and inspirational wine list. Tasting menus with or without matching wines are available. Enjoy a pre- or post-dinner drink in the visually stunning bar upstairs, with modern artwork, intricately designed bar stools, and a color-changing ceiling.

Park Hyatt Dubai. © 4/602-1234. Reservations required. Main courses AED 120–AED 240 ($33–$65/£17–£33). AE, DC, MC, V. Daily 12:30–3:30pm and 7pm–midnight.

Verre ★★★ MODERN EUROPEAN   Gordon Ramsay's contemporary European restaurant helped bring credibility to Dubai's dining scene, and remains one of the city's top culinary choices. Ramsay shares the title of holding the most Michelin stars of any chef, now with 12 at various restaurants around the globe. In Dubai, he has created an elegant dining space characterized by white minimalist decor; service is refined and very attentive. The excellent dishes vary, but among favorites typically

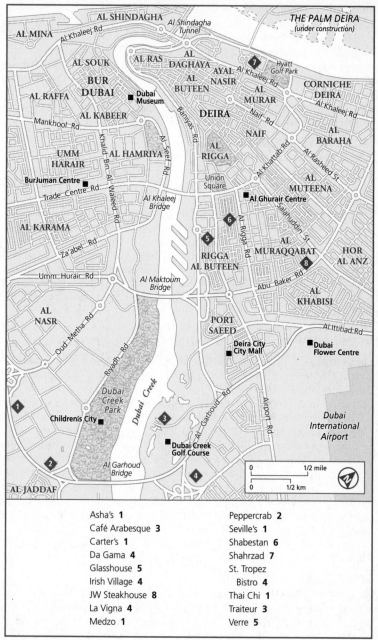

THE PALM DEIRA
(under construction)

AL SHINDAGHA
Al Shindagha
Tunnel

AL MINA
Al Khaleej Rd

AL SOUK
AL RAS
AL DAGHAYA
AYAL NASIR

BUR DUBAI

AL RAFFA
AL BUTEEN

Dubai Museum

AL MURAR

Hyatt Golf Park

CORNICHE DEIRA

AL KABEER

DEIRA

Al Khaleej Rd

Mankhool Rd

NAIF

AL BARAHA

UMM HARAIR

AL HAMRIYA

AL RIGGA

NAIF

BurJuman Centre

Union Square

AL MUTEENA

Trade Centre Rd

Al Khaleej Bridge

Al Ghurair Centre

AL KARAMA

Za'abel Rd

RIGGA AL BUTEEN

AL MURAQQABAT

HOR AL ANZ

Umm Hurair Rd

Al Maktoum Bridge

Abu Baker Rd

AL KHABISI

AL NASR

Oud-Metha Rd

PORT SAEED

Al Ittihad Rd

Riyadh Rd

Deira City City Mall

Dubai Flower Centre

Dubai Creek Park

Al Garhoud Rd

Childrenís City

Dubai Creek

Dubai International Airport

Airport Rd

Dubai Creek Golf Course

Al Garhoud Bridge

AL JADDAF

| 0 | 1/2 mile |
| 0 | 1/2 km |

Asha's **1**

Café Arabesque **3**

Carter's **1**

Da Gama **4**

Glasshouse **5**

Irish Village **4**

JW Steakhouse **8**

La Vigna **4**

Medzo **1**

Peppercrab **2**

Seville's **1**

Shabestan **6**

Shahrzad **7**

St. Tropez
Bistro **4**

Thai Chi **1**

Traiteur **3**

Verre **5**

offered are ravioli with Scottish lobster and salmon as a starter, and slow-cooked pork belly with lentils, black pudding, and pan-fried foie gras as a main dish. For dessert, choose the smooth crème brûlée or the tart *tatin* for two, with apples and cinnamon ice cream. A remarkable seven-course tasting menu is available with or without matching wines. If the food quality seems a cut above that at Dubai's other fine restaurants, it's because Ramsay uses the finest produce available locally and flies in fresh ingredients from around the world. His cookbooks are on sale at the entrance.

Hilton Dubai Creek. ℂ 4/227-1111. Reservations required. Main courses AED 150–AED 205 ($40–$55/£21–£28); fixed-price menu without wine AED 425 ($116/£59). AE, DC, MC, V. Daily 7pm–midnight.

MODERATE/EXPENSIVE

Café Arabesque ℱℱ ARABIC   If you really want to feel that you're in the Middle East (which happens less frequently than you'd think in Dubai), book a table at Café Arabesque. Some of the finest regional cuisine is served here, with specialties from Lebanon, Syria, Jordan, and Turkey. The dining room, with its open kitchen, hardwood floors, marble columns, and candlelit white linen tables, is one of the city's prettiest. Diners are greeted upon arrival with a basket of vegetables and nuts, and then begin their meal with a trip to the cold meze (appetizer) buffet. Main dishes are then ordered from the a la carte menu, accompanied by homemade flatbreads. Two of the best plates are the *shish taouk Bil Laban* (grilled chicken with yogurt) and *Adana* kebab (minced lamb kebab). The food coming out of the traditional oven is marvelous, with a rich dessert buffet awaiting you after. A trio plays live Arabic music nightly, except during Ramadan.

Park Hyatt Dubai (at Dubai Creek Golf and Yacht Club). ℂ 4/602-1234. Reservations recommended. Main courses AED 50–AED 150 ($14–$41/£6.90–£21). AE, DC, MC, V. Daily 12:30–3pm and 7:30pm–12:30am.

Peppercrab ℱ SINGAPOREAN   Located next to the tropical lobby garden of the Grand Hyatt, where big windows look out to the hotel's beautiful landscaped grounds, this delightful Singaporean restaurant is as original as it is delicious. Peppercrab is stylish but informal, and is especially popular with families. It focuses on seafood, and you can watch the cooks hard at work through the glass-enclosed kitchen, which is the centerpiece of the restaurant. Large tanks proudly display the live fish, crabs, and lobsters waiting to be ordered. Each of the restaurant's round tables is designed with sharing in mind. There's no reason to feel squeamish about the crispy, fried baby squids, a favorite Singaporean starter. The signature dish is the pepper crab, a delectable whole crab wok-fried with black pepper sauce. The welcoming staff will suit you up with an apron to protect the mess you're about to make. For dessert, the *Ice Kachang* is a curiously colorful and refreshing combination of shaved ice with palm seeds, red beans, sweet corn, black jelly, and sugar syrup.

Grand Hyatt Dubai. ℂ 4/317-1234. Reservations recommended. Main courses AED 75–AED 600 ($20–$163/£10–£83). AE, DC, MC, V. Sat–Wed 7–11:30pm; Thurs–Fri 7pm–midnight.

MODERATE

Asha's ℱℱ INDIAN   Legendary Indian singer Asha Bhosle created this superb Indian restaurant to celebrate her love for food and offer her guests a glimpse of a few regional dishes. As she explains, "Asha's only scratches the surface of the vast potential of Indian cuisine." Yet what she's managed to do in this warm namesake restaurant is remarkable, offering family recipes that give you a taste of the most authentic and at times exotic Indian cuisine. There's no beef or pork served here, but plenty of chicken, lamb, and fish selections. The menu includes delectable *tandoori* kebabs, curries, vegetarian dishes, *biryani,* and rice plates. Don't miss one of the fresh *lassies,* homemade yogurt smoothies blended with a variety of flavors. The vibrant dining room is splashed in reds, yellows, and oranges with contemporary booths and tables, and anywhere you sit affords a full view of the action. The number of Indians eating here is a strong reflection of Asha's quality.

The Pyramids Wafi City. © 4/324-4100. Reservations recommended. Main courses AED 40–AED 75 ($11–$20/£5.50–£10). AE, DC, MC, V. Daily 12:30–3pm and 7:30pm–12:30am.

Carter's INTERNATIONAL   A longtime favorite on the expatriate circuit, Carter's fills up just about every night of the week with resident Europeans in a celebratory mood. The Egyptian-themed decor interrupted by ceiling fans and wicker chairs tells you nothing about the Western, bistrolike food (alfresco dining is also available on the terrace overlooking Wafi Gardens). Among the best dishes are lamb shank served with mashed potatoes, red snapper with sautéed spinach, and the venerable fish and chips. Most of Carter's action happens inside, around the long centerpiece bar and small stage that offers live jazz and popular music most nights of the week. As the night wears on, diners should expect spontaneous dancers to surround them as the restaurant evolves into a nightclub. Of course it's possible to come just for drinks. If you're traveling alone, this is an easy and fun place to meet other Westerners.

The Pyramids Wafi City. © 4/324-4100. Reservations recommended. Main courses AED 50–AED 150 ($14–$40/£6.90–£21). AE, DC, MC, V. Mon–Sat noon–1am; Sun noon–2am.

Da Gama MEXICAN/PORTUGUESE   There's nothing particularly authentic about the Mexican or Portuguese food here, given that it's cooked by Filipinos and Indians living in the UAE. In addition, the dining room resembles a Dubai fantasy cocktail lounge more than any restaurant you'd find in Lisbon or Mexico City. Still, the relaxed outdoor seating and friendly service make this a good bet for an enjoyable and relatively inexpensive meal, and what the chefs prepare is pretty tasty. The eclectic menu mixes tacos, *mariscos* (seafood dishes), hot and cold tapas, meat skewers, rice dishes, and *cataplanas* (meat dishes baked and served in copper casseroles). The *cataplana di frango,* for example, includes chicken and sausages baked in port wine. Finish with a delicious fresh fruit crepe flambéed in cognac.

Century Village. © 4/282-3636. All dishes AED 65–AED 160 ($18–$44/£8.95–£22). AE, DC, MC, V. Daily 11am–2am.

Glasshouse 🎔🎔 MEDITERRANEAN   Although not as renowned as Verre (above) next door, the Glasshouse has a menu overseen by the same Michelin-starred British chef, Gordon Ramsay, and offers a memorable dining experience. The buzzing Mediterranean brasserie fills with a smartly dressed, mostly European crowd who come to celebrate the night. Groups of friends pack most of the tables, and the glass-intensive restaurant, including floor-to-ceiling windows and a glass floor, can become noisy as the night wears on. Ask for a table near one of the windows overlooking the Dubai Creek. An excellent way to begin your meal is with a warm tart with Mediterranean vegetables and Persian feta cheese, although the warm mackerel and vegetarian salad is every bit as tempting. Pasta and risotto dishes feature prominently on the menu, and vegetarians should not miss the tomato eggplant lasagna (there are extensive vegetarian options). Meat eaters are not excluded, and the tender sirloin, accompanied by a glass of well-bodied red wine, is the choice of cuts. Glasshouse offers one of the city's most sophisticated Friday brunches with all-you-can-drink sparkling wine or sangria.

Hilton Dubai Creek. © 4/227-1111. Reservations recommended. Main courses AED 50–AED 100 ($14–$27/£6.90–£14). AE, DC, MC, V. Daily 7am–midnight.

La Vigna ITALIAN   It's not gourmet Italian, but this delightful restaurant does an impressive job with its fresh pastas, pizzas, and hearty Italian dishes. Pizzas are tossed and then baked in a wood-fired clay oven; the best is the *quatro stagioni* with a rich tomato sauce, mozzarella cheese, ham, artichokes, mushrooms, and black olives. La Vigna has won a number of awards for its pastas, including the seafood linguine, and vegetarians will find numerous options here. The meat and vegetarian lasagnas are equally delicious, as is the chicken escalope in a mushroom sauce. The brick wall dining room attempts to re-create a scene out of the Italian countryside, and while I appreciate the decor, I prefer to sit outside on the lovely terrace. Live jazz and other music is sometimes offered evenings.

Century Village. ℂ 4/282-0030. All dishes AED 45–AED 70 ($12–$19/£6.20–£9.65). AE, DC, MC, V. Daily 11am–2am.

Medzo 🕃🕃 ITALIAN   Located inside the Wafi City pyramid, Medzo is more Mediterranean than traditional Italian, and has long been considered one of Dubai's best tables. The sleek black-and-white dining room leads to an inviting outdoor terrace, which at night transforms with candlelight into one of the city's most romantic venues (outdoor air-conditioning allows for alfresco dining year-round). Start with pan-seared scallops stuffed with gooseliver, or perhaps the homemade chili linguini with sautéed garlic prawns, lime, and fresh basil. Next, order one of the original thin crispy pizzas hot out of the wood oven. For a main course, I recommend either the grilled salmon with lobster mash, spinach, scallops and tomato relish, or beef tenderloin with balsamic-roasted shallots and Parmesan potatoes. For dessert, the white chocolate tiramisu is sublime. The purple-suited waiters offer sophisticated service.

The Pyramids Wafi City. ℂ 4/324-4100. Reservations recommended. Main courses AED 55–AED 120 ($15–$33/£7.60–£17). AE, DC, MC, V. Daily 12:30–3pm and 7:30–11:30pm.

Seville's 🕃🕃 SPANISH   With the Spanish chef turning out flavorful tapas and the servers pouring generous portions of red wine, rosé, and champagne sangrias, Seville's is as close as you'll come to finding a piece of Madrid in Dubai. Andalusian decor dominates the dining room with terra-cotta floors, Spanish archways, and wall images of bull fighting and flamenco dancing. Hot and cold tapas include fried calamari, prawns cooked in garlic and oil, and *chorizo* (Spanish sausage) flavored with cider; a rich seafood paella is offered as well. The popular terrace overlooking the Wafi rooftop gardens is one of the city's hottest hangouts on weekends, and it's possible to come just for drinks if you like. An acoustic guitarist serenades the happy diners every evening but Monday.

The Pyramids Wafi City. ℂ 4/324-4100. Reservations recommended. All dishes AED 40–AED 80 ($11–$22/£5.50–£11). AE, DC, MC, V. Sat–Mon noon–1am; Tues–Fri noon–2am.

Shabestan 🕃🕃🕃 PERSIAN   Edging past Shahrzad (below) as Dubai's best Iranian restaurant, Shabestan combines authentic cuisine with Persian hospitality. A power lunch spot by day, this fanciful restaurant inside the Radisson SAS Hotel transforms into a romantic retreat come night. The gracious staff welcomes you to an exotic dining room reminiscent of a sultan's palace, and the view of the Dubai Creek and live Persian music in the evening add to the restaurant's enchantment. Lamb is the centerpiece of the award-winning food, and I strongly recommend ordering the *chelow* kebab with marinated lamb and a large helping of saffron rice. The carefully prepared fish kebabs are equally delicious. Hot flatbread and a generous plate of raw vegetables and feta cheese accompany all selections. Ask for a table with a view of the creek, and expect to spend at least a couple hours here savoring the experience.

Radisson SAS. © 4/222-7171. Reservations recommended. All dishes AED 40–AED 150 ($11–$41/£5.50–£21). AE, DC, MC, V. Daily 12:30–3:15pm and 7:30–11:15pm.

Shahrzad ✦✦ PERSIAN   Dubai is home to one of the most significant Iranian populations outside their native country, and many will tell you that Shahrzad is unmistakably the best restaurant this side of the Persian Gulf. Named after Sultan Shahryar from the fabled *1,001 Nights*, this acclaimed Iranian restaurant, located in the Hyatt Regency Deira, offers a feast fit for kings (and don't be surprised if some of the illustrious clientele even act like kings). The exquisite dining room reveals intricate woodwork, tall columns rising to a sculpted ceiling, and a soothing fountain; a trio fills the space with Persian melodies come evening. Expect to eat a lot: The Kebab Shahrzad, for example, includes an assortment of grilled shrimp, chicken, *kofta* (minced meat), and *hammour* (a kind of grouper fish). The colorful dishes incorporate healthy amounts of herbs and mild spices, and are best accompanied by the signature saffron rice. *Doug* is a popular salty yogurt drink to go with your meal, and of course generous amounts of black tea should be consumed after the feast.

Hyatt Regency Deira. © 4/209-6707. Reservations recommended. All dishes AED 50–AED 150 ($14–$40/£6.90–£21). AE, DC, MC, V. Sun–Fri 12:30–3pm and 7:30pm–1am.

Thai Chi ✦✦ THAI/CHINESE   You get two for one at this innovative Wafi City restaurant with separate Thai and Chinese kitchens and dining rooms. The Thai kitchen has all female chefs, and its dining room is more formal and traditional, while the Chinese kitchen is all male, and its dining room casual and contemporary. Yet the menu is combined, allowing you to sample the best of both cuisines. It's common to order a large platter and place it in the center of your table to share. I recommend the Thai coconut green curry, and you can choose chicken, beef prawns, or vegetables. Many customers come especially for the coconut flavored sticky rice (with mangoes

---

Friday Brunch

Friday is to Dubai what Sunday is to the Western world, the one day set aside for rest and rejuvenation. And what better way to relax than by whiling away the afternoon over a sumptuous buffet? Friday brunch is a thriving tradition here, and many families, couples, and friends settle in for hours at the city's most popular restaurants, many of which offer brunch service. The normal time is noon to 3pm (Sat brunches are possible, too), and children often receive significant discounts off the fixed-price buffets. My recommendations ranging from most sophisticated to most family-friendly include: "Brunch in the City" at the Fairmont Dubai's **Spectrum on One** (© 4/332-5555) with free-flowing Moet & Chandon champagne; Friday Brunch at the Hilton Dubai Creek's **Glasshouse** (© 4/227-1111) with all-you-can-drink sparkling wine or sangria; Friday brunch at **Carter's** (© 4/324-4100) in Wafi City, with a complimentary Buck's Fizz on arrival; Friday brunch at **Al Qasr** (© 4/366-6730), a stunning palace hotel in Madinat Jumeirah; and "Family Friday Brunch" at **Scarlett's** (© 4/330-0000) in Emirates Boulevard with children's entertainment including a clown, face painting, and specialty balloon making.

when in season). From the Chinese side, I suggest the flavorful wok-fried beef in oyster sauce. There are also many vegetarian selections. Service, as you might expect, is gracious and attentive.

The Pyramids Wafi City. ℂ 4/324-4100. Reservations recommended. Main courses AED 60–AED 100 ($16–$27/£8.25–£14). AE, DC, MC, V. Daily noon–3pm and 7:30pm–midnight.

INEXPENSIVE

Irish Village IRISH   Expatriates love this place, and you'll find it filled with revelers just about every night of the week. The traditional Irish pub sits within the sprawling Aviation Club complex, with most of the action happening in the pub's outdoor beer garden. It sometimes seems that every Westerner in the city has descended on this spot, throwing back pints of Guinness or Kilkenny beer and spreading good cheer. The food is certainly not high-end cuisine, and includes the obligatory fish and chips, as well as Bangers in Mash (pork sausages on top of mashed potatoes with onion gravy). Sports run nonstop on the TV screens inside, and this place goes wild during football (soccer) games. The Irish village is as fun for singles as for groups of friends, since it's very easy to meet people here. Live music and other events happen regularly.

The Aviation Club. ℂ 4/282-4750. www.aviationclub.ae. Main courses AED 35–AED 60 ($9.50–$16/£4.80–£8.25). AE, DC, MC, V. Daily 11am–2am.

St. Tropez Bistro 𝒢𝒢 FRENCH   For simple charm and value, St. Tropez Bistro is unbeatable. The unpretentious restaurant consists of just a few tables surrounded by faux-French decor inside and an inviting outdoor terrace flanked by trees, fountains, and the eclectic restaurants of Century Village. You can easily linger over your meal while soothing jazz plays in the background. Come here for a fresh Niçoise salad (with tuna, eggs, potatoes, tomatoes, beans, olives, and lettuce), steak *au poivre* (tenderloin with black pepper), or perhaps chicken *cordon bleu*. In true French fashion, expect the steaks to be served rare unless you clearly specify otherwise. There's a sumptuous selection of desserts, such as chocolate mousse, banana flambé, and crème brûlée. The bistro makes a terrific choice if you're looking for an inviting atmosphere, good food, and a relatively inexpensive menu.

Century Village. ℂ 4/286-9029. All dishes AED 30–AED 60 ($8–$16/£4.10–£8.25). AE, DC, MC, V. Daily 12:30–11:30pm.

2 Sheikh Zayed Road

VERY EXPENSIVE

Amwaj 𝒢 SEAFOOD   Silver, wavelike metal sculptures, jelly fish-inspired light fixtures, and blue accents create an underwater ambience at this seafood restaurant (whose name means "waves" in Arabic) in the Shangri-La. The menu focuses on fresh seafood, such as a delicious sea bass served with grilled eggplant and pearl barley risotto, and John Dory with fennel ragout. While meat eaters have a nice selection (ranging from poached veal tenderloin to braised pigeon leg cannelloni), vegetarians are limited to a set menu (another set menu focuses on Arabic specialties). There's also an extensive selection of Iranian caviar. Save room for the Chocolate Box dessert (it's self-explanatory and decadent). After dinner, head down to the hotel's Balcony Bar for cocktails and cigars.

Shangri-La Dubai. ℂ 4/405-2703. Reservations necessary. Main courses AED 190–AED 250 ($52–$68/£26–£35); caviar AED 390–AED 1,400 ($106–$381/£54–£193); vegetarian set menu AED 195 ($53/£27); Arabic set menu 260 ($71/£36). AE, DC, MC, V. Sun–Fri 7pm–midnight.

Where to Dine on Sheikh Zayed Road

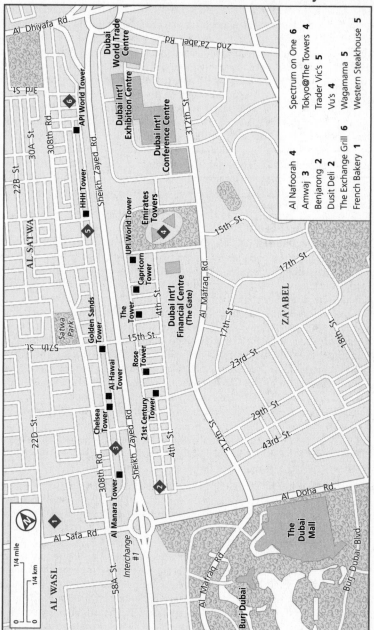

Spectrum on One **6**
Tokyo@The Towers **4**
Trader Vic's **5**
Vu's **4**
Wagamama **5**
Western Steakhouse **5**

Al Nafoorah **4**
Amwaj **3**
Benjarong **2**
Dusit Deli **2**
The Exchange Grill **6**
French Bakery **1**

The Exchange Grill ✿✿✿ STEAKHOUSE   One step inside this refined dining room, and you'll know you've arrived at one of Dubai's most exclusive restaurants. Modeled after New York's Oak Room, the setting includes just 14 tables with a single orchid at each, modern artwork, intimate lighting, and ambient music in the background. Beautifully dressed diners, often with a star or two among them, complement the restaurant's understated elegance. You may wish to start with the seafood "tower" for two, which includes a gorgeous sampling of seafood, or the wood-smoked beef carpaccio smoked by the chef. Steaks are masterfully cooked and carefully presented, with two types on offer: 1855 USDA certified Angus beef and Mayura Gold Wagyu beef. Steaks are accompanied by four different sauces and five kinds of mustard. The 7-ounce aged Angus filet mignon is outstanding, but if you're in the mood for a show, you may prefer the tableside carving of chateaubriand. The Exchange Grill offers the best steak in Dubai, and you'll pay for it.

The Fairmont Dubai. ✆ 4/311-8316. Reservations required. Main courses AED 145–AED 500 ($47–$136/£20–£70). AE, DC, MC, V. Daily 7pm–midnight.

MODERATE/EXPENSIVE
Spectrum On One ✿✿ INTERNATIONAL   Nowhere else in Dubai does such culinary diversity exist in one spot. Spectrum on One features eight innovative kitchens and distinct dining areas that let you take a gastronomic tour across Thailand, China, Japan, India, Europe, and Arabia. The result is a menu as ambitious as any you'll find, and I've chosen to highlight just a few. From the Indian menu, I love the Kashmiri *roganjosh,* tender lamb cooked in a spicy Kashmiri gravy. For Chinese, the succulent whole-roasted Peking duck is the obvious favorite. Any of the spicy green curry dishes make for an excellent meal on the Thai menu, and the black Angus beef tournedos with seared foie gras is my pick on the European side. It helps if your dinner partners are as adventurous as you, allowing you to mix and match plates across the culinary spectrum. This upscale restaurant really is one of Dubai's most interesting, and I strongly recommend you take a tour of the various open kitchens before settling into your meal. The excellent Friday brunch includes free flowing Moet & Chandon champagne.

The Fairmont Dubai. ✆ 4/332-5555. Reservations recommended. Main courses AED 65–AED 200 ($18–$54/£8.95–£28); Friday brunch AED 380 ($103/£52). AE, DC, MC, V. Daily 6:30pm–1am; Fri noon–3pm for brunch.

Vu's ✿ MODERN EUROPEAN   The panoramic view from the 50th floor of the Emirates Towers Hotel is the principal reason to dine here—floor-to-ceiling windows from one side of the elegant restaurant to the other present a spectacular view of Dubai. Come here for a special occasion, expecting to be pampered by the servers and anointed a new member of the city's elite by fellow diners. Vu's is a power lunch spot by day, and among Dubai's most romantic tables by night. While the service and view from every one of the 23 white linen tables are outstanding, the expensive menu can sometimes disappoint (this seems too often the case with restaurants content to rest on their laurels). Lean toward the caviar linguini for starters, followed by lobster or roast pigeon for your main course. Both are first-rate. The chocolate fondant is well worth the wait. Following your meal, wander up the spiral staircase to Vu's bar, an equally dazzling space serving sophisticated international cocktails.

Emirates Towers Hotel (50th floor). ✆ 4/319-8088. Main courses AED 40–AED 80 ($11–$22/£5.50–£11); 7-course fixed-price menu with matching wines AED 920 ($250/£127), without wine AED 420 ($111/£5.80). AE, DC, MC, V. Sat–Thurs 12:30–2:30pm and 7:30–11:30pm; Fri 7:30–11:30pm.

Western Steakhouse ✹ STEAKHOUSE   The re-creation of the Old West (note the wooden horses) seems a little out of place in Dubai, but this moderately priced steakhouse is a longtime favorite with consistently good food and friendly, if unhurried, service. Certified American Angus—including sirloin, tenderloin, and rib-eye—tops the menu. Surf and turf with Gulf lobster tail is another option, and you'll need to order accompaniments separately with each of the dishes. Packed most every night of the week, this restaurant draws a Western expatriate and tourist crowd, and is especially popular on weekends, when a three-course meal including traditional roast beef and unlimited champagne is offered. This must be Dubai's only establishment that includes country music as a permanent presence.

Crowne Plaza. ℂ 4/331-1111. Reservations recommended. Main courses AED 75–AED 175 ($20–$48/£10–£24). AE, DC, MC, V. Daily noon–3pm and 6–11:30pm.

MODERATE

Benjarong ✹✹✹ THAI   The Dusit Dubai's signature restaurant is in many ways the symbol of the hotel—elegant, graceful, and refined. The regal 24th-floor dining room, which sits adjacent to the champagne lounge, is decorated in dark woods with imperial pillars and moldings and large windows overlooking the rapidly expanding skyline. Diners can choose Royal Thai cuisine from the a la carte or set-course menus, and my strong recommendation is that you opt for the latter. Thais will tell you that the Tom Yam Gung (hot prawn soup seasoned with lime, lemon grass, and chili) is not to be missed, and irresistible main courses include the sweet-and-sour fish, braised beef in mild peanut curry, green curry, and assorted fried vegetables in oyster sauce. This place is worth dressing up for, and definitely a spot to impress a date. The gracious service is among the best you'll find in Dubai.

Dusit Dubai. ℂ 4/343-3333. Reservations required. Main courses AED 50–AED 100 ($14–$28/£6.90–£14); set-course menu AED 165 ($45/£23). AE, DC, MC, V. Daily 12:30–3pm and 7:30pm–12:30am.

Tokyo@The Towers ✹✹ JAPANESE   Located on the second floor of the Emirates Towers shopping arcade, this modern fusion Japanese restaurant gives you the option of sitting at the sushi bar, at a live-cooking teppanyaki table, at one of the a la carte tables, or in a private *tatami* room. Teppanyaki tables, with talented chefs creating a dazzling cooking show, are the most fun but the least intimate. Whichever section you choose, the soothing restaurant with wood columns, traditional floor cushions, and carefully placed decorative rocks creates the feeling of sitting inside the Japanese garden of an old Imperial temple. Fresh seafood is the highlight, and main dishes include teriyaki plates, tempuras, noodles, and stir-fries. The delicious ice cream, including sweet red bean or green tea, is homemade. Japanese food doesn't get better than this in Dubai, with service that is equally commendable. An upscale karaoke lounge toward the back attracts a stylish and festive crowd at night.

Emirates Towers (upper level of Shopping Blvd.). ℂ 4/319-8088. All dishes AED 40–AED 80 ($11–$22/£5.50–£11). AE, DC, MC, V. Sun–Thurs 12:30–3:30pm and 7:30pm–midnight; Fri 1–4pm and 7:30pm–midnight.

Trader Vic's ✹ POLYNESIAN   People tend to leave Trader Vic's a bit wobbly on the toes, which is perhaps an indication that the drinks matter more here than the food. And while the food's not bad, it's a fact that this well-known franchise is as much a Polynesian party as it is a restaurant. The Tiki-style Mai Thai Lounge seems to blend into the main dining room, where most every table ends up with an exotically shaped cocktail jar with mixes too strong to print. A live Cuban band fills the air with tropical rhythms, and late-night dancing is common. The colorful dining room is decorated with fishtraps and blowfish hanging from the ceiling, kitsch tapa wallpaper, and trick-ling fountains. The vaguely Hawaiian/Asian menu is heavy on seafood; the Szechuan butterfly prawns are a standout. If you want meat, the Indonesian rack of lamb with stir-fry noodles suits just fine. Whatever dish you order, though, that's probably not the part of the night you're likely to remember.

Crowne Plaza (on third floor of the commercial tower). ℂ 4/305-6399. Reservations recommended. Main courses AED 53–AED 150 ($14–$41/£7.30–£21). AE, DC, MC, V. Daily 12:30–3pm and 7pm–midnight.

INEXPENSIVE

Dusit Deli ⟨ AMERICAN/ITALIAN   This 24-hour deli off the lobby of the Dusit Dubai offers a mouthwatering selection of burgers, sandwiches, soups, and salads. It's ironic that such delicious American sandwiches are served in an Italian-style cafe inside a Thai hotel in the Middle East, but that's exactly the case here. The best are the Philly cheesesteak, bronzed chicken, and the "Louisville hot brown," mightily packed with roast turkey, crispy bacon, and tomato. There are burgers to suit every taste: the giant double-decker beef and mushroom burger, as well as lamb, vegetarian, and even crab burgers, for example. The deli also serves homemade pastries and fla-vored hot chocolates such as banana, mint, and hazelnut. Tasty breakfast sandwiches are served until noon. The rich coffee here is pure Italian.

Dusit Dubai. ℂ 4/343-3333. Sandwiches AED 30–AED 45 ($8–$12/£4.10–£6.20). AE, MC, V. Open 24 hr.

French Bakery ⟨ FRENCH   Open 24 hours, the perennially popular French Bak-ery promises a selection of homemade breads, pizzas, sandwiches, and pastries. The *salmon Viennoise* comes with salmon and capers on a fresh baguette, and I love the turkey and three-cheese sandwich packed with mozzarella, Emmental, and cheddar on sliced brown bread. The delicious, inexpensive food is proudly displayed in glass cases, so there are no surprises. You can also come here solely for one of the French pastry chef's decadent desserts, or perhaps a gourmet coffee and one of the Italian chocolates.

Sheikh Zayed Rd. at 1st Interchange. ℂ 4/343-6444. Sandwiches and snacks AED 10–AED 25 ($2.75–$6.80/ £1.35–£3.45). AE, MC, V. Open 24 hr.

The Noodle House ⟨⟨ ASIAN   This is one of my favorite lunch spots in Dubai (it's also open for dinner). The friendly eatery mixes dishes from Southeast Asia, including China, Indonesia, Singapore, Thailand, and Malaysia. The crowd here is just as diverse, giving locals and expatriates a chance to interact since seating is at long communal tables. Excellent dishes, which you'll order by checking off your selections on paper menu pads, include noodles and soups (with plenty of vegetarian options), wok-fried noodles and rice, and specialties such as Szechuan spiced beef, Thai chicken with cashew nuts, and chili prawns. Since many of the cooks hail from Indonesia, I recommend trying the *Bakmi goreng* (wok-fried Indonesian noodles) with chicken and prawns. Let your server know how spicy you want it, and order one of the exotic iced tea fusion drinks to wash it down. A creative selection of cocktails is also offered—my favorite is the creative and potent saketini. During peak hours, be prepared to wait for a short while to be seated.

Emirates Towers (lower level of Shopping Blvd.); another branch located at Madinat Jumeirah (ℂ 4/366-6730). ℂ 4/319-8757. All dishes AED 24–AED 45 ($6.50–$11/£3.30–£6.20). AE, DC, MC, V. Daily noon–midnight.

Wagamama ⟨ ASIAN   Wagamama's Dubai branch offers quick, friendly service in a delightfully casual setting. In fact, it's perfect if you don't have the time or financial will for a drawn out meal. An open kitchen surrounds the communal tables, which encourage interaction between the expatriates and local diners. For this reason, I view Wagamama as a wonderful symbol of Dubai's cultural openness. The rice bowls, noodle dishes, and teriyaki plates are generously portioned and wonderfully tasty, with delectable choices such as chicken curry, teriyaki steak, stir-fry vegetables, and noodles in coconut-based soup. The menu clearly indicates which dishes are spiciest. All are cooked to order and served the moment they're ready. Lunch tends to be much busier than dinner, and reservations are not accepted.

Crowne Plaza (on shopping level). ☎ 4/305-6060. www.wagamama.ae. All dishes AED 30–AED 45 ($8–$12/£4.10–£6.20). AE, DC, MC, V. Mon–Fri noon–midnight.

3 Jumeirah & New Dubai

VERY EXPENSIVE

La Baie ⭐⭐ SEAFOOD   The Ritz-Carlton's principal dining room is framed by a mesmerizing lobster and crab tank at one end and a white marble-top sushi bar at the other—a not-so-subtle reminder that seafood is the specialty here. Candlelit tables have elements of Asian tableware and, while elegant, the restaurant is less formal than you might expect (smart casual dress is the norm here). The pace is unhurried and not at all fussy, with attentive service befitting a Ritz. Chef Randy Joung's fusion dishes focus on seafood with Asian touches, and the produce is fresh, white, and primarily from the French Atlantic. If you want to splurge, the meat of rock lobster is softer and more tender than that of Canadian lobster, but also much more expensive. But then again, if you're eating lobster, why go budget? A mouthwatering lobster fondue is also offered.

The Ritz-Carlton. ☎ 4/399-4000. Reservations required. Main courses AED 170–AED 600 ($46–$163/£23–£83). AE, DC, MC, V. Mon–Sat 7–11pm; closed Sun.

Mezzanine ⭐⭐ MODERN ENGLISH   The acclaimed Mezzanine is every bit as pretentious as it looks, but in this case the pretense is worth it. Michelin-starred chef Gary Rhodes of London fame has brought a new level of sophistication to Dubai, his ultra-modern dining room a mesmerizing blend of white hues, baroque-style furniture, and contemporary lighting. The atmosphere is clearly celebratory and playful, yet very much refined. Rhodes's British classics taste heavenly (though he sometimes borrows a French idea to get them there); a couple suggestions include filet steak with kidney pie served on a bed of sautéed spinach, and roast monkfish on confit potatoes. If you've been to the chef's Rhodes 24 in London, then you know to expect food that is exquisitely prepared and presented. The dessert selection is just as fabulous. This is not a place for a quick meal; you should allow 2½ to 3 hours for the complete experience. Two drawbacks: The service is sharp but a bit stiff, and the wine list expensive and not particularly inventive.

The Grosvenor House. ☎ 4/399-8888. Reservations required. Main courses AED 150–AED 250 ($40–$68/£21–£34). AE, DC, MC, V. Sat–Wed 7:30pm–midnight; Thurs 7:30pm–1am; closed Fri.

Pisces ⭐⭐⭐ SEAFOOD   The city's best seafood restaurant lies in the souk area of the fantastic Madinat Jumeirah complex. Given its location on the Arabian Gulf, Dubai has longed for such world-class seafood dining, and it finally has in Pisces not just outstanding food, but chic surroundings and impeccable service. An ultra-hip crowd fills the dining room, a cool minimalist space with a chrome and glass staircase leading to a panoramic-view terrace facing the sea. Just about everything tastes wonderful here—the local *hammour*, sea bass, lobster, or any of the Pacific seafood selections. Highly recommended are the mussels *marinière* to start, followed by pan-fried scallops with foie

gras and sautéed spinach. Expect Mediterranean preparation in many dishes, with extensive use of olive oil and light herbs. The staff will be happy to accommodate special
requests, and most of the dishes can be prepared just about any way you want. The dessert
selection is fabulous, as well. Children 9 and under are not allowed.

Souk Madinat Jumeirah. © 4/366-6730. Reservations required. Main courses AED 100–AED 350 ($28–$95/
£14–£48). AE, DC, MC, V. Daily 7–11:30pm.

Zheng He's ★★★ CHINESE   Dubai's preeminent Chinese restaurant enjoys a
waterfront location within the Mina A'Salam hotel of Madinat Jumeirah. Glowing red
lanterns lead through the entrance to the exquisite dining room with dark woods and
Oriental decor. A glass kitchen looks upon the large round dining tables designed for
sharing. The view of the Arabian Gulf and Burj al Arab from the terrace will take your
breath away. Modern, progressive Chinese cuisine is carefully presented, and the food
more than holds its own to the gorgeous surroundings. If you're in the mood for something from the sea, I recommend the seafood dim sum and the marinated fish. Otherwise, set your sights on the tender beef tenderloin with wild mushrooms, or the
delectable Beijing duck served with crunchy vegetables. Save room at the end for
coconut ice cream and plum crumble. Service here is excellent. Dress is smart casual.

Mina A'Salam, Madinat Jumeirah. © 4/366-6730. Reservations required. Main courses AED 150–AED 350
($40–$95/£21–£48). AE, DC, MC, V. Daily noon–3pm and 7–11:30pm.

EXPENSIVE

The Beach Bar & Grill ★★★ SEAFOOD   Perhaps coming here has become a bit
of a cliché as far as locals are concerned, but it's still one of the most romantic dinner
spots in town, and in a casual, unpretentious way. This is one of the only venues where
you can dine by candlelight right on the beach, with a table-filled deck adjacent to the
sand. Although you should request a table outside in good weather, take a moment to
pass by the open kitchen inside. There, you will find an expertly orchestrated team of
chefs hard at work, preparing the fish and steaks with just the right timing and seasonings. In hot weather, you can still enjoy the view of the Arabian Gulf from the
cooled dining room with its stylish Moroccan decor. For fresh fish, I prefer the local
hammour filet (grilled rather than pan-fried) served with sautéed vegetables. For steak,
the Wagyu beef sirloin with thyme potatoes and asparagus is the best selection. Leave
room for a piece of warm chocolate cake served with espresso ice cream, and then take
a walk around the marvelous grounds of the Royal Mirage.

One&Only Royal Mirage. © 4/399-9999. Reservations required. Main courses AED 80–AED 180
($22–$49/£11–£25). AE, DC, MC, V. Daily 11:30am–3pm and 7–11:30pm.

Bice ★★★ ITALIAN   The Hilton Jumeirah's award-winning restaurant is also one of
Dubai's trendiest, a place to see-and-be-seen and where star-sightings are common-
place. The beautiful crowd comes largely to celebrate, and the largely Art Deco atmosphere is sexy and fun. Impressively, the restaurant has not allowed its star status to
diminish its culinary stature. Among the best dishes on the classic Italian menu created
by Chef Andrea Mugavero are fettuccini with Canadian lobster, seafood risotto, eggplant and mozzarella lasagna, and breaded veal, "Milanese" style. Many of the pasta
dishes feature truffles and wild mushrooms, and the homemade ricotta and spinach
tortelli is a house favorite. Freshly baked bread is accompanied by black olive tapenade,
sun-dried tomato paste, and olive oil with chili flakes. Bice offers an extensive wine list,
and there's an energetic bar adjacent to the main dining room. The best tables sit next

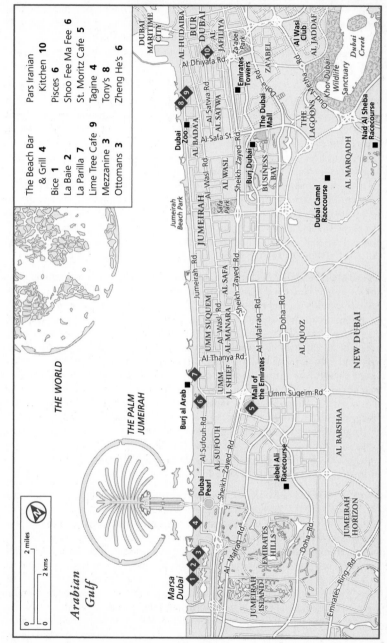

Where to Dine in Jumeirah & New Dubai

The Beach Bar
  & Grill **4**
Bice **1**
La Baie **2**
La Parilla **7**
Lime Tree Cafe **9**
Mezzanine **3**
Ottomans **3**

Pars Iranian
  Kitchen **10**
Pisces **6**
Shoo Fee Ma Fee **6**
St. Moritz Cafe **5**
Tagine **4**
Tony's **8**
Zheng He's **6**

to the huge windows overlooking the pool and gardens. Live piano music is offered nightly, and the restaurant can become quite noisy. But what's important at Bice is not what you hear but what you see and how you look, so come dressed to kill.

Hilton Dubai Jumeirah. ✆ 4/399-1111. Reservations required. Main courses AED 85–AED 155 ($23–$42/£12–£21). AE, DC, MC, V. Daily noon–3pm and 7pm–midnight.

La Parilla ✸✸ ARGENTINE   The Jumeirah Beach Hotel is a far cry from anything you'd find in Buenos Aires, but this Argentine restaurant inside Dubai's landmark wave-shape resort impressively re-creates the theme of the Argentine *pampas*. Plantation estate furniture fills the dining space, where cartwheels and other country-themed decorations cover the walls. Your main reminder that this is not South America is the room's 25th-floor panoramic view of the Arabian Gulf. The specialty, of course, is meat, and many varieties of it. The 500-gram beef tenderloin is outstanding, but if you want to sample a broader variety, then order the Espada—skewers of meat grilled on the visible *parilla* and then flambéed at your table. The food is good, but the restaurant's main draw is tango: A dancing duo grace the dining room throughout the night backed by the music of a live trio. Nowhere else in Dubai will you find such a show.

Jumeirah Beach Hotel (25th floor). ✆ 4/348-0000. Reservations required. Main courses AED 80–AED 120 ($21–$32/£11–£17). AE, DC, MC, V. Daily 6:30pm–1am.

Ottomans ✸✸ TURKISH   For a memorable night out, this exotic restaurant inside the Grosvenor House will leave you transported to another time and place. A waterfall cascades down a wall of black marble, handmade Turkish place settings and crystal glasses decorate the tables, and jewel-colored velvet cushions line the walls. Chef Ahmet has designed a creative, modern Turkish menu celebrating a multitude of flavors. The signature dish is braised lamb shank served with a tomato sauce and smoked eggplant. I also love the braised chicken with apricot, honey, saffron, vegetables, and lemon couscous. For dessert, the oven-baked rice pudding is out of this world, but you may already be overindulging with a Turkish coffee mixed with a rich chocolate sauce. The ornately costumed waitstaff provides highly attentive service, and live musicians using traditional Turkish instruments play regional music nightly. Following dinner, many guests enjoy retreating to the opulent outdoor terrace overlooking the marina, where an extensive *shisha* menu is offered.

The Grosvenor House. ✆ 4/399-8888. Reservations required. Main courses AED 70–AED 180 ($19–$49/£9.65–£25). AE, DC, MC, V. Mon–Sat 8pm–1am; closed Sun.

Shoo Fee Ma Fee ✸ MOROCCAN   Moroccans may quibble about the authenticity of Shoo Fee Ma Fee, which translates from Arabic to "what's happening," but they will agree it's still one of Dubai's most enticing dinner spots. Tucked inside the souk area of Madinat Jumeirah, the trendy restaurant and lounge is designed to resemble a Moroccan *majlis* (traditional Arabian meeting space), although the lounge beats playing in the background clearly appeal to a more European clientele. The dining room includes three levels of rich woods and elegant cushion chairs, as well as a *shisha*-friendly rooftop terrace overlooking Madinat's winding waterways. The menu mixes Moroccan, Arabic, and other regional dishes, including exotic choices such as pigeon *pastilla* (sautéed pigeon with sliced onions, butter saffron, pepper, ginger, and cinnamon stick), roasted goat's leg, lamb couscous, and camel *kofta*. Service is friendly but not especially efficient, so you may need to wait for a while before your food arrives.

Souk Madinat Jumeirah. ✆ 4/366-6730. Reservations recommended. Main courses AED 80–AED 150 ($22–$41/£11–£21). AE, DC, MC, V. Daily 7pm–12:30am.

MODERATE/EXPENSIVE

Al Nafoorah ★★★ LEBANESE   Dubai's top Lebanese restaurant sits on the ground floor of the Emirates shopping arcade, its opulent dining room leading to a lovely outdoor terrace facing the Dubai skyline. Business executives flock here by day, while romantic couples grace the restaurant by night. Al Nafoorah prides itself on its extensive selection of hot and cold meze (appetizers, such as hummus, baba ghanouj, and kibbe Nafoorah with minced lamb in ground bulgar wheat) and inventive Lebanese dishes including grilled Omani lobster, chicken livers in pomegranate, and delicious *shawarmas*. Twelve expert cooks work under award-winning Executive Chef Ali Hussein, who specializes in seafood from the Arabian Gulf. Perhaps the most exotic fish prepared is the *Hlowa Wo*, a mild white fish marinated with fresh local herbs and accompanied by cumin rice. Hussein also recommends the fusion dish with baba ghanouj and fresh crab. Friday's seafood lunch is a local favorite with Gulf delights such as *hammour*, lobster, and shrimp. Service is as inspired as the cooking.

Emirates Towers (lower level of Shopping Blvd.). ✆ **4/319-8088.** All dishes AED 50–AED 150 ($14–$40/£6.90–£21). AE, DC, MC, V. Sat–Thurs 12:30–5pm and 8pm–midnight; Fri 1–5pm.

Tagine ★★★ MOROCCAN   Indisputably Dubai's best Moroccan restaurant, Tagine lies in the spectacular One&Only Royal Mirage. The exotic dining room is pure Moroccan, with an incense-filled, candlelit atmosphere as enchanting as any you'll find in Dubai. Come ready to sink into one of the satin cushions and stay hypnotically planted for the evening. The signature dish is couscous *Bidaoui*, steamed semolina served with tender lamb or chicken and garnished with fresh cooked vegetables. My favorite is the couscous *fassia*, a giant platter topped with lamb or chicken and sweet raisins, sweet onions, and honey. Equally delicious are the lamb *kofta* and the mixed kebab with a variety of tender meats. If you can possibly find any more room, top off your meal with an assortment of Moroccan pastries baked with almond. Tagine is as much about sharing a memorable experience as about the food, with live music offered most nights. When you're finished, take a stroll through the stunning hotel grounds.

One&Only Royal Mirage. ✆ **4/399-9999.** Reservations required. Main courses AED 75–AED 80 ($20–$22/£10–£11). AE, DC, MC, V. Tues–Sun 6pm–midnight.

INEXPENSIVE

Lime Tree Cafe ★ DELI   Casual beach-close eateries are almost a thing of the past in Dubai, as construction of luxury properties continues nonstop, but the bright green villa housing the Lime Tree Cafe stays secure in its place with a committed expatriate following. Think San Francisco in the summer, where being cool means eating healthy and wholesome. The adorable cafe is best for breakfast, offering such delights as ricotta hotcakes with blueberry sauce or toasted bagels with eggs. With a refreshingly creative menu that changes daily, the homemade lunch selections include canapés, soups, salads, and sandwiches, and there's a wonderful variety for vegetarians. Rich cakes, cookies, ice creams, fresh juices, and smoothies on their own are enough to merit a visit. The Lime Tree Cafe offers casual seating inside or on the charming outdoor patio. During peak hours you may have a short wait. There is a second location in Ibn Battuta Mall.

Jumeirah Beach Rd. (next to Jumeirah Mosque). ✆ **4/349-8498.** www.thelimetreecafe.com. All dishes AED 20–AED 35 ($5.50–$9.50/£2.75–£4.80). AE, MC, V. Daily 7am–6pm.

Pars Iranian Kitchen ⟨✦⟩ IRANIAN   Pars is widely viewed as the best inexpensive Iranian restaurant in the city. This branch, located next to the Rydges Hotel in an area called Satwa (there's another branch inside the Mall of the Emirates), is the most popular—a place where half the city seems to gather late at night. Most of the tables are outdoors, where the food is also cooked on an enormous coal-filled barbecue. Inexpensive, traditional fare includes the mixed grill of chicken and lamb with rice, Persian stew, *chelow* kebab *barg* (with lamb filet), and *chelow koobideh* (with minced meat). The kebabs served with succulent lamb and flat bread are as tasty as you'll find anywhere, and come with a heaping plate of rice and an assortment of cold vegetables, goat cheese, and mint leaves. As the night wears on, the multicultural eatery fills with the smell of *shisha* pipes alongside the delicious Persian fare.

Satwa Roundabout (next to Rydges Plaza). ⟨✆⟩ 4/398-4000. All dishes AED 35–AED 45 ($9.50–$12/£4.80–£6.20). No credit cards. Daily 7pm–1am.

St. Moritz Cafe INTERNATIONAL ⟨Kids⟩   Families will love the St. Moritz Cafe, located in the Mall of the Emirates. With giant glass windows, the cafe stares into Ski Dubai, the unbelievable indoor ski resort. The restaurant decor, including a faux fireplace in the center, re-creates (with a bit of imagination) the warmth of a Swiss chalet—never mind that it may be more than 100°F (37°C) outside. Simple but strangely diverse dishes include pastas, crepes, and fondues. A sharing platter features fried calamari, potato wedges, barbecue chicken wings, and vegetable spring rolls. Just about everything seems to be available on the menu. This is not a place for an intimate meal, but it's good fun for the kids.

Mall of the Emirates (in front of Ski Dubai). ⟨✆⟩ 4/409-4000. Main courses AED 30–AED 60 ($8–$16/£4.10–£8.25). AE, DC, MC, V. Daily 10am–midnight.

Tony's DELI   Located inside the Village Mall, Tony's is as close as you'll get to a Manhattan deli in Dubai. The food is pretty tasty, and alongside the soups, salads, pizzas, and pastas, you'll find American-style burgers, sandwiches, and wraps. Sandwiches are served on panini or baguette bread, and I was delighted to find Philly cheesesteak, Reuben, and pastrami sandwiches offered. The deli gets a little off topic by suggesting a few stir-fry and wannabe Mexican dishes, and there's no reason for you to go that route. Most of what's available is written on the blackboard, and the fresh produce is on display through glass cases. Breakfasts are also yummy here, including French toast, pancakes, and eggs cooked to order.

Jumeirah Beach Rd. (in the Village Mall). ⟨✆⟩ 4/349-9034. Main courses AED 18–AED 35 ($5–$9.50/£2.50–£4.80). MC, V. Daily 8am–11pm.

4 Outside Dubai

EXPENSIVE

Al Hadheerah ⟨✦✦⟩ ARABIC   Located about 45 minutes outside Dubai at the idyllic Bab al Shams desert resort, Al Hadheerah offers an unforgettable dining experience under the stars. The open-air scene is that of an Arabian fort with natural stone, rock walls, and sunken seating areas surrounded by endless sand dunes. The fixed-price evening includes falcon displays, henna artists, live music, and belly dancing. Camel and horse rides alongside Bedouin Arab horsemen are available. As for the food, the extensive menu includes cold Arabic meze served at the table with freshly baked breads; a selection of hot meze from the buffet; and a choice of main courses from the live cooking stations. Among the latter are beef or chicken *shawarma,* Arabic and Iranian kebabs, lamb chops, whole *ouzi* cooked on the spit, and many other meat and fish possibilities. A rich selection of desserts, coffees, and teas rounds out the meal. This is a wonderful outing for families, and more refined than some of the desert safaris offered near Dubai.

Bab Al Shams Desert Resort and Spa (located 45 min. outside Dubai). ℂ **4/809-6195.** Reservations required. All-inclusive buffet including show AED 375 ($102/£52) adults, AED 225 ($61/£31) children 12 and under (those 4 and under eat free). AE, DC, MC, V. Daily 7–11:30pm.

7

Exploring Dubai

Until recently, Dubai and culture seldom came together in the same sentence. But things are changing on this front, and today there is more than just the Dubai Museum to give you a feel for Dubai's heritage and culture. Although there are not so many must-see cultural attractions, the **Bastakiya** ✯✯ neighborhood is a picture-perfect restoration of an early Arabian neighborhood, and a walk through here will give you a strong sense of Dubai's history. Spend a little time walking or taking a boat along the creek, the city's lifeline where dhows haul their traditional trade. Be sure to visit the Gold and Spice souks, where business is conducted in the same traditional way that Arabian markets have done for centuries. And in case you were worried that Dubai isn't paying attention to culture, know that it has contracted a branch of the Louvre to open here in 2010.

Dubai is recognized around the world for its unbelievable tourism development. Everything seems to be larger and glitzier than anywhere else. The massive **Dubailand** complex, which will be twice the size as Disney World, will upon completion have the largest collection of amusement parks in the world, with about half expected to be open by 2010. These will include Six Flags Dubai, Universal Studios Dubai, Paramount Studios Theme Park, Dubai Snowdome, and one of the world's largest water parks, among many other entertainment, shopping, and sports attractions.

Dubai's attractions are meant to impress. The fact that the indoor **Ski Dubai** was built is an accomplishment in its own right; that it's located in one of the world's hottest deserts almost exceeds imagination. Yet Ski Dubai, located in the Mall of the Emirates, will be dwarfed in size by the Snowdome. Mall of Arabia, also located in Dubailand, will become the world's biggest shopping center. And of course this city will soon open the world's tallest building, the Burj Dubai, which will be surrounded by its own entertainment complex.

Dubai is a paradise for outdoors and sports enthusiasts, particularly for beach activities, golf, and tennis. All of the major beach resorts offer water sports activities, and there are also a number of excellent parks where you can walk, jog, rollerblade, or go for a bicycle ride. **Camel and horse racing** are important aspects of Dubai's heritage, and the emirate today hosts championship races as well as international golf and tennis tournaments. A **desert safari** is one of the most fun activities you can do outside the city, complete with dune bashing in a 4WD, camel riding, delicious dining under the stars, and Arabian entertainment. Those who have more time may want to consider an overnight camping adventure in the desert to get a more in-depth perspective of Arabic life outside the booming Dubai metropolis.

WALKING TOUR: HISTORIC DUBAI

Start:	Herib Bin Harib Mosque
Finish:	Perfume Souk
Time:	4 hours
Best Time:	Early morning or early evening
Worst Time:	In the heat of the middle of the day

The best way to visit the historic areas of Bur Dubai and Deira is to walk. Each neighborhood can be visited in half a day, and especially in hot weather the most sensible approach is to visit one side in the early morning and the other in the evening. During this daylong walking tour, you'll discover the city's old quarters, survey the traditional architecture of Emirati homes and mosques, visit cultural centers, ride a water taxi across the creek, and interact with local merchants in the souks. There's no better way to get to know the original heart and soul of Dubai.

❶ Herib Bin Harib Mosque

Begin your tour in Bur Dubai at the **Herib Bin Harib Mosque,** near the mouth of the creek just before the Al-Shindagha Tunnel. The construction of this and five other mosques in the neighborhood dates back to the early 1900s, and all of them were restored in 2001. These simple structures were crucial in helping develop the Islamic consciousness of the early Bedouin community.

Facing the creek from the mosque, turn right and walk a short distance to the

❷ Heritage and Diving Village

Located side by side, these showcase Dubai's maritime and pearl-diving traditions. In addition to photographs and exhibits focused on Dubai's maritime past, there are potters and weavers selling Arabian handicrafts, local women serving traditional Emirati food, and vendors offering afternoon camel rides.

Continuing along the edge of the creek, you will next come to the

❸ House of Sheikh Obaid bin Thani

This is one of the first residential buildings in Dubai. Next to it stands the historically important **House of Sheikh Saeed Al-Maktoum.** This carefully restored courtyard home of Dubai's former ruler is a good example of the 19th-century architectural style of the Gulf coast, and includes an excellent collection of photographs from Dubai's pre-oil days.

Walking a bit farther along the creek pathway, you'll find the Bin Zayed Mosque. Adjacent to it is the

❹ House of Sheikh Joma'a Al-Maktoum

This home is characteristic of the traditional architecture of the Al-Shindagha area, where the ruling family lived. Facing inland lie two more houses of worship, the **Al-Mulla Mosque** and the **Al-Otaibat Mosque.**

Continuing along the creek path, you'll pass an example of a watchtower used for defense of the early city, the

❺ Al-Shindagha Square Fort

Keep walking past it along the water's edge until you reach the **Wakeel House,** a two-story structure overlooking the creek that was the first administrative building in Dubai.

From there, the **Grand Souk Bur Dubai** stretches out before you and blends in with the broader textiles souk, which some people refer to as "Little India." An incredible selection of fabrics from South Asia is sold here. Just in front along the water's edge is **Dubai's Creek Frontage,** where water taxis *(abras)* make their way back and forth across the channel from the Dubai Old Souk Abra Station.

At this point, turn right (away from the creek) and walk past the Grand Mosque to the

⑥ Al Fahidi Fort (Dubai Museum)

This key cultural museum can be visited in just a couple hours and offers the emirate's best opportunity for discovering the history, culture, and traditions of Dubai.

Just east of the Dubai Museum is the pristinely restored **Bastakiya** area ✿✿★. Wander the old quarter's meandering pathways surrounded by wind towers and traditional Arabian homes. Check in at the **Sheikh Mohammed Center for Cultural Understanding** to gather information about Emirati culture (the Center also arranges walking tours of the old quarter). You can visit the **Majlis Gallery,** which was Dubai's first art gallery, stop for a coffee at the **Basta Art Café,** and check out the **XVA Hotel & Art Gallery.** Within this historic quarter, pedestrian paths also lead to a preserved fragment of the **Dubai Wall,** which was built in the early 19th century to protect the old city from outside attack. The original wall extended 840m (2,756 ft.) and was 2.5m (8¼ ft.) high.

Exit Bastakiya on the creek side and take a 10-minute *abra* ride across to Deira. The short water taxi ride across the creek will drop you off in the dhow wharfage area of Deira, just in front of Baniyas Road. Here you can watch the colorful dhows as they make their way back and forth along the creek to the Arabian Gulf. Take the pedestrian underpass to the left that will take you to the

⑦ Grand Souk Deira

This is Dubai's oldest and busiest bazaar, where merchants have been selling their wares for centuries. Just behind the Grand Souk lies the **Spice Souk,** where the fragrant smells of Arabian spices and seasonings beckon.

From the Grand Souk, make your way toward Al-Ahmadiya Street in the heart of *Al Ras,* where you'll find the square with the

⑧ Heritage House

The fully restored Heritage House is an excellent example of late-19th-century Arabian architecture and furnishings. Next door is the **Al-Ahmadiya School,** which sheds light on the history of education in Dubai. You will also see the Bin Lootah Mosque, dating from 1910, in front of the Al-Ahmadiya School.

Heading back on Sikkat Al-Khail Road and crossing over Old Baladiya Street, you will see, on the left, the glittering

⑨ Gold Souk

The best time to visit is after 4pm, since most shops close during the heat of the afternoon. Nighttime is especially busy. Spend as much time here as your wallet can afford, but be sure you're ready to haggle if you're going to buy. Just beyond the Gold Souk lies the fragrant **Perfume Souk,** which sells Arabian *attars* (perfume oils) and *oud.*

1 Museums & Cultural Sights

Al-Ahmadiya School ✿   A visit here affords a chance to learn about the history of education in Dubai. Teaching in the UAE was originally done by religious men called "Al-Muttawa" in private homes and was limited to the religious teachings of the Holy Koran, writing, arithmetic, and Arabic calligraphy. In the early 20th century, the Al-Ahmadiya and other semi-formal schools began to open, offering students instruction in literature and various sciences, in addition to religion. Students were grouped by their age and ability to memorize the Koran, and typically sat on mats rather than at desks. In 1956, Dubai adopted a formal education system, and the Al-Ahmadiya school introduced classrooms and more subjects, such as English, sociology, and science. The

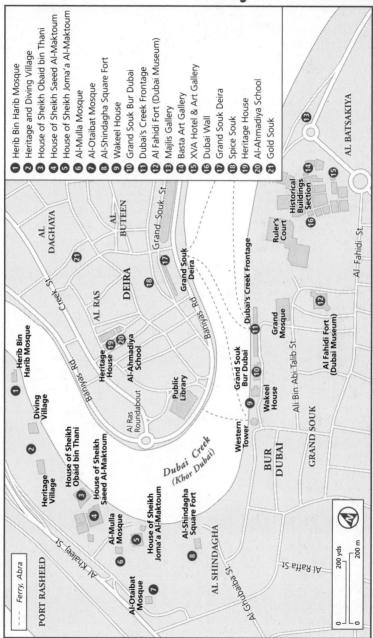

1. Herib Bin Harib Mosque
2. Heritage and Diving Village
3. House of Sheikh Obaid bin Thani
4. House of Sheikh Saeed Al-Maktoum
5. House of Sheikh Joma'a Al-Maktoum
6. Al-Mulla Mosque
7. Al-Otaibat Mosque
8. Al-Shindagha Square Fort
9. Wakeel House
10. Grand Souk Bur Dubai
11. Dubai's Creek Frontage
12. Al Fahidi Fort (Dubai Museum)
13. Majlis Gallery
14. Basta Art Gallery
15. XVA Hotel & Art Gallery
16. Dubai Wall
17. Grand Souk Deira
18. Spice Souk
19. Heritage House
20. Al-Ahmadiya School
21. Gold Souk

What to See & Do in Dubai

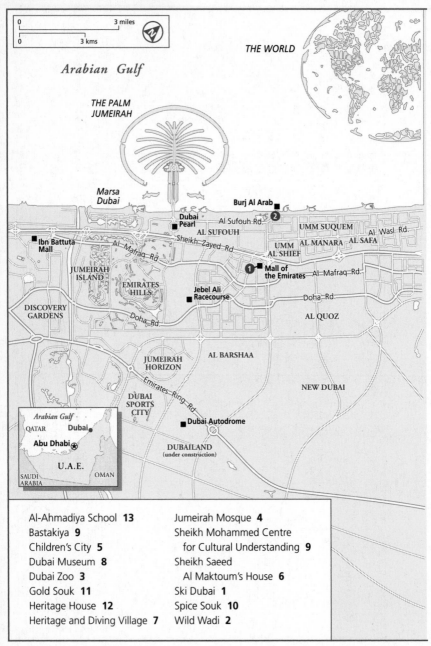

Al-Ahmadiya School **13**	Jumeirah Mosque **4**
Bastakiya **9**	Sheikh Mohammed Centre
Children's City **5**	for Cultural Understanding **9**
Dubai Museum **8**	Sheikh Saeed
Dubai Zoo **3**	Al Maktoum's House **6**
Gold Souk **11**	Ski Dubai **1**
Heritage House **12**	Spice Souk **10**
Heritage and Diving Village **7**	Wild Wadi **2**

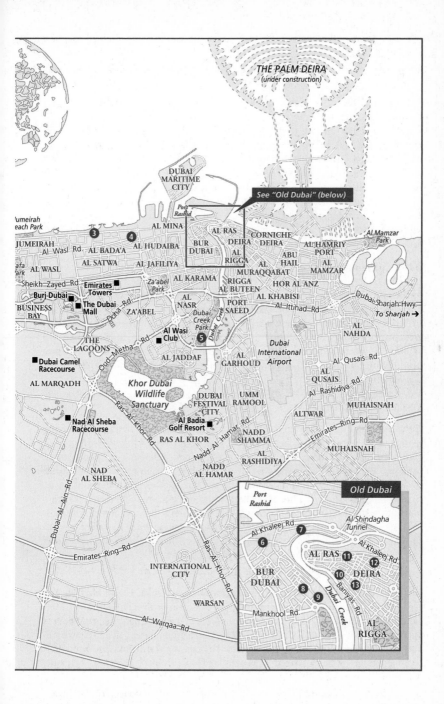

number of students rapidly expanded after this time, and the school moved to a new location to accommodate more pupils.

Al Khor St., Al Ras, Deira. © **4/226-0286.** www.dubaitourism.ae. Free admission. Sat–Thurs 8am–7:30pm; Fri 2:30–7:30pm.

Bastakiya ✦✦✦   A complete restoration of Dubai's early settlement for wealthy Persian merchants, Bastakiya is an idyllic neighborhood of meandering lanes, traditional Gulf houses, and ornate wind towers. The coral stone and cement wind towers once lined the Dubai Creek, keeping the historic houses cooled using innovative air current systems. Although the area dates from the late 1800s, it was completely restored in recent years. The village includes the Sheikh Mohammed Centre for Cultural Understanding (p. 101), Dubai Museum (see below), the Majlis Gallery with traditional ceramics, jewelry, and art, and XVA Gallery (p. 117) with contemporary paintings, sculptures, and installations from regional artists. There are a number of shops and restaurants in this walking village, as well.

Bastakiya, Bur Dubai. www.dubaitourism.ae. Free admission. Daily 9am–8pm.

Dubai Museum ✦✦   For many years, the Dubai Museum was the emirate's only real effort to prove that Dubai has a culture beyond sand, sea, and shopping. Seated in the late-18th-century Al Fahidi Fort that over time served as the ruler's palace, a prison, and a garrison, this became a museum in 1970 and has been expanded over the years. Life-size dioramas represent Dubai life in its pre-oil days with re-creations of a souk, early Arabian homes, mosques, and date gardens. There are exhibits of desert and marine life, including a realistic depiction of underwater pearl diving. The main fort is a military museum, and there's a large replica dhow outside the museum.

Al Faheidi Fort, Bastakiya, Bur Dubai. © **4/353-1862.** www.dubaitourism.ae. Admission AED 3 (80¢/40p) adults; AED 1 (25¢/15p) children under 10. Sat–Thurs 8:30am–8:30pm; Fri 2:30–8:30pm.

Gold Souk ✦✦✦   Street after street glitters with gold in this famous shimmering market, a must-see while you're in town. Dubai is the world's largest re-exporter of gold, and its Gold Souk features original and design copies—including rings, bracelets, earrings, necklaces, and gold ingots. Winding through a maze of paths, wall-to-wall shops with vendors from around the world sell yellow and white gold, silver, pearls, and other gems. Because of the heat and fact that many shops close between 1 and 4pm, it's best to avoid visiting the Gold Souk in the middle of the day. The most fun—although also most crowded—time to visit is at night, when it's cooler out and the lighted shops sparkle with their gold and precious stones. Combine an excursion here with a walk through the nearby Spice Souk (p. 101).

Baniyas Rd., Deira. www.dubaitourism.ae. Free admission. Sat–Thurs 9:30am–1pm and 4–10pm; Fri 4–10pm.

Heritage and Diving Village ✦   Near the mouth of Dubai Creek, Heritage and Diving Village showcase Dubai's history as a pearl-diving and trading post. In addition to photographs and exhibits focused on Dubai's maritime past, there are potters and weavers selling Arabian handicrafts, local women serving traditional Emirati food, and vendors offering afternoon camel rides. Heritage and Diving Village lies within walking distance of Sheikh Saeed Al Maktoum's House (below). The most lively time to visit is in the evening.

Near Shindagha Tunnel, Al Shindagha. © **4/393-7151.** www.dubaitourism.ae. Free admission. Daily 8am–10pm.

Heritage House ★★   Next to the Al-Ahmadiya School, the Heritage House was built in 1890 and fully restored in 1994. It contains two floors overlooking an authentic Arabian courtyard. Rooms are traditionally furnished, with displays explaining the original purpose of items in each room. You can see the *majlis* (the area of the home designated for receiving visitors), as well as the main living room, where the family would come together. The architecturally significant courtyard home is one of Dubai's most interesting.

Al-Ahmadiya Street, Al Ras, Deira. ✆ 4/226-0286. www.dubaitourism.ae. Free admission. Sat–Thurs 8am–7:30pm; Fri 2:30–7:30pm.

Jumeirah Mosque ★★   You'll likely hear the mosques before you see them—the call to prayer can be heard in the morning as the sun starts to seep into your hotel room—and a trip to Dubai isn't complete without a visit to this mosque, the only one in the emirate that's open to non-Muslims. Tours are organized by the Sheikh Mohammed Centre for Cultural Understanding, and they educate visitors about Islamic religion and culture. The 1½-hour tour starts at 10am, but be sure to get there about 30 minutes before to ensure you have a spot. Men and women should dress modestly, and while kids 4 and under are not admitted, cameras are.

Jumeirah Beach Rd., Jumeirah. ✆ 4/353-6666. www.cultures.ae. Admission AED 10 ($2.70/£1.40). Tours Sat–Sun, Tues, and Thurs 10am.

Sheikh Mohammed Centre for Cultural Understanding ★   Who are the people of the Emirates? What are the Five Pillars of Islam? Does daily life change during Ramadan? What is the significance of the date palm tree? Find the answers to these and other questions at this excellent cultural organization, established to promote inter-cultural awareness and understanding. The knowledgeable staff offers free written information about the history of the Emirates and its people, local customs, Islam, religious and other celebrations, traditional food, and other insights into UAE culture. The Centre's activities, based on the theme of "open doors, open minds," include cultural breakfasts, lunches, and dinners; Arabic language courses; Bastakiya walking tours; specialized cultural events; and home visits that bring UAE nationals and expatriates together. Visits to the Jumeirah Mosque (see above) are also arranged by the Sheikh Mohammed Centre for Cultural Understanding.

Bastakiya, Bur Dubai. ✆ 4/353-6666. www.cultures.ae. Free admission. Sun–Thurs 9am–3pm.

Sheikh Saeed Al Maktoum's House ★   The home of Dubai's former ruler, this is a good example of the 19th-century architectural style of the Gulf coast characterized by vaulted high-beam ceilings, arched doorways, and sculpted window overhangs. You can visit the downstairs *majlis* (meeting room), living room, kitchen, and courtyard, as well as the upstairs bedrooms and balconies. The house exhibits rare photographs of Dubai in its pre-oil days, as well as paintings, lithographs, and art objects that capture the emirate's development. There is also a collection of rare coins, stamps, and historical documents. A national monument, Sheikh Saeed Al Maktoum's House was once the center of local government.

Next to Heritage and Diving Village, Al Shindagha. ✆ 4/393-7139. www.dubaitourism.ae. Admission AED 2 (50¢/30p) adults; AED 1 (25¢/15p) children under 10. Sat–Thurs 8am–8:30pm; Fri 3–9:30pm.

Spice Souk ★★   The Spice Souk is what comes to mind when people think of Dubai as it was not so long ago, before skyscrapers, highways, and mega-malls took over much of the landscape. Although smaller than it once was, the market features winding alleyways of stalls packed with exotic fragrances and Arabic seasonings. Set in the heart of Deira, this is one of Dubai's most authentic sights, and you'll discover a remarkable variety of spices, nuts, dried fruits, incense herbs, and perfume oils here. Combine a trip here with a visit to the Gold Souk (p. 100).

Near the Gold Souk, Deira. www.dubaitourism.ae. Free admission. Sat–Thurs 9am–1pm and 4–9pm; Fri 4–9pm.

2 Just for Kids

Children's City 🏕🏕   Located in Creekside Park, Children's City is a fun educational center for kids ages 5 to 15. Gallery and exhibition spaces include a planetarium to explore the night skies, a discovery space to understand the human body, an international culture gallery depicting the experiences of children across the globe, an exhibit celebrating local heritage, and a nature center with information about land and sea environments. There's also a theater, play area, and computer learning stations.

Creekside Park, Umm Hurair. ✆ 4/334-0808. www.childrencity.ae. Admission AED 15 ($4.10/£2.05) adults; AED 10 ($2.70/£1.35) children 15 and under. Sat–Thurs 9am–8:30pm; Fri 3–8:30pm.

Dubai Zoo 🏕   The Dubai Zoo has two claims to fame: It's the oldest zoo in the Arabian Peninsula, and it breeds the rare chimpanzee and Arabian wildcat. Beyond that, the zoo holds little claim to greatness. Its size is inadequate to the number of animals, too often kept in small cages, and it's often just too plain hot here. The good news is the zoo's located in a shaded area of Jumeirah surrounded by a number of trees. There are about 200 species of mammals, birds, reptiles, and fish at the zoo, including some Arabian and endangered species. Many of the exotic animals housed here were actually seized in Dubai's ports.

Jumeirah Beach Rd., Jumeirah. ✆ 4/349-6444. www.dubaitourism.ae. Admission AED 3 (80¢/40p). Wed–Mon 10am–5pm; closed Tues.

Wild Wadi 🏕🏕🏕   This is one of my favorite places in Dubai, a refreshing oasis in the midst of a scorched if glitzy and developed desert. Themed around the legend of Wild Wadi, including the adventures of Juha and Sinbad, the water park features 30 thrilling rides and attractions that are equally fun for kids and adults. Among them are wild rapid rides, a lazy river, a wave pool for body-boarding and surfing, and Jumeirah Sceirah—the terrifyingly fun 33m-high (108-ft.) monster ride that drops you at 80kmph (50 mph) to the earth below. There are a number of games for kids, two fast-food restaurants, lockers, and VIP cabanas for adults available for a small fortune. Wild Wadi is located next to the Jumeirah Beach Hotel.

Jumeirah Beach Rd., between Jumeirah Beach Hotel and Burj Al Arab. ✆ 4/409-4000. www.wildwadi.com. Admission AED 180 ($49/£25); AED 150 ($41/£21) children under 1.1m (3 ft. 7 in.). Sept–May daily 11am–7pm; June–Aug daily 11am–9pm.

3 Parks & Beaches

Al Mamzar Beach Park 🏕   Situated in the Al Hamriya area, Al Mamzar Beach Park has four inviting beaches with protected swimming areas and lifeguards as well as open grass spaces with picnic and barbecue areas, children's playgrounds, and an amphitheater with shows for kids. You can walk along winding paths, rent a bicycle, or take a train tour through the park, which also has food kiosks, two swimming pools, and air-conditioned bungalows for rent. Wednesdays are for women and children only.

Past Al Hamriya Port, Al Hamriya. ✆ 4/296-6201. www.dubaitourism.ae. Admission AED 5 ($1.35/70p) per person or AED 30 ($8.15/£4.10) per car. Daily 8am–10:30pm.

Creekside Park ⭐⭐   This is my top choice for jogging, rollerblading, and bicycling in the city. Situated along the creek in the heart of the city, Creekside Park offers waterfront pathways with fishing piers, botanical gardens, playgrounds, barbecue sites, restaurants, and an amphitheater. Concerts and other special events are often held here on holidays and during Dubai Shopping Festival. A 30m-high (98-ft.) **cable car** operates along 2.5km (1½ miles) of the park. Children's City (p. 102) is also located here.

Next to the creek, Umm Hurair. 🕿 **4/336-7633**. www.dubaitourism.ae. Admission AED 5 ($1.35/70p); cable car AED 25 ($6.80/£3.45); AED 10 ($2.70/£1.35) children 15 and under. Daily 8am–11pm.

Jumeirah Beach Park ⭐⭐   Spanning 1km (¾ miles) of coastline in the Jumeirah residential area, this is the city's best public beach. You can rent a lounge chair and umbrella, play beach volleyball, grab an ice cream or snack, or even bring your own food to barbecue. In addition to sand and sea, there's a grassy area with landscaped gardens and a playground. The beach park has lifeguards on duty from 8am until sunset, after which swimming is not allowed. Mondays are exclusively for women and children.

Near Jumeirah Beach Club, Jumeirah. 🕿 **4/349-2555**. www.dubaitourism.ae. Admission AED 5 ($1.35/70p) per person; AED 20 ($5.45/£2.75) per car. Daily 8am–10:30pm.

Safa Park ⭐   This is one of Dubai's largest, most appealing parks. Tree-lined pathways wind their way across green lawns, past an Arabic garden, and to a fountain-filled lake, where small boats are available for rent. Safa Park is an excellent spot for recreational activity, offering bike riding, volleyball, basketball, soccer, and tennis. A low-impact jogging track runs along the perimeter, and rollerblading is allowed in the park. Al Safa also has a traditional Ferris wheel, giant trampoline, bumper cars, and other games for kids and teenagers. A mini-train offers tours through the park if you'd prefer to just relax. Tuesdays are for ladies only.

Al Wasl Rd., Jumeirah. 🕿 **4/349-2111**. www.dubaitourism.ae. Admission AED 3 (80¢/40p) per person; free for children 2 and under. Daily 8am–11pm.

4 Organized Tours

CITY TOURS

London it's not, but Dubai has a handful of open-air double-decker buses roaming its streets. The **Big Bus Company** ⭐ (🕿 **4/324-4187**; www.bigbus.co.uk) offers city tours with two different routes: one focused on sights in Old Dubai, including the Dubai Museum and Sheikh Saeed Al Maktoum House, and the other focused on Jumeirah Beach, with a trip to the Jumeirah Mosque, Burj Al Arab, and Ski Dubai. The tours include the hop-on, hop-off bus routes, a dhow river cruise, and a walking tour, with commentary in English. Prices are AED 165 ($45/£23) for adults and AED 99 ($27/£14) for children 15 and under. Tours depart every hour from 9am to 5pm. Another option is **Wonder Bus Tours** (🕿 **4/359-5656**; www.wonderbusdubai.com), featuring amphibious buses that are as happy in the water as on the road. The 2-hour trips visit Creekside Park and Dubai Creek Golf and Yacht Club before hitting the water. Prices are AED 161 ($44/£22) for adults and AED 103 ($28/£14) for children 15 and under.

If you'd prefer to see the city by boat, **Tour Dubai** ⭐⭐ (🕿 **4/336-8409**; www.tourdubai.com) offers 1-hour excursions along the creek in traditional dhows with four departures per day and hotel pickup available. Prices are AED 130 ($35/£18) for adults and AED 65 ($18/£8.95) for children 11 and under. The same company also offers dinner dhow cruises and other tours. A more traditional, less expensive way to cross the creek is by **water taxi** ⚓, known as *abra*. These little motorized boats connect Deira and Bur Dubai at the dhow wharfage area on the Deira side or the Al Seef Road area on the Bur Dubai side. The fee for the 10-minute ride is negligible (50 fils/15¢/8p).

Another way to visit Dubai is by air. Experience the city and its surroundings with a hot-air balloon ride, with departures every morning from Dubai Internet City and Fossil Rock. The trip takes you over desert and mountains and lasts a little more than an hour. Hot-air balloon rides with **Voyagers Xtreme** (© 4/345-4504; www.turner traveldubai.com) leave every morning and cost AED 780 ($213/£108) per person; the whole excursion with travel time and instruction is about 5 hours. For an expensive, luxury helicopter tour, contact **Aerogulf Services Company** (© 4/220-0331; www.aerogulfservices.com), which offers 30-minute rides for AED 3,200 ($872/£441), with a maximum of four passengers.

DESERT SAFARIS

A trip to Dubai is not complete without a trek into the desert, and there are numerous tour operators offering a range of desert and mountain safaris. Options include half-day, full-day, and overnight excursions; the most popular are evening desert safaris. These dune dinners begin around 4pm with a thrilling ride over the dunes in a 4WD followed by a visit to a camel farm, and then continue with a sunset dinner and Arabian campsite with live entertainment, including belly-dancing and *henna* artists. Most end around 9pm and include transportation to and from one's hotel. Full-day safaris typically involve visits to traditional Bedouin villages, Fossil Rock, and the Hajar Mountains. Overnight safaris let you sleep under the stars at a Bedouin-style campsite. Another popular all-day trip goes to the traditional Arabian village of Hatta, located in the foothills of the Hajar Mountains with freshwater rock pools perfect for swimming. Among the most reputable companies offering a range of desert safaris are **Arabian Adventures** (© 4/303-4888; www.arabian-adventures.com), **Off-Road Adventures** (© 4/321-1377; www.arabian tours.com), and **Orient Tours** (© 4/282-8238; www.orienttours.ae). Dune dinners cost approximately AED 300 ($82/£41) per person, day safaris approximately AED 325 ($89/£45), and overnight safaris about AED 450 ($123/£62).

5 Staying Active

ACTIVITIES A TO Z

BEACH CLUBS

If you're not staying at a beach resort but want to have access to one, there are several excellent beach clubs that offer day passes for nonguests. All have private beaches with watersports, pools, health clubs, restaurants, and bars. These include the clubs at **Le Méridien Mina Seyahi** (© 4/399-3333), **Dubai Marine Beach Resort & Spa** (© 4/346-1111), **Sheraton Jumeirah Beach Resort & Towers** (© 4/399-5533), **Oasis Beach Hotel** (© 4/315-4029), **Jumeirah Beach Hotel** (© 4/406-8800), and the **Ritz-Carlton Dubai** (© 4/399-4000). Rates range from AED 120 to AED 400 ($33–$109/£17–£5.50) depending on the resort and time of year.

BOWLING

When it's just too hot to be outside, there's always bowling. A popular Dubai pastime, particularly in summer, options include **Al Nasr Leisureland** (© 4/337-1234; www.alnasrleisureland.ae), **Dubai Bowling Centre** (© 4/296-9222; www.dubai bowlingcentre.com), and **Thunderbowl** (© 4/343-1000). Games typically cost AED

15 to AED 20 ($4.10–$5.45/£2.05–£2.75) per person, or AED 80 to AED 100 ($22–$27/£11–£14) per hour.

DEEP-SEA FISHING AND YACHT CHARTERS

Dubai's fishing season extends from September to April, and requires a permit or a charter with a licensed tour guide. Common catches include sailfish, barracuda, king-fish, bonito, cobia, dorado, king mackerel, and tuna. **Dubai Creek Golf and Yacht Club** (© 4/295-6000; www.dubaigolf.com) operates a 9.8m (32-ft.) Hatters vessel that carries up to six passengers and includes the crew, tackle, bait, ice, and fuel. Rates are AED 3,500 ($954/£483) for 4 hours, AED 4,000 ($1,090/£552) for 6 hours, and AED 4,500 ($1,226/£621) for 8 hours. **Dubai Voyager** (© 4/348-1900; www.dubaivoyager.com) is located at the Fishing Village in Umm Suqeim and oper-ates a fleet of fully equipped fishing boats at slightly less expensive rates.

GOLF

With fairways extending along the creek, the par 71 championship course at the **Dubai Creek Golf and Yacht Club** (© 4/295-6000; www.dubaigolf.com) is open to players holding a valid handicap certificate. Greens fees are AED 645 to AED 760 ($176–$207/£89–£105) for 18 holes (excluding cart). The Club also has a floodlit par 3 (9-hole) course. The **Montgomerie** (© 4/380-1333), located at Emirates Hills, is a par 72 course boasting the world's largest greens. Fees are AED 300 ($82/£41, including cart) for 18 holes, or AED 180 ($49/£25) for 9 holes. **Emirates Golf Club** (© 4/380-2222; www.dubaigolf.com) is home of the Dubai Desert Classic and fea-tures two 18-hole championship courses: Majlis (AED 825/$225/£114) and Wadi (AED 645–AED 760/$176–$207/£89–£105). Each of these clubs offers professional instructors and world-class facilities.

HORSEBACK RIDING

Another popular sport in Dubai, recreational riding is available with or without an instructor. Two options are the **Jebel Ali Equestrian Club** (© 4/884-5485) and the **Jebel Ali Golf Resort & Spa** (© 4/883-6000). Lessons cost AED 60 ($16/£8.30) for 30 minutes or AED 100 ($27/£14) for 1 hour; desert or beach hacks cost AED 150 ($41/£21) and up per hour.

SKIING

Ski Dubai (&&) (© 4/409-4000; www.skidxb.com) is one of Dubai's modern icons. This 22,500-sq. m (242-sq. ft.) indoor ski resort, equivalent in size to three football fields, accommodates skiing, snowboarding, and tobogganing at temperatures just below freezing. Never mind that it may be hot as Hades outside, Ski Dubai is a win-ter wonderland packing 6,000 tons of artificial snow. A tow lift and quad chairlift service the five runs, the longest of which is 400m (1,312 ft.) with a 60m (197-ft.) vertical drop. Snowboarders have access to a quarter-pipe freestyle zone, and ski and snowboard lessons are available for beginners. Lift tickets include winter clothing (except for hats and gloves) along with ski or snowboard equipment. There's also a fun snow park for kids to play in—think snowballs. The 25-story high Ski Dubai is con-nected to the Mall of the Emirates (p. 116). Snow park admission AED 70 ($19/£9.65); ski slope (2 hr.) AED 150 ($41/£21), additional hour AED 40 ($11/£5.50); ski slope day pass AED 279 ($76/£38); children 12 and under AED 220 ($60/£30). Open Sunday to Wednesday 10am to 11pm and Thursday to Saturday

10am to midnight. An even more spectacular indoor ski resort called the Dubai Sunny Mountain Ski Resort (Snowdome) is due to open in Dubailand in late 2008.

SNORKELING & SCUBA DIVING

Although the diving is even better on the UAE's east coast, the clear waters off Jumeirah Beach are home to a fascinating variety of marine life, such as barracuda, clownfish, eagle rays, moray eels, sea snakes, sea horses, and stingrays. Cement Barge, *Mariam Express,* and the *MV Dara* are popular wreck dives near Dubai. Reputable dive shops include **Pavillion Dive Centre** (© 4/406-8827; www.thepavilliondive centre.com) at the Jumeirah Beach Hotel, where prices range from AED 250 to AED 4,000 ($68–$1,090/£35–£552), and **Al Boom Diving** (© 4/342-3993; www.al boomdiving.com) on Al Wasl Road. Most beach resorts and dive shops rent snorkeling equipment.

TENNIS

Most Dubai resorts have lighted tennis courts and available instructors. Among the city's best tennis clubs are the **Aviation Club** (© 4/282-4122; www.cftennis.com) at Al Garhoud, **Dubai Tennis Academy** (© 4/344-4674; www.dubaitennisacademy.com) at the American University in Dubai, and **Emirates Golf Club** (© 4/380-2222; www.dubaigolf.com) at Emirates Hills, which all offer lessons. Prices vary.

SPECTATOR SPORTS
CAMEL RACING

The most traditional local sport is camel racing, which takes place across the UAE in Dubai, Ras Al Khaimah, Umm Al Quwain, Al Ain, and Abu Dhabi. The controversial use of children as camel jockeys is now prohibited by law, and robotic jockeys are used instead with operators following in 4WDs guiding them with remote controls. In Dubai, races take place during the winter months (usually late Oct to early Apr) on Thursdays and Fridays at the course at **Nad Al Sheba** (© 4/336-3666). There are usually two races per day, with one beginning at 7:30am and the other in the early afternoon. The sheikhs' camels typically compete in the morning race. Admission is free.

GOLF

The **Dubai Desert Classic** is the emirate's preeminent golf tournament, which Tiger Woods won in 2008. The European PGA tour event, boasting $2.5 million in prize

---

And the Sexiest Camel Is . . .

As part of an annual Camel Festival, Abu Dhabi has begun to stage an international beauty pageant for camels in the spring called "Ship of the Desert." Expert camel judges choose the most beautiful from among 10,000 camels brought from Bahrain, Kuwait, Oman, and Saudi Arabia in a contest worth almost $10 million. Judges look at the contestants' big brown eyes, long lashes, and extra long necks as they choose who will reign above all others. The contest is meant to showcase the region's heritage, in which camel ownership has long been a sign of prestige among Bedouin society. To compete, the camels must be pure-bred and free of any diseases. And the best part is you can take home one of these beauties if you're willing to pay the price. In 2008, Dubai's crown prince took home a winner for a modest $2.7 million.

---

money, runs from late January to early February at **Emirates Golf Club** (© 4/380-1777; www.dubaidesertclassic.com). Admission is AED 175 ($48/£24) per day, and tickets sell out quickly.

HORSE RACING

Dubai takes horse racing seriously, although gambling is not part of it. The Dubai ruling family has one of the world's best racing operations, called Goldolphin (www.godolphin.com), which it sends around the globe to compete in the world's top races. Dubai's racing season brings top jockeys from Europe, the U.S., and Australia, and lasts from October to April, with races taking place at night at **Nad Al Sheba** (© 4/327-0077; www.dubairacingclub.com). General admission is free. **Dubai Racing Carnival** is a 9-week festival of top-class racing beginning in late February and culminating in the $6 million **Dubai World Cup** (www.dubairacingclub.com/dubai worldcup), the world's richest race, which takes place in late March.

RUGBY

The **Dubai Rugby 7s** (© 4/321-0008; www.dubairugby7s.com) is one of the year's most popular social events, attracting tens of thousands of spectators to the new **Dubai Rugby Grounds.** Usually the last weekend in November, the Dubai Rugby 7s marks the opening round of the IRB Sevens World Series, in which 16 of the best Sevens nations compete.

TENNIS

The **Dubai Tennis Open** (© 4/282-4122; www.dubaitennischampionships.com) takes place each year from late February to early March at the **Aviation Club** in Garhoud. The million-dollar event includes men's and women's tournaments. Andy Roddick took the men's title in 2008.

8

Shopping

There's no doubt about it: Dubai is a shopper's paradise. One could argue that all of the international fashions offered here are available in London, New York, or Milan, that Dubai actually isn't any less expensive than elsewhere except for during a couple festival periods, and that if you're really looking for authentic Middle Eastern goods, Dubai is hardly at the center of production and you're better off elsewhere. But there's something about shopping here that goes well beyond this being just a hot consumer market. I consider it more like a city of Shoppers Gone Wild, with an Arabian flair. Sure, this is the result of deft marketing, glitzy malls, duty-free prices, and wide consumer selection, but it's also what you get when millions of people fly in from around the world each year to purchase items from every corner of the globe.

It sometimes seems the whole Dubai culture revolves around spending money. This is just as true for locals and expatriates as for visitors. Emiratis may be a minority in their own land, but you will see them en masse at the malls, since shopping is a favorite family pastime. In summer, the heavily air-conditioned shopping centers are among the only places people want to go, since it's hot as Hades outside. So, the whole population ends up shopping through the summer, particularly during **Dubai Summer Surprises** (p. 109), with only a marginal decrease come fall. And then there's **Dubai Shopping Festival** (p. 109), the apex of the year-round shopping frenzy that grows larger year by year, as people pour into Dubai from all directions to fill their bags, get some sun, and return home with more photos but diminished savings.

The diversity of goods at the many fanciful malls, markets, stores, and shops is truly amazing, the result of Dubai's heritage as an expanding center of trade. There are traditional souks selling everything from textiles and carpets to antiques, handicrafts, electronics, food, and spices. There's Dubai's world-famous **Gold Souk** (p. 112), where skillful bargaining can lend you an excellent deal. There are mega-malls and shopping centers that resemble amusement parks, world-class department stores selling the latest international fashions, and independent stores and eclectic boutiques offering goods to suit particular tastes. You'll easily find recognizable American, European, and Asian products, but make sure not to overlook what Dubai more uniquely offers: jewelry of Middle Eastern design, local fashion, Arabian perfumes, carpets and tapestries, antiques, *shisha* pipes, and other regional goods.

Despite the hype, you may not find prices much lower than you would during sales periods in the U.S. and Europe, except during the shopping festivals, when prices really are temptingly low. The obvious savings comes from the absence of a sales tax. The best day-to-day bargains are found in the bazaars—if you're a skillful negotiator. Bargaining is

Dubai Shopping Festivals

The **Dubai Shopping Festival** ★★★ (www.mydsf.com) began in 1996 as an effort to boost retail sales in what was then a slow period at the beginning of the year. The plan worked. Today, roughly three million annual visitors come for DSF, as it's known locally, which takes place for 1 month between late January and February. DSF has evolved into an international tourist extravaganza in which more than 2,300 Dubai retail stores participate with impressive bargains and store giveaways under the theme "One World, One Family, One Festival." Everything is on sale at discount prices—gold, jewelry, perfume, haute couture, electronics, handicrafts, textiles, you name it. In 2007, the festival earned more than AED 10 billion in sales, making it among the most intense shopping sprees ever recorded.

One of the major attractions during DSF is **Global Village** ★ *Kids* (www.globalvillage.ae), a large outdoor complex where art and fashion from across the world are showcased in 67 international pavilions with life-size replicas of famous monuments. World cuisine, live cultural performances, and carnival rides are also offered. Global Village is open from December to March from around 4pm to midnight or 1am, depending on the day; 1 day a week is reserved for families only. Tickets are AED 5 ($1.35/70p), cash only. *Note:* Those wishing to pay by credit card here should be sure to bring along their passport for identification. Otherwise, there are ATMs scattered throughout the event. Another favorite attraction during DSF is the **Night Souk,** which takes place on the streets of Al Riqqa, Al Muraqab-bat, and Al Seef, where vendors stay open past midnight, the smell of authentic Arabian food fills the air, and street performers dance into the night.

Raffles of anything from luxury cars to pots of gold and large cash prizes happen throughout the festival—you'll find these ongoing at Global Village, the major malls, and Dubai airport. The entertainment extends to children's events, fashion shows, film festivals, music events, and nighttime light shows and fireworks displays. In years past there have been balloon festivals, performances by Cirque du Soleil, and other cultural events all planned around DSF. There's even a water and light show at the Creek Park. The **Dubai World Cup** ★★★ (p. 107), the richest horse race in the world with a $12-million purse, also takes place during the Shopping Festival. Hotels and some airlines, including Emirates Airlines, offer discounted rates during DSF, adding further appeal to visiting during this time.

A second, smaller shopping festival happens in summer called **Dubai Summer Surprises (DSS)** *Kids*. Created to lure visitors to Dubai during the unbelievably hot summer, it lasts for 10 weeks between June and August and includes impressive shopping discounts and heavily reduced hotel rates. Since kids are out of school, DSS has a particular emphasis on family events, including children's entertainment and educational activities.

Where to Shop in Dubai

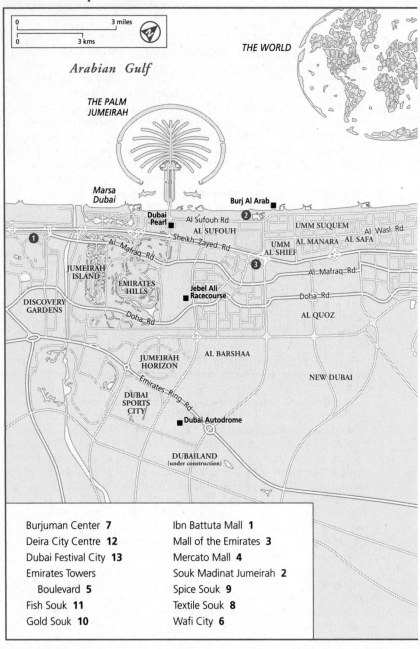

Burjuman Center **7**

Deira City Centre **12**

Dubai Festival City **13**

Emirates Towers
   Boulevard **5**

Fish Souk **11**

Gold Souk **10**

Ibn Battuta Mall **1**

Mall of the Emirates **3**

Mercato Mall **4**

Souk Madinat Jumeirah **2**

Spice Souk **9**

Textile Souk **8**

Wafi City **6**

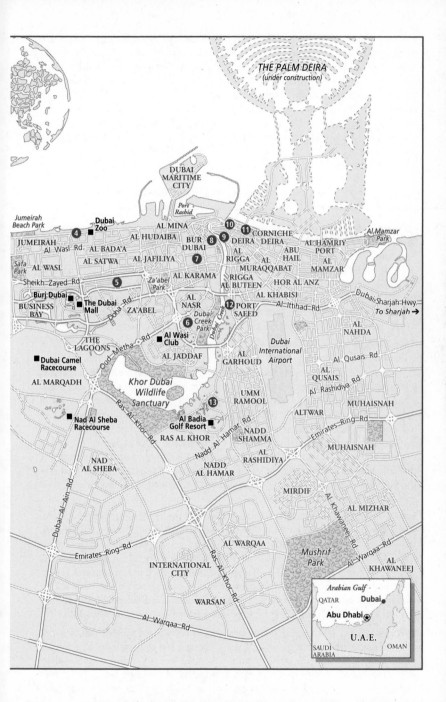

common in the souks, but not the malls or established stores. Don't expect to get a refund when you buy from anywhere other than an established international store, and even in those check the policy carefully, as refunds are often heavily restricted. Most stores in Dubai are open until 10pm (many malls stay open until midnight on Thurs–Fri), and accept all major credit cards; cash is the usual method of payment in the souks.

Dubai's traditional shopping areas include Al Riqqa Road, Al Dhiyafa Road, Bani Yas Square, and Karama—which sells mostly pirated and counterfeit goods. Higher-end fashions are available along Jumeirah Beach Road, at the many large shopping centers (of which Mall of the Emirates is the largest), and in the duty-free complex at the airport. Once complete, the Dubai Mall at Burj Dubai will become the world's largest shopping complex, a 1.1 million-sq.-m (12 million-sq.-ft.) area with 15 individual malls or niches, more than 1,000 retail outlets, and the world's largest gold souk.

1 Souks

Fish Souk Unless you're a resident here or have a particular passion for cooking fish while on vacation, you're unlikely to open your wallet in the fish souk. If it's particularly hot outside, you're unlikely to want to open your nose here, either. But in early morning and again in the evening, just as the dhows are returning from sea, the fish market is an interesting place to explore the marvelous selection of seafood on display. You'll find a small fishing museum and seafood restaurant here, too. Deira, near Shindagha Tunnel.

Gold Souk ★★★ The Gold Souk is amazing for its sheer size and diversity. Dubai is the world's largest re-exporter of gold, and its famous Gold Souk features just about every jewelry design you can fathom—including rings, bracelets, earrings, necklaces, and gold ingots. Winding through a maze of paths, wall-to-wall shops sell yellow and white gold, silver, pearls, and other gems. Bargaining is expected: Although the price of gold is set (based on weight) according to the daily international rate—and no more or less expensive here than anywhere else in Dubai—there is leverage in price over the quality of the design and craftsmanship of each particular piece of jewelry. Because of the heat and fact that many shops close between 1 and 4pm, it's best to avoid visiting the Gold Souk in the middle of the day. The most fun—although also most crowded—time to visit is at night, when it's cooler out and the lighted shops sparkle with their gold and precious stones. Baniyas Rd., Deira.

Souk Madinat Jumeirah ★★ Dubai's version of Venice, Madinat Jumeirah exemplifies the emirate's role as a fantasyland in the Arabian desert. Its beautiful though artificial souk replicates an ancient Middle Eastern marketplace with winding alleys and handsome boutiques selling Arabian art, sweets, jewelry, and upscale souvenirs. The bazaar includes 75 shops and galleries, and more than 20 waterfront cafes, restaurants, and bars. Items are far more expensive here than at Dubai's traditional souks in the old town, but it's worth visiting just to window-shop and enjoy the extraordinary scenery. Open daily 10am to 11pm. Madinat Jumeirah in Umm Suqeim. ℰ 4/366-8888.

Spice Souk ★ The Spice Souk is what comes to mind when people think of Dubai as it was not so long ago, before skyscrapers, highways, and megamalls took over much of the landscape. Although smaller than it once was, the souk features winding alleyways of stalls packed with exotic fragrances and Arabic seasonings. Set in the heart of Deira, this is one of Dubai's most authentic sights, and you'll discover a remarkable variety of spices, nuts, and dried fruits here. Deira, near the Gold Souk.

Textile Souk (Meena Bazaar)   Dubai is home to a large Indian immigrant community, who brought their textiles and tailoring along with them. The textile souk carries colorful fabrics from various countries, which can all be fashioned into traditional dress (saris and tunics) or basics (dress shirts and pants). The number of choices, such as the Gold Souk, can seem overwhelming, but if you have a few days, you can walk away with some affordable fit-for-you pieces. Bur Dubai, across the creek from the Spice Souk.

2 Malls & Shopping Plazas

BurJuman Centre ⚑⚑   BurJuman dresses the A-list of celebrities (and wannabe celebrities) seeking designer fashions, cosmetics, and jewelry. Stores such as Saks Fifth Avenue, Calvin Klein, DKNY, Versace, Dior, Prada, and Guess are here, and the three-story mall with 300 retail outlets is also filled with gourmet cafes and restaurants. There's no better place in Dubai for haute couture. Families will appreciate Planet Sega and Toby's Jungle Adventure, both located here. Open Saturday to Thursday 10am to 10pm, Friday 4 to 10pm. Trade Centre Rd., located next to Citibank in Bur Dubai. ⒞ 4/352-0222.

Deira City Centre ⚑   City Centre has long been one of Dubai's leading shopping plazas, although it's been overshadowed somewhat by the larger and glitzier Mall of the Emirates. Among City Centre's 350 stores are Burberry, Debenhams, Gap, H&M, Karen Millen, Mango, New Look, Massimo Dutti, and Zara. There are shops selling traditional Arabian perfumes, handicrafts, and carpets, as well as local and international jewelry stores such as Damas and Tiffany & Co. City Centre also has an 11-screen cinema, 55 restaurants outlets, and kids' games, rides, and activities at Magic Planet. Open Saturday to Thursday 10am to 10pm, Friday 2 to 10pm. Located across from the Dubai Creek Golf and Yacht Club. ⒞ 4/295-1010. www.deiracitycentre.com.

Dubai Festival City ⚑   Misleadingly named, Festival City is actually another of Dubai's enormous malls. It has 600 stores and 100 restaurants and cafes, as well as five hotels, a marina and yacht club, fitness center, 12-screen cinema, and 10-lane bowling alley. As many locals as foreigners shop here, and the stores are a mix of international and regional brands. The Power Centre—part of Festival City—is a household shopping complex that includes a giant IKEA. It's connected by way of a gold marketplace to the Festival Waterfront Centre, which offers high-street brands and waterfront alfresco dining. Open Sunday to Wednesday 10am to 10pm, Thursday to Saturday 10am to midnight. Located in Garhoud off the Garhoud Bridge. ⒞ 4/232-5444. www.dubaifestivalcity.com.

Emirates Towers Boulevard ⚑   Situated in the iconic Emirates Towers, the elegant Boulevard houses two floors of fashion-forward shops, restaurants, and bars. It's both smaller and more exclusive than Dubai's other shopping centers. Among the well-known international shops are Yves Saint Laurent, Giorgio Armani, Bulgari, Damas, Gucci, Cartier, and Ermenegildo Zegna. Local stores such as Ajmal Eternal and the Persian Carpet House are also here. The Boulevard connects to Emirates Towers Hotel. Open Saturday to Thursday 10am to 10pm, Friday 4 to 10pm. Sheikh Zayed Rd. in the Emirates Towers Hotel and Office Tower. ⒞ 4/319-8999.

Ibn Battuta Mall ⚑   This enormous mall on the way to Jebel Ali was designed with six distinct shopping courts celebrating the travels of Arab explorer Ibn Battuta through Andalusia, China, Egypt, India, Persia, and Tunisia. The China Court showcases a life-size Chinese *junk* ship, and there's a tempting ice-cream shop next to it called Marble Slab Creamery. Wander the maze of walkways leading through the other shopping courts, but be careful not to get lost. Department stores include H&M,

Mall of the Emirates

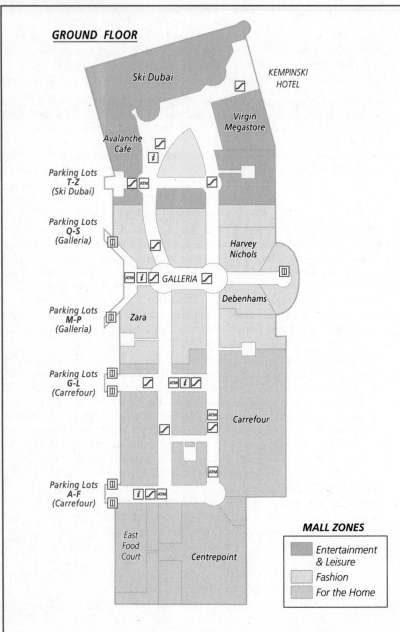

GROUND FLOOR

Ski Dubai

KEMPINSKI HOTEL

Virgin Megastore

Avalanche Café

Parking Lots T-Z (Ski Dubai)

Parking Lots Q-S (Galleria)

Harvey Nichols

GALLERIA

Debenhams

Parking Lots M-P (Galleria)

Zara

Parking Lots G-L (Carrefour)

Carrefour

Parking Lots A-F (Carrefour)

East Food Court

Centrepoint

MALL ZONES

Entertainment & Leisure

Fashion

For the Home

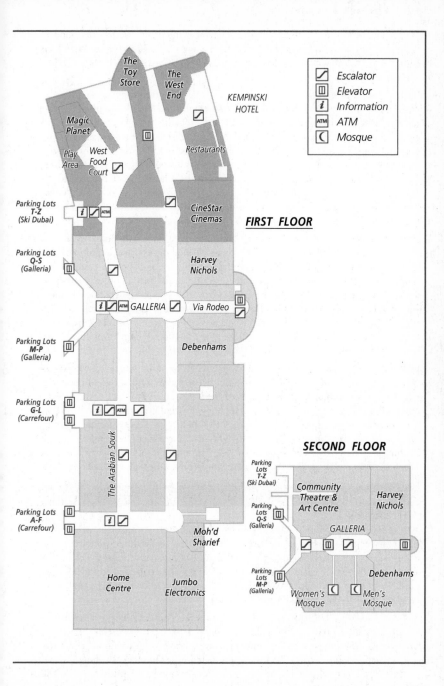

Escalator
Elevator
Information
ATM
Mosque

KEMPINSKI HOTEL

The Toy Store

The West End

Magic Planet

Play Area

West Food Court

Restaurants

CineStar Cinemas

FIRST FLOOR

Parking Lots T-Z (Ski Dubai)

Parking Lots Q-S (Galleria)

Harvey Nichols

GALLERIA

Via Rodeo

Parking Lots M-P (Galleria)

Debenhams

Parking Lots G-L (Carrefour)

The Arabian Souk

SECOND FLOOR

Parking Lots T-Z (Ski Dubai)

Community Theatre & Art Centre

Harvey Nichols

Parking Lots Q-S (Galleria)

GALLERIA

Parking Lots M-P (Galleria)

Debenhams

Parking Lots A-F (Carrefour)

Moh'd Sharief

Women's Mosque

Men's Mosque

Home Centre

Jumbo Electronics

Debenhams, and Fitz & Simons, and most major name-brand retailers are found in the mall. The plaza also holds an IMAX theater, along with a 20-screen cinema. Open Saturday to Thursday 10am to 10pm, Friday 2 to 10pm. The Gardens at Jebel Ali. ℂ **4/362-1900.** www.ibnbattutamall.com.

Mall of the Emirates ✸✸✸ This spectacular mall takes the shopping experience to new heights, offering not just world-class department stores and retail outlets, but also the unbelievable **Ski Dubai** (p. 105), two world food courts, a community theater and arts center, a 14-screen cinema, and a fun zone including a large arcade and bowling alley. Mall of the Emirates is the largest shopping center outside North America, boasting more than 400 stores and 65 restaurants. Retailers include Harvey Nichols, Debenhams, Louis Vuitton, Mango, and Zara. The **Kempinski hotel** (p. 66) connects to the mall and ski resort. Why not ski and shop, then go back to your hotel for a swim? Open Sunday to Wednesday from 10am to 10pm, Thursday to Saturday from 10am to midnight. Sheikh Zayed Rd., at Interchange 4. ℂ **4/341-4747.** www.malloftheemirates.com.

Mercato Mall ✸ One of the flashier additions along Jumeirah Beach Road, this ornate Renaissance-style mall houses 90 stores, 16 food outlets, and a multiplex cinema. A favorite hangout for the young and wealthy, the Italianesque complex has shops selling arts, antiques, carpets, jewelry, perfume, and men's and women's fashions. Internationally known stores such as Armani, Cerrutti, Hugo Boss, Mango, Massimo Dutti, and Topshop are all found here, as is a Virgin Megastore stocked with the latest music and games. The mall's giant glass ceiling gives this mall a refreshingly open feel. Open Saturday to Thursday from 10am to 10pm, Friday from 2 to 10pm. Located opposite the beach on Jumeirah Beach Rd. ℂ **4/344-4161.**

Wafi City ✸✸ The recently expanded Wafi City is one of the emirate's most impressive malls, part of an expansive leisure complex where **Raffles Dubai** (p. 60) opened in late 2007. The innovative shopping center houses more than 350 high-end stores, an outstanding collection of restaurants and bars at the adjacent Pyramids complex, and the luxurious **Cleopatra's Spa** (p. 119). Among the shops here are Versace, Jaeger, La Senza, Chanel, Mont Blanc, and Tag Heuer. Wafi City is also appealing for families, and the Encounter Zone offers entertainment for teens and tots. Open Saturday to Thursday 10am to 10pm, Friday 4:30 to 10pm. Sheikh Rashid Rd. ℂ **4/324-4555.** www.wafi.com.

3 Shopping A to Z

ART GALLERIES

Art Space One of the city's most sophisticated galleries, Art Space showcases contemporary Middle Eastern art and artists. Painting and sculpture exhibitions change every 3 weeks, with champagne opening nights. Recent shows have featured well-known artists from the Gulf, Levant, and North Africa. The gallery is located on the 9th floor of the Fairmont Dubai. Open Saturday to Thursday 10am to 8pm. Fairmont Hotel, Sheikh Zayed Rd. ℂ **4/332-5523.** www.artspace-dubai.com.

B21 Art Gallery Located in a warehouse in the Al Quoz area, where a number of quality art galleries have recently been popping up, B21 promotes emerging talent from across the Arab region. The contemporary art exhibits here tend to be innovative and at times provocative. It's located just behind the Spinney's warehouse. Open Saturday to Thursday 10am to 7pm. Al Quoz 3, off Sheikh Zayed Rd. at Interchange 3. ℂ **4/340-3965.** www.b21artgallery.com.

Majlis Gallery   The Majlis Gallery in the Bastakiya quarter features traditional ceramics, jewelry, paintings, sculptures, Islamic calligraphy, and other works by regional artists. It's the oldest commercial gallery in Dubai, situated in a lovely courtyard house typical of this area 100 years ago. The Majlis Gallery exhibits well-known international and regional artists. Hours vary. Al Fahidi St., Bastakiya, Bur Dubai. ℂ 4/353-6233. www. majlisgallery.com.

Third Line   Off Sheikh Zayed Road at Interchange 3, Third Line promotes Middle Eastern artists who push the boundaries of contemporary Islamic art through various mediums. A recent exhibit by Susan Hefuna explored her German-Egyptian heritage through works in wood, bronze, textiles, and drawings. Another by Pouran Jinchi revealed a line of postmodern headgear incorporating patterned fabrics with traditional calligraphy and Islamic design. Open Saturday to Thursday from 11am to 8pm. Al Quoz 3, off Sheikh Zayed Rd. at Interchange 3. ℂ 4/341-1367. www.thethirdline.com.

XVA Gallery   XVA is a boutique hotel and gallery in the center of Bastakiya, behind the Basta Art Café and the Majlis Gallery. Owned by Mona Hauser, the gallery displays an excellent collection of Middle Eastern artwork through changing exhibits, including contemporary paintings, sculptures, and installations by regional artists. From September to June on Wednesday evenings, free film screenings are shown. There's also a shaded vegetarian cafe and a small gift shop here. Open Saturday to Thursday 9am to 7pm, Friday 10am to 5pm. Bastakiya, Bur Dubai. ℂ 4/353-5383. www.xvagallery.com.

CARPETS

Persian Carpet House ⭐   Persian carpets are considered by many to be the best carpets in the world, often holding or increasing their value with time. They are known for their calligraphic nature and often have elaborate curvilinear or floral designs. Persian Carpet House is a trusted place to buy high quality carpets, not just from Iran but from Afghanistan, Pakistan, Kashmir, and elsewhere in the region. Open Saturday to Thursday 10am to 10pm, Friday 4 to 10pm. Emirates Towers Blvd., ground level. ℂ 4/330-3277.

Pride of Kashmir   Hand-knotted pure-silk carpets from Kashmir are sold along with Persian carpets from Qum, Kashan, Isfahan, Nain, and Tabriz. In addition to the extraordinary rugs, this store sells gorgeous cashmere, *pashmina, shahmina,* and *jamawar* shawls, cashmere jackets and pullovers, and classic and antique furniture. Did you know it takes three goats and up to 3 years to complete a single *pashmina* shawl? Open Saturday to Thursday from 10am to 10pm, Friday from 2 to 10pm. Mercato Mall. ℂ 4/342-0270. www.prideofkashmir.com.

The Sultani   Located in an open area of Dubai Festival City, the Sultani offers an impressive selection of richly patterned Persian, Afghan, Pakistani, and Kashmir carpets. The shop also sells *pashminas,* antiques, jewelry, furnishings, and lifestyle accessories. As with other carpet stores, bargaining is expected. Open Sunday to Wednesday 10am to 10pm, Thursday to Saturday 10am to midnight. Dubai Festival City. ℂ 050/587-2430. www.thesultani.com.

DEPARTMENT STORES

Debenhams   Another excellent department store out of Britain, Debenhams is known for quality goods and excellent customer service. Here you'll find an extensive selection of reasonably priced designer clothes for men, women, and children, as well as beauty products and homeware. Debehams has branches at Deira City Centre, Ibn

Battuta Mall, and Mall of the Emirates. Open Saturday to Thursday 10am to 10pm, Friday 2 to 10pm. Deira City Centre. ☎ **4/294-0011**. www.debenhams.com.

Fitz & Simons   The first branch of this cutting edge European department store to open in the Middle East, Fitz & Simons offers a range of stylish men's and women's fashions, lingerie, cooking ware, home decor, contemporary jewelry, and lifestyle accessories. Among the established European brands offered are Gerry Weber, Stre-nesse, Luisa Cerano, Wolford, Georg Jensen, and Royal Copenhagen. Open Saturday to Thursday 10am to 10pm, Friday 2 to 10pm. Ibn Battuta Mall, India Court. ☎ **4/368-3700.** www.fitzandsimons.com.

Harvey Nichols 🦴   This very stylish London-based department store sells high-end fashions. Its clothing line tends to be younger and sexier than that of its British com-petitor, Harrods. This is the largest Harvey Nichols outside the British Isles, and there's a chic Arabian-style cafe on the second floor called Almaz by Meno, which has a selection of simple dishes and desserts, as well as 18 flavors of *shisha*. The only prob-lem is this Harvey Nichols tends to be more expensive than the one in London. Open Sunday to Wednesday from 10am to 10pm, Thursday to Saturday from 10am to mid-night. Mall of the Emirates. ☎ **4/409-8888**. www.harveynichols.com.

Marks & Spencer   A favorite in the U.K., Marks & Spencer sells quality lines of men's and women's clothes, including swimwear and lingerie, as well as shoes, beauty products, and gourmet food. This is the largest Marks & Spencer outside the U.K. Open Sunday to Wednesday 10am to 10pm, Thursday to Saturday 10am to midnight. Dubai Festival City. ☎ **4/206-6466**. www.marksandspencerme.com.

Saks Fifth Avenue   The BurJuman Centre may be a long way from New York City's Fifth Avenue, but this Saks promises all the shopping elegance of the Manhat-tan original. The largest luxury goods store in the Middle East, Saks Fifth Avenue sig-nificantly expands Dubai's selection of designer and boutique products. In addition to high-end brands such as Gucci, Prada, and Juicy Couture, Saks features exquisite jew-elry, cosmetics, fragrances, and accessories for men and women. Open Saturday to Thursday 10am to 10pm, Friday 4 to 10pm. BurJuman Centre. ☎ **4/351-5551**. www.saks fifthavenue.com.

FASHION

Boutique 1   This deluxe-fashion store combines multiple high-end brands under one roof. A favorite among locals, Boutique 1 offers elegant and edgy selections, as well as some exclusive pieces designed just for it. Among the brands sold here are Mul-berry, Chloé, Oscar de la Renta, Blumarine, Missoni, Stella McCartney, Rachel Roy, and Elie Saab. Open Saturday to Thursday 10am to 10pm, Friday 4 to 10pm. Emirates Towers Blvd. ☎ **4/330-4555**. www.boutique1.com.

First Lady   If you didn't think *abayas* (the traditional Islamic dress worn by many Arab women) could be glitzy, think again. First Lady sells a variety of fashionable and even sparkling black *abayas*. Open Sunday to Wednesday 10am to 10pm, Thursday to Saturday 10am to midnight. Dubai Festival City. ☎ **4/232-6222**.

H&M   This Swedish clothing company has more than 1,200 stores in 22 countries, and three of the only four in the Middle East are in Dubai at Deira City Center, Mall of the Emirates, and Ibn Battuta Mall. H&M offers high-street fashion and accessories for men and women of all ages, and boasts more than 100 in-house designers. It tends to be less expensive than competitor stores, making it a kind of "IKEA" of the fashion world. Open Sunday to Wednesday from 10am to 10pm, Thursday to Saturday from 10am to midnight. Mall of the Emirates. ℂ 4/341-5880. www.hm.com.

Ounass   Designer women's fashions are sold at this local company, including dresses, bags, shoes, and other accessories. Some of the brands retailed here are Catherine Malandrino, Elle Tahari, Juicy Couture, Manouch, Rock & Republic, Theory, and Pinko. Open daily 10am to 11pm. Madinat Jumeirah in Umm Suqeim. ℂ 4/366-8888.

JEWELRY

Ahmed Seddiqi & Sons   The UAE's top seller of Swiss watches, Seddiqi & Sons features quality timepieces and jewelry. Well-known luxury Swiss watches include quartz, battery, shockproof, and waterproof options. The store will custom design watches with jewelry. Service is meticulous. Open Saturday to Wednesday from 10am to 10pm, Thursday and Friday from 10am to midnight. Wafi City (also in Diera City Centre, Grand Hyatt, Jumeirah Beach Hotel, and Le Royal Méridien). ℂ 4/324-1010.

Al Liali   Among the many jewelry stores you'll find in Dubai, many of international fame, Al Liali stands out as one of the top local options. This Dubai-based jeweler offers Arabian and European designs, including custom handcrafted jewelry. It specializes in 18-carat gold, certified diamonds, silver, and precious and semi-precious stones. Open Saturday to Thursday from 10am to 10pm, Friday from 2 to 10pm. Mercato Mall (also in BurJuman Centre, Madinat Jumeirah, Mall of the Emirates, and Ibn Battuta Mall–Egypt Court). ℂ 4/344-5055.

Damas   You'll find this UAE-based jeweler just about everywhere in Dubai, and it's worth a look just to know how wealthy locals like to wear their gems. Classic and contemporary jewelry and watches include well-known international brands as well as in-house designs. Open Saturday to Thursday from 10am to 10pm, Friday from 2 to 10pm. Mercato Mall (also in BurJuman Centre, Deira City Centre, Festival City, Ibn Battuta Mall, and Mall of the Emirates). ℂ 4/349-8833. www.damasjewel.com.

PERFUMES

Ajmal Eternal   This distinctive fragrance store sells non-alcohol based perfumes characteristic of the traditional Gulf region. The showroom displays an exotic selection in fanciful glass perfume bottles ranging in sizes, shapes, and colors, as well as other artistically designed glass pieces and decorative plates. Open Saturday to Thursday 10am to 10pm, Friday 4 to 10pm. Emirates Towers Blvd. ℂ 4/330-0600. www.ajmaleternal.com.

Al Arabiya Al Swissriya   Swiss Arabian Perfumes, as it is called in English, sells premium and authentic *ood* (alcohol-free, concentrated perfume oil), along with a range of French and Arabian perfumes. Come here to learn which fragrances locals traditionally use and see the beautifully designed perfume bottles that encase them. Brands include Divina, Mukhalat Malaki, and Kashkha. Open Sunday to Wednesday 10am to 10pm, Thursday to Saturday 10am to midnight. Dubai Festival City. ℂ 6/577-4451.

SPAS

Cleopatra's   The largest day spa in the UAE, Cleopatra's will restore your body with a tantalizing array of treatments. Choose between massages, scrubs, wraps, aromatic baths, and facials. In the mood for a Middle Eastern mud bath? Ask for the exotic Rasul Therapy. Attached to the Wafi City shopping and entertainment complex, Cleopatra's features separate men's and women's spa areas, each with its own treatment rooms, sauna, Jacuzzi, steam room, and plunge pool. Clients with spa packages also have access to the wonderful "lazy river" surrounding the adjacent Pharaoh's Club pool. Female spa open daily 8:30am to 8pm; male spa open daily 9:30am to 10pm. Wafi City. ℭ 4/324-7700. www.wafi.com.

H20 The Male Spa The contemporary male spa of the Jumeirah Emirates Towers hotel is designed with jet-lagged business travelers in mind. The rejuvenating spa offers massages, facial treatments, and tanning facilities, as well as two particularly innovative concepts. One is the oxygen bar, where clients de-stress in Italian shiatsu massage chairs while hooking up to oxygen and watching movies with 3-D glasses. The other is a saltwater flotation pool, in which the management promises 1 hour equals 8 hours of deep sleep. Open daily 9am to 11pm. Jumeirah Emirates Towers hotel. ℭ 4/319-8181. www.jumeirahemiratestowers.com.

Ritz-Carlton Spa Like the Ritz-Carlton it's housed in, this Balinese-inspired spa is a great place to get away from the fast-paced, skyscraper-filled Dubai. Treatments range from Balinese-influenced body rituals performed by native therapists to European-style facials that incorporate ingredients from the Dead Sea; my favorite is the Degrees Hot Stone Massage. There are two female-only treatment rooms, and the spa also offers bath treatments in your guest room (women are treated with champagne and chocolate-covered strawberries, while gents enjoy a cigar and cognac). Open daily 9:30am to 7:30pm. Ritz-Carlton Dubai, Jumeirah. ℭ 4/399-4000. www.ritzcarlton.com.

Willow Stream Spa The Fairmont Dubai is heavily influenced by its proximity to the Gulf waters, and the Willow Stream Spa follows suit with separate sunrise and sunset pools, marine-based treatments and products (Phytomer), and water features including Jacuzzis, Turkish hammam-style steam rooms, ice showers, and footbaths. The Romanesque-style spa is divided between male and female areas (the latter even has its own gym) and the health club. Choose from a variety of massages, facials, body wraps, and more; signature treatments include the Energy of the Sea body treatment, which combines a sea-salt scrub with Thai massage techniques. Spa open daily 9am to 9pm, health club 6am to midnight. Fairmont Dubai, Sheikh Zayed Rd. ℭ 4/311-8800. www.fairmont.com.

SWEETS

Bateel Dates are a staple of this part of the world, and the best dates in the UAE are sold here. Bateel has its own farm that grows more than 20 varieties of dates, as well as a processing plant and chocolate factory. The result is what you find at the retail outlet: chocolate-covered dates and other Arabian sweets, gourmet Arabic coffee, and more tempting treats. Open Saturday to Thursday 10am to 10pm, Friday 4 to 10pm. BurJuman Centre. ℭ 4/355-2853. www.bateel.ae.

Patchi Mouthwatering Arabian chocolates and elegant sweets are sold at this famous Lebanese confectionary shop in Emirates Towers and elsewhere. Ask for a mixed arrangement to buy as a gift, and be sure to purchase some for yourself. The beautiful store also sells decorative plates, glasses, and crystal. Open Saturday to Thursday 10am to 10pm, Friday 4 to 10pm. Emirates Towers Blvd. ℭ 4/330-4222. www.patchi.com.

9

Dubai After Dark

Dubai has been called the world's "new Ibiza" and without question boasts the hottest nightlife in the Middle East. The many nationalities living in and visiting this wealthy emirate ensure a diversity that gives Dubai a unique richness. While the performing arts remain underdeveloped, the bar and clubbing scene puts Dubai on par with other leading resort cities. The action here revolves around hotels, since with only a few exceptions these are the places that have liquor licenses to serve drinks in restaurants, bars, and clubs. Whereas drinking is not allowed in many Arab countries, and even in some parts of the UAE such as neighboring Sharjah, non-Muslims are free to drink in Dubai. An evening at a *shisha* cafe, most of which do not serve alcohol, is the more traditional nighttime activity for Emiratis.

The expanding after-dark scene includes beach bars, pubs, wine bars, cocktail lounges, and nightclubs. The venues cater to crowds from both East and West. Thursday is the biggest night (the weekend here is Fri–Sat), but there's something going on every evening of the week. Special promotions often target women, and Tuesdays and Sundays are ladies' nights at many establishments. Bars usually close at 1am or 2am, while clubs are empty before 11pm and stay open until 3am. Door policies and cover charges vary. The drinking age is 21, but some clubs require patrons be at least 25 to enter. Most don't allow beach attire, and many bouncers selectively allow entrance based on appearance. Among the clubs that say "members only," exceptions are often made for groups that include women.

Among the liveliest areas with multiple restaurants, bars, and clubs housed in one location are Madinat Jumeirah, the Pyramids at Wafi City, the Boulevard at Emirates Towers, and the Dubai Marine Beach Resort & Spa. The largest hotels and resorts offer multiple entertainment options, as well. Choosing one of these entertainment complexes allows you to visit multiple establishments in a one-stop night on the town. It also minimizes your need to deal with traffic and finding parking, which can be difficult on weekend nights.

Live music is not permitted during Ramadan, and nightclubs remain closed during this period. Still, there's plenty to do at night during this holy month. Restaurants are full starting at sundown, and Ramadan tents stay open until 2 or 3am with people talking, sipping non-alcoholic drinks, and smoking *shisha*. Many hotel bars do serve alcohol during this period, but only after dark. They're typically much quieter than during the rest of the year.

Dubai After Dark

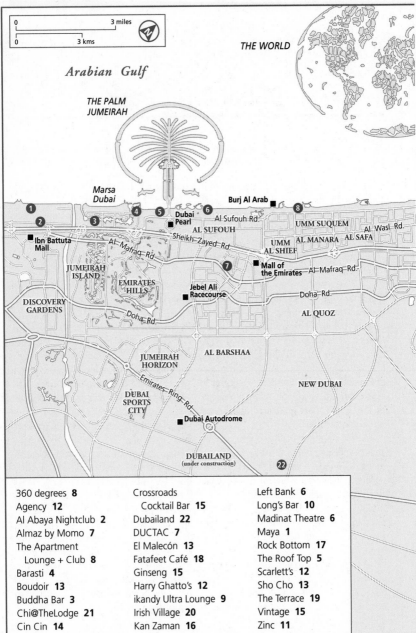

0 ——— 3 miles
0 ——— 3 kms

Arabian Gulf

THE WORLD

THE PALM JUMEIRAH

Marsa Dubai

Burj Al Arab

Dubai Pearl

Al Sufouh Rd.

AL SUFOUH

Sheikh Zayed Rd.

Ibn Battuta Mall

UMM SUQUEM

Al Wasl Rd.

UMM AL MANARA AL SAFA

UMM AL SHIEF

Al Mafraq Rd.

JUMEIRAH ISLAND

EMIRATES HILLS

Mall of the Emirates

Al Mafraq Rd.

Jebel Ali Racecourse

DISCOVERY GARDENS

Doha Rd.

Doha Rd.

AL QUOZ

JUMEIRAH HORIZON

AL BARSHAA

Emirates Ring Rd.

NEW DUBAI

DUBAI SPORTS CITY

Dubai Autodrome

DUBAILAND
(under construction)

22

360 degrees **8**
Agency **12**
Al Abaya Nightclub **2**
Almaz by Momo **7**
The Apartment
  Lounge + Club **8**
Barasti **4**
Boudoir **13**
Buddha Bar **3**
Chi@TheLodge **21**
Cin Cin **14**

Crossroads
  Cocktail Bar **15**
Dubailand **22**
DUCTAC **7**
El Malecón **13**
Fatafeet Café **18**
Ginseng **15**
Harry Ghatto's **12**
ikandy Ultra Lounge **9**
Irish Village **20**
Kan Zaman **16**

Left Bank **6**
Long's Bar **10**
Madinat Theatre **6**
Maya **1**
Rock Bottom **17**
The Roof Top **5**
Scarlett's **12**
Sho Cho **13**
The Terrace **19**
Vintage **15**
Zinc **11**

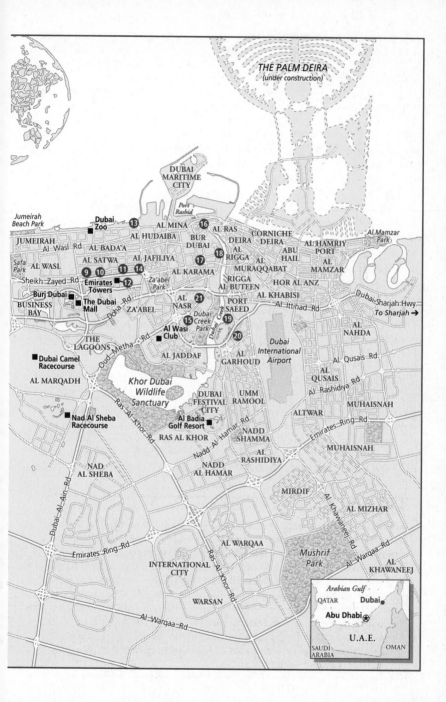

THE PALM DEIRA
(under construction)

Jumeirah
Beach Park

DUBAI
MARITIME
CITY

Port
Rashid

**Dubai
Zoo** ⑬ AL MINA ⑯ AL RAS

JUMEIRAH AL HUDAIBA BUR DEIRA CORNICHE
AL Wasl Rd. DUBAI DEIRA

AL BADA'A ⑱ AL AL HAMRIY
Safa AL SATWA RIGGA ABU PORT
Park AL WASL AL JAFILIYA ⑰ AL HAIL AL
Sheikh Zayed Rd. ⑨ ⑩ ⑪ ⑭ AL KARAMA MURAQQABAT MAMZAR
**Emirates ⑫ Za'abel RIGGA HOR AL ANZ
BURJ Dubai** Towers Park AL BUTEEN
The Dubai AL AL KHABISI
BUSINESS Mall ZA'ABEL NASR ㉑ Al-Ittihad-Rd.
BAY PORT
Dubai SAEED AL
THE Creek ⑲ NAHDA
LAGOONS Park ⑮ ⑳
**Dubai Camel Al Wasi Dubai
Racecourse** Club AL International AL Qusais-Rd.
AL JADDAF AL Airport QUSAIS
AL MARQADH GARHOUD Al-Rashidiya-Rd.
Khor Dubai UMM MUHAISNAH
Nad Al Sheba Wildlife RAMOOL ALTWAR
Racecourse Sanctuary DUBAI Emirates-Ring-Rd.
FESTIVAL MUHAISNAH
NAD **Al Badia** CITY NADD
AL SHEBA **Golf Resort** SHAMMA
RAS AL KHOR AL MIRDIF AL MIZHAR
RASHIDIYA
NADD
AL HAMAR
AL WARQAA Mushrif AL
Emirates-Ring-Rd. Park KHAWANEEJ
INTERNATIONAL
CITY Arabian Gulf
QATAR **Dubai**●
WARSAN Al-Warqaa-Rd. **Abu Dhabi**⊕
SAUDI U.A.E.
ARABIA OMAN

123

1 The Performing Arts

In the midst of such unbelievable growth, it's surprising that Dubai has moved at a snail's pace to establish a performing arts scene. There are finally a couple of theaters in town, but performances remain sporadic, and there are no standing production companies based in Dubai. This should change with the construction of the Royal Hall in the Dubai Pearl development, which with 1,500 seats will become the largest performing arts center in the region.

Dubai Community Theater and Arts Center (DUCTAC)   Located on the second floor of Mall of the Emirates, DUCTAC houses the larger Centerpoint Theater and smaller Kilachand Studio, which together offer plays, operas, classical music concerts, comedy, and children's shows. Check the website for event information. The complex includes a cafe, library, exhibition halls, classrooms, and workshops with training in acting, scriptwriting, and costume design. Mall of the Emirates. ℂ **4/341-4777**. www.dubai theatre.org.

Jumana–Secret of the Desert ⓐ   *Jumana–Secret of the Desert* is a dazzling outdoor show that takes place in the Al Sahra Desert Resort of Dubailand. It's one of the first attractions to open in Dubailand (p. 15), the enormous entertainment resort, most of which is still under construction. Created to celebrate the history and culture of Arabia, the production involves a large cast of dancers, acrobats, camels, and horses. The stage uses water-projected imagery, lasers, and pyrotechnics to link Arabian folklore to the desert and sea. The result is a spectacular evening performance under the stars. It takes place Tuesday to Saturday at 9pm and costs AED230 ($63/£32) for adults, AED115 ($31/£16) for children 12 and under. Al Sahara Desert Resort in Dubailand. ℂ **4/367-9500**. www.alsahra.com.

The Laughter Factory   Without a permanent home but with lots of laughs and good cheer, the Laughter Factory brings to Dubai and elsewhere in the region professional stand-up comedians from English-speaking countries. Shows can be racier than you might expect in the Middle East. Locations include the Aviation Club, Crowne Plaza, and Le Méridien Mina Seyahi. They typically start at 9pm, and admission is AED100 ($27/£17). Locations vary. ℂ **4/355-1862**. www.thelaughterfactory.com.

Dubai Cinemas

World-class movie theaters have sprung up in most of Dubai's major malls, such as the 14-screen cinema in Mall of the Emirates (which has two "gold class" theaters staffed with waiter service) and the 21-screen cinema at Ibn Battuta Mall (which has an IMAX theater). Major Hollywood films are shown in English with Arabic subtitles, and are censored. **Bollywood films,** adored by Dubai's resident Indian population, are shown at Lamcy Plaza and some other theaters around town. Movie information is available in each of the major daily newspapers. The **Dubai International Film Festival,** which began in 2004, takes place for a week each December and offers a selection of full features, short films, and documentaries from around the globe, including Arab cinema. For more information, visit www.dubaifilmfest.com.

Madinat Theatre   Designed to resemble an ancient Arabian citadel, this 424-seat theater is the first of its kind in Dubai. It's located in the dazzling Madinat Jumeirah complex, and you could easily combine dinner at one of the surrounding restaurants with a show. Performances include plays, musicals, and comedies. In the same complex, the Madinat Arena features sports tournaments, concerts, and other special events, such as *The Nutcracker.* Madinat Jumeirah. ℭ 4/366-8888. www.madinattheatre.com.

2 Clubs & Discos

Al Abaya Nightclub   Most of Dubai's nightlife is Western in orientation, but this is one of the city's traditional Arabian nightclubs with Arabic singers and dancers, including belly dancers. Al Abaya, curiously named after the traditional dress women in the Gulf wear, is a great place to come if you'd like to remind yourself you're actually in the Middle East. The club also offers tasty Lebanese food, including mixed grills and meze. Open 10:30pm to 3am. The Palm Hotel, Sheikh Zayed Rd., at Interchange 5. ℭ 4/399-2222.

The Apartment Lounge + Club ⚔⚔   Designer-dressed patrons pack Dubai's most exclusive club, a two-room "apartment" featuring a swanky martini-style lounge and a raging dance floor. Music varies by night, and may include Latin rhythms on Tuesdays, house, hip-hop, and R&B on Wednesdays, and funky house on Thursdays and Fridays. A mix of local and international DJs work the sound system, and ladies often receive free drinks before midnight. Open Tuesday to Saturday 9pm to 3am. Jumeirah Beach Hotel. ℭ 4/406-8000. Cover varies.

Boudoir ⚔   One of the hardest nightspots to get into, Boudoir's reward is an opulent Parisian-style lounge catering to a beautiful, if pretentious, clientele. While dinner is served here earlier, the action starts after 11pm, when cutting-edge lounge beats and dancing take over. This is one of Dubai's trendiest late-night bars. Open daily from 7:30pm to 4:30am. Dubai Marine Beach Resort & Spa. ℭ 4/345-5995. www.myboudoir.com.

Chi@The Lodge   A favorite of the expatriate set, Chi@TheLodge is an enormous club with indoor and outdoor dance floors, a celebrity-attracting VIP area, and other distinct entertainment rooms. The disco, which has hints of Thai decor, regularly hosts theme nights and occasionally music concerts; check the website for event details. Thursday nights tend to be best. Daily 8pm to 3am. Al Nasr Leisureland, Oud Metha. ℭ 4/337-9470. www.lodgedubai.com.

Zinc ⚔   This recently expanded nightclub in the Crowne Plaza attracts a smart casual crowd mesmerized by the ultra-modern lighting, high-tech sound system, and innovative drink selection. The resident DJ occasionally brings in international DJ celebrities. This is one of the hottest dance clubs in Dubai, and music includes R&B, house, and hip-hop. Daily 8pm to 3am. Crowne Plaza, ground floor. ℭ 4/331-1111.

Tips **Dress the Part**

Women are best not dressing provocatively and going alone to clubs, where in some places they might receive unwanted attention. Call girls work in some Dubai nightclubs, and although prostitution is technically illegal, it's a booming industry in some parts of the city—particularly at bars in lower-end hotels in Deira and Bur Dubai. I've avoided including any clubs where this is common.

3 Bars

Buddha Bar ✦✦✦   The famed Buddha Bar of Paris origin has opened in the posh Grosvenor House hotel. A giant Buddha stands guard over the stunning main room, red-lit with floor-to-ceiling windows overlooking the Dubai Marina. An amazing sound system plays the avant-garde lounge beats of the Buddha Bar music series. The venue includes a Vietnamese lounge, sushi bar, and Japanese private rooms, and attracts a mixed-age, international crowd. Come here dressed to kill. Open Sunday to Wednesday 7pm to 2am, Thursday and Friday 7pm to 3am; closed Saturday. Grosvenor House, Dubai Marina. ✆ 4/345-5995. www.grosvenorhouse.lemeridien.com.

Ginseng ✦   This Asian-inspired cocktail lounge in the Pyramids complex is perfect for starting out the night. Murals with Asian calligraphy decorate the contemporary lounge frequented by fashionably dressed young professionals. New-age cocktails fuse exotic fruits and premium spirits, although Ginseng's celebratory crowd frequently opts for champagne cocktails and Oriental martinis. The kitchen offers Asian tapas as well as tempting vegetarian plates. Open daily 7pm to 2am. The Pyramids Wafi City. ✆ 4/324-8200. www.ginsengdubai.com.

Harry Ghatto's *Finds*   Almost hidden at the back of Tokyo@TheTowers restaurant, Harry Ghatto's is an upscale karaoke bar attracting a diverse, non-professional singing crowd. It's possible to come just for a drink and to watch, but the fun is in singing. The cover charge is simply, "no drink no song." A microphone is passed around the bar, so there's no need to perform on stage. The talented waitstaff participates in the action, and there are more than 1,000 songs to choose from. Light Japanese fare, including sushi, is served along with an international selection of drinks. Open daily 8pm to 3am. Emirates Towers (upper level of the shopping boulevard). ✆ 4/330-0000. www.jumeirah.com.

Left Bank ✦   Left Bank takes its name from *La Rive Gauche,* the romantic and intellectual district in Paris that includes the Latin Quarter. This stylish brasserie, bar, and terrace attracts Dubai's more creative crowd, and is a trendy place in Madinat Jumeirah for early evening drinks and conversation. As the night wears on, a resident DJ pumps up the volume and the music takes over. Open daily noon to 1am. Souk Madinat Jumeirah. ✆ 4/368-6171.

Long's Bar   This no-nonsense American bar in the Towers Rotana hotel attracts a beer-guzzling, cocktail-clinking group. Western expatriates come here to drink, flirt, and get a little rowdy. There's no reason to dress up, just come as you are. Long's offers tasty pub food, one of the city's most popular happy hours, and sports screens switched on for big games. Open daily noon to 2:30am. Towers Rotana, Sheikh Zayed Rd. ✆ 4/343-8000.

Tips Dubai Drinking Laws

Dubai's drinking age is 21, and bars and nightclubs regularly check IDs (a passport is best). There's zero tolerance for drinking and driving or disorderly behavior in Dubai, and drivers caught behind the wheel with even a trace of alcohol are sent to jail. If you're going to drink, it's best to do so at establishments in your hotel. If you go elsewhere, take a taxi or go with a designated driver.

Bars with a View

Bar 44 ✭ (① 4/399-8888), on the 44th floor of the swanky Grosvenor House hotel, has a view of both the city and the marina and Gulf beyond. The action happens around the circular bar placed strategically in the center, and there is often live jazz music. Hours are Friday to Wednesday 6pm to 2am and Thursday 6pm to 3am. **New Asia Bar & Club** (① 4/324-8888) is housed at the top of the pyramid at Raffles in Wafi City, and offers a great view of old Dubai's glittering lights along with DJ-spun international music, cigars, and specialty cocktails; the upstairs **China Moon Champagne Bar** is open to members and hotel guests only. Hours are 7pm to 3am. A place to impress, **Vu's** ✭✭ (① 4/319-8088) is located on the 51st floor of the Emirates Towers hotel. This intimate space is designed so each of the plush tables and bar stools stares out at Dubai's expanding skyline. It's open daily from 6pm to 3am. Even more extravagant, **Skyview Bar** ✭ (① 4/301-7600) at the Burj al Arab is suspended 200m (656 ft.) over the sea and features a "mixology trolley"—a mobile bar that slides from table to table as a "mixologist" prepares specially designed cocktails tailored to individual tastes. It's open daily from noon to 2am, and is a clever way to visit this famous hotel if you're not a guest.

Scarlett's ✭   Although Scarlett's serves Tex-Mex food, its appeal is distinctly European. The restaurant-bar seems to blend into one, and a DJ spins R&B and top 40 every night but Sunday. There's a small dance floor, and Tuesday is "ladies night." Crowds also swarm to Scarlett's for major sports events and for Sunday brunch. Open daily noon to 3am. Emirates Towers Blvd. ① 4/330-0000.

4 Live Music

El Malecón ✭✭   This spirited Cuban restaurant and bar is a blast, an unpretentious place with live Latin music and salsa dancing most nights of the week. The decor is meant to resemble Havana's La Bodeguita del Medio, where scribbles and photos of Che Guevara adorn the walls. Order a *mojito*, and get ready to swing those salsa hips. Open daily 7pm to 3am. Dubai Marine Beach Resort and Spa. ① 4/346-1111.

Rock Bottom ✭   Live rock and an eclectic mix of party music are performed every night at this no-frills American bar, popular with bikers, rock 'n' rollers, and unpretentious partyers. The drink of choice is the "bulldog," packed with Red Bull and high potency spirits. A restaurant by day, Rock Bottom gets kicking after 10pm when the in-house band hits the stage. Dress casually, and be prepared to dance. With a closing hour of 3am, this is one of the latest bars open in Dubai. Regent Palace Hotel. ① 4/396-3888.

5 Outdoor Bars & Lounges

Barasti ✭✭   Dubai's best happy hour takes place at Barasti, a casual beach bar at Le Méridien Mina Seyahi. Locals and expatriates pack the large wood deck that has beachside beds and tables, a downstairs bar, and sports screens for the big games. Each evening brings a different theme, ranging from Tuesday "moonlight acid jazz" and Wednesday "love Latino" to Thursday funky dance and weekend beach parties. This is a place to wear your flip-flops, breathe in the salty air, and settle in for some good beachside fun.

Crossroads Cocktail Bar   This Balinese-inspired bar sits at the edge of Raffles' 1-hectare (2.5-acre) garden, affording great views of some of the more than 129,000 plants. Night revelers can converge under a wood gazebo outside, or sip their Dubai Sling cocktail in the warmly lit indoor space. Open 5pm to 2am. Raffles Dubai. ℭ 4/324-8888.

ikandy Ultra Lounge   This poolside lounge at the Shangri-La is a great place to get the party started or to unwind before you call it a night. Lounge music mingles in the air with *shisha* smoke, and drinks, like the crowd, are worldly, including the Babmu (Miami), Zuka (Rio de Janeiro), and Jimmy Liks (Sydney). Ikandy also serves a bar menu that includes a selection of meze. Open 6pm to 2am. Shangri-La Hotel. ℭ 4/343-8888.

Irish Village ⟨⟩   An institution among Western expatriates living in Dubai, Irish Village includes a cozy pub-style interior and a large outdoor sitting area. The action happens outside, where the crowd gives this the feeling of an everyday festival. Throw back a pint or two of Guinness, or any of the other dozen beer types on tap, and order some fish and chips if you're in the mood for a snack (p. 82). This is an especially popular spot for watching sports events, and it's easy to meet people here. Check the website for live music events that happen periodically. Open daily 11am to 1:30am. The Aviation Club, Al Garhoud. ℭ 4/282-4750. www.irish village.ae.

Maya   Although Dubai is a long way from Mexico's Yucatán Peninsula, Maya succeeds in creating a refined Mesoamerican atmosphere tucked away in the tropical gardens of Le Royal Méridien Beach Resort & Spa. The Maya lounge sits on top of the modern Mexican restaurant created by acclaimed chef Richard Sandoval, in a soothing outdoor atmosphere looking out to the Gulf. Champagne cocktails and other innovative concoctions line the drink list—I recommend a *margarita Maya* or a *mojito Cuzco.* The limited lounge menu includes tacos, seviches, and guacamole. Open 6pm to 2am. Lounge menu available to 1am. Le Royal Méridien Beach Resort & Spa. ℭ 4/316-5550.

The Roof Top   This enchanted rooftop bar is designed in the style of a *majlis,* a traditional Arabian meeting place adorned with silk cushion seating areas, regional art objects, Oriental carpets, and candles. It's located in the beautiful grounds of the One&Only Royal Mirage, well worth a visit for its extraordinary Arabian architecture and landscaped grounds. The Roof Top bar offers a "chill out" ambience with traditional cocktails and Arabic meze, such as hummus and *kibbeh.* The crowd tends to be more classic than trendy. Open daily 5pm to 1am. One&Only Royal Mirage. ℭ 4/399-9999.

Sho Cho ⟨⟩   Situated on the jetty extending from the Dubai Marine Beach Resort & Spa, Sho Cho enjoys a coveted location at the end of a row of restaurants and bars. It's worth a walk out here just to see the view. Sho Cho includes both a chic indoor lounge with a sushi bar, aquarium, and long cocktail bar, as well as a cool outdoor deck adjacent to the water. A model-quality crowd packs this place on Tuesday and Sunday nights, when acclaimed DJs come to rock the house. Open 7pm to late. Dubai Marine Beach Resort & Spa. ℭ 4/346-1111.

The Terrace ⟨⟩   This is where the urban elite comes to unwind, an idyllic spot set on the edge of Dubai Creek. The menu includes premium wines and vodkas, as well as a number of sophisticated cocktails, and for those who want to snack there's a tempting raw bar. The stylish outdoor deck looks right over bobbing yachts, with the entire city skyline in the distance. This is my favorite place for watching the sunset in Dubai. If you prefer to sit in the air-conditioning inside, floor-to-ceiling windows guarantee an equally spectacular view. Open daily noon to 2am. Park Hyatt Dubai. ℭ 4/602-1234.

6 Wine Bars

Agency ✦✦   This sophisticated wine bar in the Boulevard shopping area of Emirates Towers attracts a well-heeled 30- and 40-somethings crowd. The chic modern space houses roughly 400 types of wine, including 60 options by the glass. There are frequent wine promotions and tastings, and the atmosphere is as lively before as after dinner. Saturday to Thursday 12:30pm to 1am, Friday 3pm to 1am. Ground level of Emirates Blvd. ✆ **4/330-0000.**

Cin Cin ✦✦✦   This ultra-chic champagne and wine bar, named after the Italian call to toast, is the city's most fashionable lounge. A beautiful crowd gathers to admire each other amid the ultra modern decor of leather lounge chairs, reflective white paneling, and decorative mood lights. The wine rack on the wall displays 2,000 bottles, and Cin Cin offers the largest selection of fine wines in Dubai. There's a cigar bar next door with a walk-in humidor and excellent cognacs. Open daily 6pm to 2am. Fairmont Dubai, Sheikh Zayed Rd. ✆ **4/332-5555.**

Vintage ✦   This wine bar sits on the upper floor of the Pyramids at Wafi City and is a civilized space serving international wines, cheese plates, and fondues. This is where to go if you're seeking intimate conversation in a refined setting rather than booming music in a late-night party. Tasting flights are typically offered. Open Friday to Wednesday 4pm to 1am, Thursday 4pm to 2am. The Pyramids Wafi City. ✆ **4/324-4100.** www.waficityrestaurants.com.

7 *Shisha* Cafes & Lounges

It goes by many names, including narghile, hubbly bubbly, and hookah, but all you need to know here is *shisha*. This tradition is enjoyed at various cafes and lounges throughout Dubai (and most of the Middle East). Although the pastime is most common among locals, it's popular among expatriates and visitors, men and women, smokers and nonsmokers. The *shisha* water pipe works by water filtration and indirect heat, and is used for smoking flavored tobaccos. *Shisha* comes in a variety of flavors such as apple, grape, and strawberry, and is meant to be shared with everyone at the table, usually over an afternoon coffee or following a nighttime meal. Smoking *shisha* is particularly popular during Ramadan nights, when people sit and chat under tents erected throughout the city.

Almaz by Momo   Eighteen flavors of *shisha* are served in a stylish Arabian room on the second floor of Harvey Nichols. The cafe also offers simple Moroccan dishes and desserts, as well as non-alcoholic drinks including delicious mocktails and alcohol-free champagne. Open Sunday to Tuesday 9am to 1am, Wednesday to Saturday 9am to 2am. Harvey Nichols, Mall of the Emirates. ✆ **4/409-8877.**

Fatafeet Café ✦   This is among the best known *shisha* joints in town. The traditional cafe offers Egyptian food, Lebanese music, and a broad selection of *shisha*. Among the flavors for leisurely puffing are apple, anise, coffee, grape, strawberry, and vanilla. Patrons have a great view across the creek to Deira. Open daily 10:30am to midnight. Al-Seef Rd., Bur Dubai. ✆ **4/397-9222.**

Kan Zaman   Located in Heritage Village, this traditional Arabic cafe is an idyllic spot to smoke *shisha* and snack on meze or other Arabic food. The ambience is distinctly local, with Arab friends and families seated on the large waterfront outdoor area. Open daily 11am to 3am. Heritage and Diving Village, Al Shindagha, Bur Dubai. ✆ **4/393-9914.**

360 degrees ★★   The rooftop deck atop the Marina restaurant boasts a spectacular view of the Gulf, Burj Al Arab, and Jumeirah Beach Hotel. The crowd is a mix of beachgoers and fashionistas, with the atmosphere becoming more bling as the night wears on. If you arrive early enough, relax on one of the loungy leather sofas or malleable beanbags after a day in the sun, ordering some *shisha* and perhaps a cocktail to go with it. DJs spin house music during the weekends. Open Saturday to Wednesday 5pm to 2am. Jumeirah Beach Hotel. © 4/316-5550.

Side Trips from Dubai

In many ways, Dubai is about as unreal a city as they come. It's a flashy desert metropolis that many have compared to Las Vegas without gambling, a place where people from around the world come to bask in the sun, have fun, make money, and be part of a fascinating urban experience. You can easily spend all your time in Dubai and not run out of things to do. In fact, Dubai offers so much to visitors—luxury resorts, beautiful beaches, incredible shopping, endless indoor and outdoor activities, great dining, exciting nightlife—that it's unlikely you'll want to leave. But for all its appeal, Dubai is not the only place you should visit while in the UAE.

For starters, you'll need to sign up for a desert safari. Whether it's an evening dinner in the sunset-lit dunes or an overnight trip to a Bedouin camp under the stars, an outing to the Arabian Desert (p. 151) should be front and center on your itinerary. A trip to the picturesque mountain enclave of Hatta, with its traditional village and freshwater rock pools, makes for another wonderful day trip. And you'll love Musandam, the peninsula near the UAE border with Oman in which dhow boats for hire weave their way along beautiful waterways set between jagged cliffs of the Western Hajar Mountains. Each of these destinations feels like a trip back in time, offering a sense of serenity in the region's most scenic areas.

You'll find other Emirati towns worlds removed from Dubai, as well. Abu Dhabi is the wealthy capital with a pristine and less hedonistic air than Dubai. It's here that you'll get the best sense of traditional Emirati life in a cosmopolitan setting. Sharjah, by contrast, is the cultural capital of the UAE, a city steeped in conservative values and most different from neighboring Dubai. Come here to understand more about the country's religious and cultural influences. If you want to visit a true desert oasis offering more moderate temperatures than elsewhere in the country, travel to Al Ain in the emirate of Abu Dhabi. This and other Emirati cities tend to share little resemblance with Dubai and are far more like the traditional hamlets you'll find elsewhere in the Arabian Gulf.

The UAE is relatively small, and most places can be reached as day or overnight trips. Tour companies offer excursions to each of the destinations discussed below. If you want to do it on your own, the UAE's highway network is excellent, petrol is comparatively inexpensive, and traveling by car is generally safe. Just watch out for extremely fast drivers, occasional blowing sand, and lost camels checking out the road.

1 Abu Dhabi ⍟

Abu Dhabi is the somewhat curious cousin of Dubai and the second-most-visible emirate and city in the UAE. It offers a more relaxed pace than Dubai, which one local described to me as "Las Vegas on speed." It's certainly far less Westernized. In fairness to people who prefer Dubai, Abu Dhabi can seem a little slow and perhaps even a bit boring. But its beaches are just as beautiful, there's less traffic and more greenery, and the character is distinctly Emirati, preserving much of the conservative heritage that its northeastern neighbor has begun to toss off.

Although Dubai has firmly established itself as the region's tourist hub, Abu Dhabi is the actual capital of the UAE, as well as the largest and by the far wealthiest emirate. It is the seat of government and the heart of the UAE's oil wealth. Abu Dhabi is both the name of a city and of the larger emirate that surrounds it, and in fact occupies more than 85% of UAE territory.

Although Abu Dhabi doesn't seek to compete directly with Dubai in terms of tourist and entertainment infrastructure, it is making impressive advances. Take a walk along the Corniche, the road that runs along the water's edge, and you'll see a picture-perfect city rising behind it. Construction is booming, skyscrapers are going up everywhere, and more people are visiting. The Emirates Palace (p. 137) hotel sets the standard for unadulterated luxury, the most expensive resort ever built. The Sheikh Zayed Grand Mosque (p. 135) is the world's third-largest mosque, and the Cultural Foundation is an impressive arts center. The malls are as enticing as any you will find, and Abu Dhabi boasts outstanding beach and sports facilities, as well.

ESSENTIALS
GETTING THERE & DEPARTING
BY PLANE   Etihad (℃ **888/838-4423** in the U.S., or 6/505-8000; www.etihad airways.com), the outstanding national airline, flies nonstop to Abu Dhabi from JFK airport in New York. The flight takes a little more than 12 hours. Other airlines flying into Abu Dhabi include **British Airways** (℃ **800/247-9297** in the U.S. and Canada, or 2/622-5777; www.british-airways.com); **Emirates Airlines** (℃ **800/777-3999** in the U.S., or 2/575-7474; www.emirates.com); and **Northwest/KLM** (℃ **800/225-2525** in the U.S., or 2/632-3280; www.klm.com).

BY CAR   You'll need a valid international driving license issued by the country where your national driving license is from to operate a car in the UAE (visitors are not allowed to use their national driving license here). Abu Dhabi lies 166km (103 miles) from Dubai, a roughly 2-hour drive from Dubai on the Sheikh Zayed Highway, depending on how fast you travel. Although the highway is well-paved and marked, watch out for other drivers often traveling at very high speeds. Rental-car agents in Abu Dhabi include **Avis** (℃ **800/331-1212** in the U.S. and Canada, or 2/621-8400; www.avis.com); **Budget** (℃ **800/527-0700** in the U.S., or 2/633-4200; www.budget.com); **Hertz** (℃ **800/654-3001** in the U.S., or 2/672-0060; www.hertz.com); and **Thrifty** (℃ **800/367-2277** in the U.S., or 2/634-5663; www.thrifty.com).

VISITOR INFORMATION   Abu Dhabi's **Tourism Authority** (℃ **2/444-0444;** visitabudhabi.ae) is part of a ministry, and does not typically serve the public. Check the website for visitor information.

CITY LAYOUT   The capital of the UAE is an island city connected by bridges to the mainland and surrounded by the Arabian Gulf. It's designed on a grid system built around a central "T," with the Corniche running along the coast and the Airport Road traversing the length of the island. Streets that parallel the Corniche (which is the same as 1st St.) have odd numbers, and those that parallel the Airport Road (the same as 2nd St.) have even numbers. The city's main tourist areas are as follows: Al Ras Al

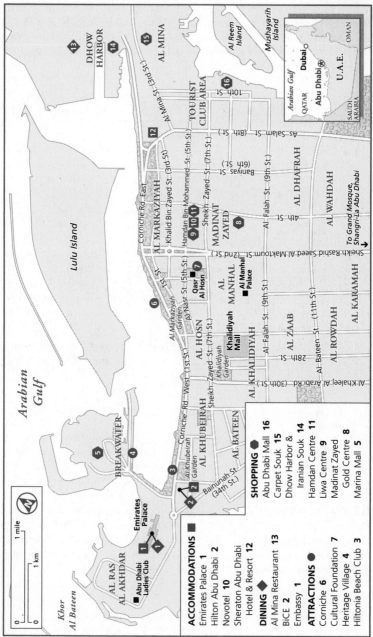

Abu Dhabi

ACCOMMODATIONS ■
Emirates Palace **1**
Hilton Abu Dhabi **2**
Novotel **10**
Sheraton Abu Dhabi
Hotel & Resort **12**

DINING ◆
Al Mina Restaurant **13**
BiCE **2**
Embassy **1**

ATTRACTIONS ●
Corniche **6**
Cultural Foundation **7**
Heritage Village **4**
Hiltonia Beach Club **3**

SHOPPING ⬡
Abu Dhabi Mall **16**
Carpet Souk **15**
Dhow Harbor &
Iranian Souk **14**
Hamdan Centre **11**
Liwa Centre **9**
Madinat Zayed
Gold Centre **8**
Marina Mall **5**

Akhdar, at the northwestern tip; the nearby Breakwater, an area of reclaimed land connected by a causeway to the west Corniche; Corniche West; Corniche East and central Abu Dhabi; Al Meena and the so-called Tourist Club area, at the island's northeastern tip; and finally the southern end of the island, which includes the areas of Al Matar, Al Maqtaa, and Al Safarat.

FAST FACTS: Abu Dhabi

Area Code The telephone area code for Abu Dhabi is **2**.

Banks Banks are generally open Sunday to Thursday 8am to 1:30pm (and some again 4:30–6:30pm), morning only on Saturday, and closed Friday. There is a large network of local and international banks regulated by the UAE Central Bank, and most have 24-hour ATMs.

Drugstore Most pharmacies are open from 8:30am to 10:30pm. For a list of 24-hour pharmacies, call ✆ **2/677-7929**, or check for the "pharmacies on duty" listed at **www.adpolice.gov.ae**.

Hospital For medical emergencies, dial ✆ **998**. Corniche Hospital (✆ **2/672-4900**) is on the Corniche, near the Sheraton Abu Dhabi Hotel and Resort.

Internet For a list of places to access the Internet in Abu Dhabi, visit www.visit abudhabi.ae/en/practical.information/telecommunication.and.internet.services. aspx.

Police For 24-hour police assistance, dial the ✆ **999** hot line or 2/446-1461.

Post Office The Abu Dhabi Central Post Office (✆ **2/621-1611**) is near the Madinat Zayed Shopping Centre and Gold Centre. It's open Saturday through Thursday from 8am to 10pm.

EXPLORING ABU DHABI

Corniche 🏵🏵   One of the best ways to explore Abu Dhabi is to take a drive or a stroll along the park-lined Corniche. As you travel the coastal boulevard, you'll come across parks with picnic areas, walkways, and bicycle paths. It's a great way to get to know the city from the water's edge, with the gleaming city skyline on one side and the sparkling Gulf on the other.

Cultural Foundation 🏵🏵   Located on the grounds of the old fort, called Qasr Al Hosn (not open to the public), the Cultural Foundation houses the National Archives, National Library, and the Institute of Culture and Art. There is a weekly art exhibition, theater, and lecture rooms, making this the cultural heart of the city and one of the most impressive cultural facilities in the Arabian Gulf.

Sheikh Zayed First St. (the same as 7th St.), at the corner of 2nd St. ✆ 2/621-5300. www.cultural.org.ae. Admission AED 3 (80¢/40p). Sat–Wed 8am–2pm and 5–9pm; Thurs 9am–noon and 5–8pm; closed Fri.

Dhow Harbor and Iranian Souk 🏵   The harbor is the one place you can watch the traditional dhows return from sea, and sunset is the best time to do this. A number of dinner dhow cruises depart from here, and there are a couple restaurants at Al Dhafra (see below). You will also find the fish souk here. Next to the harbor is the

Iranian souk, where mostly houseware goods and potted plants are sold. The UAE developed as a merchant nation, and trade with Iran has long been one of its principal economic activities. This Iranian market is an authentic if not very charming look into the traditional way of doing business here. Note that photography is not allowed anywhere inside the port area.

Al Meena.

Grand Mosque (Sheikh Zayed Bin Sultan Al Nahyan Mosque) 𝔸𝔸𝔸 The Grand Mosque gets its name for a reason: It's the third-largest mosque in the world (the first two are in Saudi Arabia), and it's got enough marble, gold, and silver to make the Taj Mahal jealous. Seven giant Swarovski crystal chandeliers hang from the ceilings (more than one million crystals were used to create them), where silver looks like fine needlework; a giant Iranian carpet, handmade by hundreds of artisans, stretches from one end of the main prayer hall to the next; and marble with colorful stone and gold makes up the walls and floors. The mosque, which opened in 2008, holds three places in the Guinness Book of World Records: the largest chandelier (10m/33 ft. in diameter and 15m/49 ft. high); the largest carpet 7 sq. m (77 sq. ft.); and the largest dome of its kind (the mosque has 82, but the main one is 32 m/105 ft. in diameter and 70m/230 ft. high).

The mosque can accommodate almost 41,000 worshipers at once, and offers free guided 60- to 90-minute tours at 10am Sunday to Thursday. Be sure to take your camera and dress modestly (if need be, the ladies near the shoe lockers can loan you something).

Between the Al Maqtaa and Al Mussafah bridges. zayedmosquetour@adta.ae. Free admission.

Heritage Village 𝔸𝔸 This mock village gives visitors an idea of what Abu Dhabi was like before the high-rise hotels and megamalls. The workshop area and museum are highlights. The former has stalls for everything from pottery and glass to leather and carpentry; my favorite is the spices/perfume stall, not only for the friendly shopkeeper, but for the AED 5 ($1.40/70p) items such as cardamom and a wonderfully fragrant rose soap. All the stalls sell their wares, and there's also a small marketplace near the entrance, though I didn't find anything other than cheap trinkets here.

It's worth spending about 30 minutes here on your way to Marina Mall (the Heritage Village is on the outskirts of the mall, so you can easily walk over if the weather is pleasant). If you're in a taxi, tell them to take you to the large flag at the end of the Breakwater; otherwise, you might end up at a private condo complex with a similar name.

Near the Breakwater. ℭ 2/681-4455. Fax 2/681-6003. Free admission. Mon–Thurs and Sat 9am–1pm and 5–9pm; Fri 5–9pm; closed Sun.

Hiltonia Beach Club 𝔸𝔸 If a day at the beach is what you want, the Hiltonia Beach Club is the city's best beach club open to non-hotel guests. In addition to lounge chairs and umbrellas in the sand, there's a range of extra-fee watersports; these include water-skiing, windsurfing (including lessons), snorkeling, and fishing, as well as kayak and sailboat rentals (for catamarans and lasers). There's a cafe here, too.

Corniche Rd., across from the Hilton Abu Dhabi. ℭ 2/692-4368. Open to non-Hilton guests during weekdays for AED 100 ($27/£14). Nonguests are not allowed on weekends or holidays.

Abu Dhabi: From Cultural Vacuum to Cultural Capital

Culture is not the first attribute people usually ascribe to Abu Dhabi, a long-time sleepy town best known for its endless sand, enticing sea, and unimaginable amounts of oil. But with an ambitious $27-billion project underway to create an enormous tourist and cultural development on Saadiyat Island—located just 500 meters (1,640 ft.) off the coast of Abu Dhabi—the capital's reputation will soon change for the better. The most talked about aspect of the Saadiyat Island project is the construction of the Louvre Abu Dhabi, anticipated to fully open by 2012. For a modest $1.3 billion, Abu Dhabi has acquired the right to use the Louvre's name for 30 years, as well as rotate artwork from the world's most famous museum in Paris. Jean Nouvel, the architect of the stunning 24,155 sq. m (260,000 sq. ft.) complex, designed it in the shape of a floating web-patterned dome (like a giant umbrella that allows the sun to filter through), and was awarded the 2008 Pritzker architecture prize for his talent. The Louvre Abu Dhabi will showcase art across time and regions, and will be administered by an international agency of French museums that includes some of Paris's best known art destinations, such as the Musée d'Orsay, Pompidou Center, Musée Rodin, and, of course, the Louvre.

Besides bringing in the granddaddy of all museums, the cultural district of Saadiyat Island includes plans for a national museum, performing arts center, classical arts museum, maritime museum, and the Guggenheim Abu Dhabi. The Guggenheim, designed by Frank Gehry, will, like its New York twin, celebrate modern and contemporary art. At 30,000 sq. m (323,000 sq. ft.), this will be the only Guggenheim museum in the region and will be larger than any existing Guggenheim in the world. And the project's ambition doesn't stop there. The 27 sq. km (10 sq. miles) Saadiyat development will also feature residential, business, and leisure components, including 8,000 villas, 38,000 apartments, 29 hotels, two championship golf courses, miles of beaches and mangrove forests, and three marinas. The enormous project will be completed in three phases, with the full opening scheduled for 2018. No doubt, the coming decade will see a number of additional ideas for this visionary project.

WHERE TO STAY
VERY EXPENSIVE
Beach Rotana Abu Dhabi 🏨🏨 *(Kids)* Although far less opulent than Emirates Palace, Beach Rotana is one of my favorite hotels in Abu Dhabi. The family-friendly resort sits on a pristine white-sand beach in the Tourist Club Area and features an excellent beach club with water sports, beautiful swimming pools for children and adults, a pool bar, and a fun-filled kids club. Other activities include the contemporary "Zen" spa with a full range of treatment rooms, relaxation areas, and classes (such as yoga), tennis and squash facilities, and a diving center offering dive trips and PADI courses. A passageway links the hotel to the enormous Abu Dhabi Mall. Guest rooms

and suites face the sea and are spacious and generously appointed; club rooms have walk-in showers and Jacuzzi baths, as well as extra touches such as fresh fruit and carefully arranged flower designs. The resort is home to 10 restaurants and bars, including the tropical feeling Trader Vic's and cook-at-your-table Benihana; the latter may not be authentic Japanese, but it sure is fun. Service at this Rotana is known to be friendly and professional. You can easily arrange desert, island, and fishing trips; shopping excursions; and golf or other sports outings from here.

Tourist Club Area, P.O. Box 45200, Abu Dhabi. © 2/644-3000. Fax 2/644-2111. www.rotana.com. 413 units. AED 1,500 ($408/£208) and up double. AE, DC, MC, V. **Amenities:** 10 restaurants; 3 bars; large outdoor pool and kids pool; beach club with water sports; dive center; spa with fitness center, sauna, steam room, and yoga classes; tennis and squash courts; kids club; babysitting; business center; multilingual concierge; executive level rooms; car rental; currency exchange; laundry service; dry cleaning. In room: A/C, minibar, safe, high-speed Internet.

Emirates Palace ★★★   During a visit to the Emirates Palace in January 2008, fellow guests included President George W. Bush and U.S. Secretary of State Condoleezza Rice, which, if the palatial surroundings don't give it away, tells you this isn't your average hotel. The size of the hotel can be intimidating to some (it's easy to get lost here), but everywhere you turn there's someone to point you in the right direction. Upon check-in, a butler arrives at your room to explain everything from the complimentary minibar and Internet service to the in-room entertainment and lighting systems (trust me, you need the tutorial). Rooms are swathed in buttery wood and heavy brocaded duvets, and all have balconies that offer various views, including the 1.3km (¾-mile) hotel beach, outfitted with imported Algerian sand.

The hotel, with its 114 mosaic tile-covered domes, Swarovski crystal chandeliers, and gold-plated lobby is gorgeous, and the **Anantara Spa** is just as impressive. The decor is influenced by Morocco, with arched walkways and bright mosaic-tile work. The crown jewel of the spa is its signature **Gateway to Arabia** treatment ★★, which includes a traditional Moroccan hammam.

The hotel is within close proximity to Marina Mall (p. 140) and the Heritage Village (p. 135).

P.O. Box 39999, West End Corniche, Abu Dhabi. © 2/690-9000. Fax 2/690-9999. www.emiratespalace.com. 394 units. AED 2,800 ($762/£387) and up double. AE, DISC, MC, V. **Amenities:** 8 restaurants; 2 bars; nightclub/lounge; 2 pools; 4 tennis courts; 1.3km (¾ mile) private beach; spa; 2 fitness centers; kids' playground; boutiques; dive center. In room: A/C, plasma TV, free Wi-Fi, complimentary minibar, hair dryer, private butler service, personalized check-in, laptop (in suites only).

Shangri-La Abu Dhabi ★★   This is what you expect from a hotel in the Middle East—latticed archways, fortresslike doors made from local wood, and a spectacular view of the palatial **Sheikh Zayed Bin Sultan Al Nahyan Mosque** (p. 135). While this hotel looks much different that its sister property in Dubai, it has the same superb service and amenities, all in a peaceful and beautiful setting.

Rooms are elegantly outfitted and, like the hotel, are decorated with Arabic touches, and all have an outdoor terrace or balcony affording views of the mosque across the strait. Bathrooms have walk-in monsoon showers and are embellished with mosaic tiles.

The hotel is part of a larger complex, Qaryat Al Beri, which, when entirely completed this year, will include Venetian-like canals to transport guests between the hotel, CHI spa (open at press time), souk, and Trader's Hotel (the company's business hotel outlet). The Shangri-La houses four restaurants, including **Shang Palace** (p. 139), the all-day Sofra bld, which has a decadent dessert bar, and the Vietnamese Hoi An.

Between the bridges, P.O. Box 128881, Abu Dhabi. © 2/509-8888. Fax 2/558-5999. www.shangri-la.com. 214 units. AED 2,400 ($653/£331) and up double; AED 6,800 ($1,852/£939) and up suite. AE, DC, MC, V. **Amenities:** 4 restaurants; bar; 5 pools; private beach; health club; spa; salon; 24 hr. room service. *In room:* A/C, flatscreen TV, DVD player, video games, Internet, minibar, hair dryer, tea/coffeemaker, safe.

EXPENSIVE

Hilton Abu Dhabi ⭐⭐ *Kids*   Much of the excitement that goes on in Abu Dhabi happens at the Hilton, a beach resort and spa with excellent facilities. The Hiltonia beach club lies across the Corniche from the hotel and offers swimming pools and a private beach with numerous watersports, including windsurfing, water-skiing, sailing, kayaking, and fishing. The Hilton also features tennis and squash courts, a health club and spa, and children's activities and a day care center. Spacious guest rooms have garden or sea views and are decorated in warm tones with large windows and marble bathrooms. Some rooms have sofa beds. Executive-level rooms include express check-in, breakfast, evening refreshments, and complimentary Internet access. Quite a few of the city's best restaurants and bars are located at the Hilton, including **BiCE** (p. 139) and the **Jazz Bar.** Shopping lies within close proximity, and the concierge will help arrange city tours upon request.

Corniche Rd., P.O. Box 877, Abu Dhabi. © 2/681-1900. Fax 2/681-2734. www1.hilton.com. 325 units. AED 1,200 ($327/£166) and up double. AE, MC, V. Free parking. **Amenities:** 9 restaurants; 2 bars; dance club; outdoor pool; 2 lighted tennis courts; 3 squash courts; spa and health club; Hiltonia beach club w/watersports activities; kids' activities; concierge; business center; babysitting; laundry service; executive-level rooms. *In room:* A/C, TV, hair dryer, Wi-Fi.

MODERATE

Novotel   Located in the city center, on what comes closest to being Abu Dhabi's main street, this is one of the capital's best moderate options. The French-chain hotel has a deserved reputation for being comfortable, efficient, and reasonably priced. There are a number of restaurant (including French) and entertainment options, such as a piano lounge and sports bar. The outdoor pool leads to a fitness center, Jacuzzi, and sauna, and guests are just a few minutes' drive from the beach. Hamdan Street lies in the heart of Abu Dhabi's business and shopping district, which becomes very busy during peak hours.

Hamdan St., P.O. Box 47136, Abu Dhabi. © 2/633-3555. Fax 2/634-3633. www.novotel.com. 272 units. AED 850 ($232/£117) and up double. AE, MC, V. Free parking. **Amenities:** 4 restaurants; 3 bars; outdoor pool; fitness center; concierge; business center; salon; babysitting available; laundry service; dry cleaning. *In room:* A/C, TV, minibar, Wi-Fi.

Sheraton Abu Dhabi Hotel & Resort   This Sheraton sits on a small private beach and is a good choice if you want to stay on this side of Abu Dhabi, close to the port. Although the hotel is not one of the city's newest, its rooms remain among the most comfortable, with "Sweet Sleeper" beds, spacious bathrooms, and luxury touches such as evening turndown service. Opt for a city- or sea-view room, with executive club rooms only slightly more expensive. One of the best things about staying here is the extensive list of beach activities, including water-skiing, wakeboarding, sea kayaking, paddle boats, beach volleyball, fishing trips, and Corniche cruises. There's also an extensive selection of restaurants and two fun beachside bars.

Corniche Rd., P.O. Box 640, Abu Dhabi. © 2/677-3333. Fax 2/672-5149. www.sheraton.com/abudhabi. 272 units. AED 750 ($204/£103) and up double. AE, MC, V. Free parking. **Amenities:** 5 restaurants; 2 bars; small beach club w/watersports activities; outdoor pool; 2 lighted tennis courts; health club w/large fitness center and massage services; kids' activities; concierge; business center; salon; laundry service; executive level rooms. *In room:* A/C, TV, dataport, minibar, coffeemaker, hair dryer, in-room safe.

WHERE TO DINE
VERY EXPENSIVE

Embassy EUROPEAN   When you take a Michelin star chef (Gary Hollihead) and put him in a "seven star" hotel, you get Embassy, based on the London outpost of the same name. The restaurant/lounge/nightclub is super-chic, fusing Arab design elements with touchstones of Embassy London's look; glasswork, marble, gold, and silver abound; and there's also a small outdoor terrace. The menu changes regularly, but the focus remains on seafood with starters such as lobster ravioli with seafood minestrone and entrees such as monkfish tail with sautéed goat-cheese gnocchi. Non-seafood fans can choose from a variety of beef dishes such as Venison Wellington with foie gras and truffles; vegetarians should probably eat elsewhere.

The club, which is members-only, is open Monday and Wednesday 7pm to 1am, Tuesday and Thursday through Friday 10pm to 3am; closed Saturday and Sunday.

Inside the Emirates Palace. ✆ 2/690-89260. www.embassyabudhabi.com. Main courses AED 75–AED 175 ($20–$48/£10–£24). Reservations recommended. AE, MC, V. Mon–Fri noon–3pm and 7–11:30pm; closed Sat–Sun.

Shang Palace 🟉 CANTONESE   This is the Shangri-La chain's signature restaurant, and focuses on Cantonese cuisine served in an elegant setting. Large red and cream lanterns hang from the ceiling, and large windows afford a nice view of the strait and the mosque. It's no surprise that crispy duck is on the menu, and a small window at the restaurant's entrance where you can see the duck roasting gives you a sneak peak. My favorite dishes here include the spring rolls, which are crisp and light; the mushroom dumplings; and the noodles with giant shrimp.

Inside the Shangri-La Abu Dhabi. ✆ 2/509-8888. Reservations required. Main courses AED 70 ($20/£10) and up. AE, DC, MC, V. Daily 11:30am–2pm and 7–11pm.

EXPENSIVE

BiCE 🟉🟉 ITALIAN   Like its trendy counterpart in Dubai, BiCE is one of the hottest restaurants in Abu Dhabi. Head chef Luciano Gandolfo's modern Italian menu includes a number of homemade pastas, risottos made with Carnaroli rice Ferron, and tempting steak and seafood selections. My favorite pastas include veal-stuffed ravioli bathed in a wild-mushroom sauce, and small potato gnocchi in a light Gorgonzola fondue with walnuts. The champagne risotto with asparagus and black truffles is a creative if indulgent dish. The best steak here is a medium-cooked Angus filet in a red-wine sauce. For dessert, the tiramisu suits just fine. Ask for a table near one of the floor-to-ceiling windows that looks out to the Gulf. People tend to dress up for BiCE, and a piano singer is on hand nightly to warm the celebratory crowd.

Inside the Hilton Abu Dhabi. ✆ 2/692-4160. Reservations recommended. Main courses AED 55–AED 185 ($15–$50/£7.60–£26). AE, MC, V. Daily noon–3pm and 7–11pm.

MODERATE

Al Mina Restaurant 🟉 ARABIC   This casual restaurant along the Dhow Harbor has an old Arabian-style dining room as well as outdoor patio seating next to the water. It's one of the city's more picturesque settings for local and Iranian cuisine. To start, consider a plate of hummus, tabbouleh, and stuffed vine leaves. Local seafood includes lobster, squid, and *hammour,* and among the Iranian specialties are *chelow* kebab and kebab *Sultani* (grilled mutton tenderloin served with saffron rice). If you want a more extravagant Arabian feast, walk across the road to **Al Arish,** which offers an open buffet for AED 100 ($27/£14) and is open daily from 1:30 to 5pm and

7:30pm to midnight. The same owners also offer a 2-hour Arabian **dinner dhow cruise** that leaves from next to Al Mina restaurant nightly at 9pm. The fixed menu includes salad and Arabic appetizers followed by seafood and mixed grill, dessert, fruit, and tea or coffee. The cost is AED 135 ($37/£19), and you can pay at the dhow.

Al Dhafra, Dhow Harbor. ⓒ 2/673-2288. Iranian cuisine and mixed grills AED 20–AED 50 ($5.45–$14/£2.75–£6.90); seafood AED 80–AED 180 ($22–$49/£11–£25). AE, MC, V. Daily 4–11:30pm.

SHOPPING

While it may be overshadowed by its glitzy neighbor of Dubai, Abu Dhabi offers its own impressive shopping scene. From traditional products sold at local markets around the dhow area and in the Iranian and carpet souks, to modern fashions displayed in the capital's sophisticated malls, this wealthy emirate offers a compelling mix of goods from the East and West. You can find antiques, gold, carpets, and an array of Arabian souvenirs alongside mainstream items and top international brands. Bargaining is the expected way of doing business in the souks and traditional stores. For gold and jewelry, head to the **Madinat Zayed Gold Centre** (ⓒ 2/631-8555), located near the main post office on East Road. The Madinat Zayed Gold Centre houses some of the largest jewelry shops in the Gulf, featuring all colors of gold, diamonds, pearls, and other treasures. On **Hamdan Street,** the closest Abu Dhabi comes to having a "main street," you will find the **Liwa Centre** (ⓒ 2/632-0344), which sells, among other things, discount jewelry and perfumes. Nearby, the **Hamdan Centre** (ⓒ 2/632-8555) is a practical stop for discount clothing, shoes, handbags, and Arabian souvenirs. Bargaining is possible here, too. You will find beautiful carpets from Iran, Afghanistan, Pakistan, Turkey, and China at the **carpet souk** (also known as the Afghan souk) located off Al Meena Road near the Dhow Harbor. The traditional **fish, vegetable, and fruit souks** are also in the Al Meena area. The souks are typically open Saturday to Thursday from 8am to 1pm and 4 to 9pm, and Friday from 4 to 9pm. The top malls in the city are the **Marina Mall** 🏵🏵 (ⓒ 2/681-8300; www.marinamall.ae) in the Breakwater area, and the **Abu Dhabi Mall** (ⓒ 2/645-4858; www.abudhabimall.com) in the so-called Tourist Club area.

ABU DHABI AFTER DARK

Abu Dhabi's nightlife is very quiet compared with that of Dubai, but there are a few good options. The **Beachcomber** (ⓒ 2/697-0235), located on the small beach of the Sheraton Abu Dhabi Hotel & Resort, is a friendly alfresco bar that's fun for a sunset cocktail and—if you're so inclined—some puffs of *shisha.* It's open Sunday to Thursday from 4pm to 1am, and Friday and Saturday from noon to 1am. Upstairs is **Bravo** (ⓒ 2/697-0235), a Spanish tapas bar serving pitchers of sangria. It's open daily from 6:30pm to 12:30am. At the Hilton (ⓒ 2/681-1900), you'll find **Hemingway's** (open nightly until 12:30am) and the **Jazz Bar** (open nightly until 1:30am), both with live music, as well as **Cinebar,** the Hilton's popular nightclub. Cinebar is open nightly from 6pm to 3am. The city's most exclusive nightclub, which is by reservation only, is the **Embassy** (p. 139; ⓒ 2/690-8960) at the Emirates Palace. It's open Monday and Wednesday 7pm to 1am, Tuesday and Thursday through Friday 10pm to 3am.

2 Sharjah 🏵

Although just next door to Dubai, the emirate and city of Sharjah seems a world removed. Crowded, conservative, and lacking in Dubai's fashion-conscious modernity, Sharjah offers a journey into the traditional Emirati way of life. If Abu Dhabi is

Decent Proposal

Since September 2001, Sharjah has implemented rules consistent with the emirate's conservatism—rules that are far stricter than anywhere else in the UAE. Men and women who are not in a "legally acceptable" (read family or spouses) relationship are not supposed to be alone in public or commercial places, including vehicles. Men may not wear short shorts or go bare-chested in public. Women may not wear clothes that expose the stomach or back, skirts above the knee, or tight and transparent clothing that reveals the body. Swimsuits are only allowed at beaches or pool areas. Men should not visit "ladies only" places. Fines for breaking these rules range from warnings to possible jail time. Enforcement of the decency laws seems to vary.

the UAE's political center and Dubai the commercial hub, then Sharjah is the federation's cultural and historic heart.

Settlement in Sharjah dates back 6,000 years, and it was the key port on the lower Arabian Gulf into the first half of the 19th century. Not so long ago, Sharjah was among the richest cities in the Gulf, a fishing, pearling, and trading hub that eclipsed Dubai in prestige and wealth. But while Dubai's leaders in recent decades have embraced globalization with a kind of frenetic engagement, Sharjah's rulers have opted to focus on preserving the emirate's heritage and conservative values. The result is a traditional Arabian lifestyle that contrasts sharply with Dubai's more modern, Western approach.

In 1998, UNESCO designated Sharjah the Cultural Capital of the Arab Region. The emirate's rulers successfully restored old buildings and districts to their authentic architectural past, established museums and cultural organizations, opened universities, and organized regular art exhibitions and events. The museums here are dedicated to the arts, sciences, Islamic history, natural history, and traditional Arabian crafts. For some, this makes Sharjah more interesting than the other emirates, which tend to lack cultural offerings. Islam lies at the heart of this cultural life. Mosques show up on just about every block, a testament to the importance of religion in this society. Sharjah takes its conservatism seriously, and visitors are expected not to wear revealing clothing or engage in behavior that could be interpreted as disrespectful of Islam.

As Dubai rents have skyrocketed, Sharjah—with its significantly more affordable housing—has become the main residential suburb for workers commuting to Dubai. The downside is intense traffic during the morning and evening rush hours within the city and on the road to Dubai. If you're going to visit, it's best to travel on the weekend or outside peak commuter hours. Otherwise the only culture you may see is that related to the automotive industry.

ESSENTIALS
GETTING THERE & DEPARTING

BY CAR Travelers on a visit visa can use a valid international driving license or obtain a temporary driving license to drive a private or hired vehicle. Temporary licenses valid for 1 month are issued at the Sharjah Traffic and Licensing Department, on Al Ramtha Road (© **6/538-1111**), at a cost of AED 80 ($22/£11). Sharjah lies less than 20km (12 miles) from Dubai, but because of the enormous number of commuters who work in Dubai and live in Sharjah's more affordable housing, it can take more than 2 hours to reach during peak times along the E11 Al Ittihad Road linking the two cities. You may find it more convenient to take a taxi rather than driving yourself.

VISITOR INFORMATION   The **Sharjah Commerce and Tourism Development Authority** (© 6/556-6777; www.sharjahtourism.ae) is part of a ministry, and does not typically serve the public. Check the website for visitor information.

CITY LAYOUT   Sharjah developed around the creek, also called the Khalid Lagoon. The Corniche runs along the water's edge and is an appealing spot for walking in nice weather. The Heritage Area is the old walled city, home to numerous museums and the Souk Al Arash. There are two main areas dedicated to arts: The Arts Area in Al Shuwaiheen, and that on the other side of Al Bourj Avenue in Al Sheyoukh, where the Arabic Calligraphy Square and Sharjah Institute of Theatrical Arts are located. The Arts Area is home to a number of art institutes and galleries, including the Sharjah Arts Museum. Qanat Al Qasba (www.qaq.ae) is another popular area with a canal, waterfront restaurants, and performance spaces that often feature concerts, film festivals, and performing arts.

FAST FACTS: Sharjah

Area Code   The telephone area code for Sharjah is **6.**

Banks   Banks are generally open Saturday to Thursday 8:30am to 1pm (or later) and closed Friday. ATMs can be found at the main banks and in most shopping malls.

Drugstore   Most pharmacies are open 9am to 1:30pm and 4:30 to 10pm, closing earlier on Fridays. All government and private hospitals have on-site pharmacies. For a list of 24-hour pharmacies, ask your hotel concierge.

Hospital   Al Qassimi Hospital (© 6/538-6444), on Wasit Road, is the government-run hospital offering a full range of medical and healthcare services.

Post Office   Sharjah's Central Post Office (© 6/572-2219) is in Al Soor and open Saturday through Thursday from 8am to 8pm.

Police   © **999** or 6/563-3333.

EXPLORING SHARJAH

Heritage Area   Sharjah's old city was restored just a decade ago, transforming the former homes of prominent families into museums showcasing the region's heritage. Today's Heritage Area includes the Souk Al Arash, Bait Al Naboodah, Al Midfaa House, and Sharjah Fort (Al Hisn). Once the meeting place for Bedouins and their camels, the now air-conditioned **Souk Al Arash** ☞☞ features covered alleys with old-time vendors selling antiques, carpets, jewelry, and handicrafts. The **Al Naboodah** ☞ family home is a reconstruction of an Arabian home surrounding a large courtyard as was common in the mid–19th century, with rooms displaying traditional Arabian furnishings, jewelry, clothes, toys, and kitchen wares. The **Al Midfaa House** offers another glimpse into what was a peaceful Arabian family home. The **Sharjah Fort** (Al

Sharjah

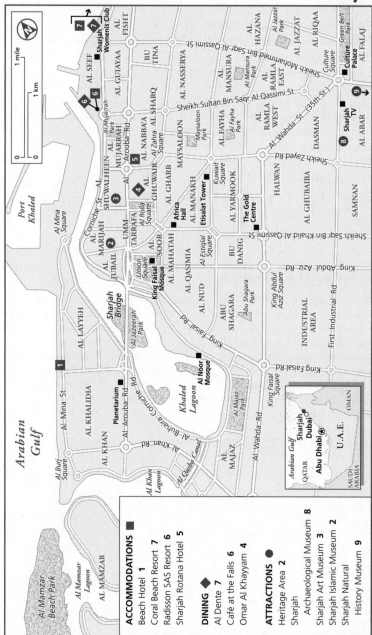

ACCOMMODATIONS ■
Beach Hotel **1**
Coral Beach Resort **7**
Radisson SAS Resort **6**
Sharjah Rotana Hotel **5**

DINING ◆
Al Dente **7**
Café at the Falls **6**
Omar Al Khayyam **4**

ATTRACTIONS ●
Heritage Area **2**
Sharjah
 Archaeological Museum **8**
Sharjah Art Museum **3**
Sharjah Islamic Museum **2**
Sharjah Natural
 History Museum **9**

Hisn) served as the traditional residence of the emirate's ruling family dating back more than 200 years. Displays inside trace the history and development of Sharjah.

Heritage Area, Al Merraija. © 6/568-0006. www.sharjahtourism.ae. Free admission. Tues–Sat 8am–8pm; closed Fri am and Mon.

Sharjah Archaeological Museum ★★ This educational museum reveals human development across the Arabian Peninsula over time. Among the artifacts displayed are jewelry, coins, pottery, tools, and ancient weapons. One museum section focuses on the latest discoveries unearthed from regional excavation sites. Public computers offer detailed information about each of the displays. Wednesdays are for ladies only.

Al Abar, near Cultural Square. © 6/566-5466. www.sharjahtourism.ae. Admission AED 5 ($1.35/70p). Mon–Sat 9am–1pm and 5–8pm; closed Fri am and Sun.

Sharjah Art Museum ★★ The centerpiece of the Arts Area, this is the largest art museum in the Arabian Gulf. It houses the personal collection of more than 300 paintings and maps belonging to Sharjah's ruler, HH Dr. Sheikh Sultan bin Mohammed Al Qassimi, as well as other permanent displays of Arabian art. In addition, the museum offers frequently changing art exhibitions. There's an arts library, bookshop, and cafe here, as well. Wednesday afternoons are for ladies only.

The Arts Area, Al Shuwaiheen. © 6/568-8222. www.sharjahtourism.ae. Admission AED 5 ($1.35/70p). Tues–Sat 9am–1pm and 5–8pm; closed Fri am and Mon.

Sharjah Islamic Museum ★★★ Providing an outstanding opportunity to learn about the cultural history of Islam over the past 1,400 years, the Sharjah Islamic Museum houses impressive collections of antiques, manuscripts, and artifacts. Arts and crafts celebrating the Islamic civilization include pottery, glass, and metallic handicrafts, jewelry, textiles, ornamentation tools, and Islamic mints. The **Holy Kaaba Hall** features an exquisite collection of gold-plated Qurans as well as a copy of the same curtain that covers the Kaaba Stone at Mecca. Other rooms include the Islamic Mints Hall, China and Pottery Hall, Arabesque Hall, Manuscripts Hall, Archaeology Hall, Metallic Handicrafts Hall, and Science Hall—where one of earliest world maps is shown.

Heritage Area. © 6/568-3334. www.sharjahtourism.ae. Admission AED 5 ($1.40/70p). Tues–Sat 9am–1pm and 5–8pm; closed Fri am and Mon.

Sharjah Natural History Museum ★★ Looking beyond the man-made skyscrapers and other constructions that have popped up with increasing speed in recent years, you may not have thought the UAE's habitat amounted to much more than sand and sea. But this natural history museum puts the spotlight on the region's unique flora and fauna. Interactive exhibits reveal the UAE's desert and marine ecosystems, and there is also a botanical center, children's farm, and Arabian Wildlife Centre. The latter houses an impressive display of indigenous and endangered Arabian animals, such as the Arabian leopard, which is on the verge of extinction.

Junction 8, East Coast Rd. © 6/531-1411. www.sharjahtourism.ae. Admission AED 15 ($4.10/£2.05). Tues–Sat 11am–5:30pm; closed Fri am and Mon.

WHERE TO STAY
EXPENSIVE
Radisson SAS Resort ★★ *Kids* If you've decided to spend your beach holiday in Sharjah, the Radisson SAS Resort should be your top option. The attractive modern

resort overlooks the sparkling blue waters of the Arabian Gulf and features its own private beach and bay. Guest rooms are generously appointed with contemporary furnishings, and each has a view of the sea. A number of uniquely designed "boutique cabana" rooms have been set up poolside; business-class rooms are larger and include breakfast and other special amenities. Resort activities include a high-tech fitness center, spa, and beach club, with swimming, windsurfing, and tennis lessons all offered. There's also a children's fun zone with an impressive array of games and activities. The signature restaurant, **Café at the Falls** (p. 146), sits within the enchanted indoor forest filling up the hotel's atrium lobby. The Radisson SAS resort is a self-contained oasis where just about everything you might want, except alcohol, is available.

Corniche Rd., P.O. Box 3527, Sharjah. © **800/201-1718** in the U.S. and Canada, or 6/565-7777 in the UAE. Fax 6/565-0090. www.radissonsas.com. 300 units. AED 1,300 ($354/£179) and up double. AE, MC, V. Free parking. **Amenities:** 6 restaurants and cafes; 2 outdoor pools; 2 lighted tennis courts; full-service spa w/coed and ladies-only fitness centers; private beach w/watersports; kids' activities; concierge; tour desk; business center; babysitting; laundry service. *In room:* A/C, TV, minibar, safe, free Wi-Fi.

MODERATE

Coral Beach Resort 🌟 *Kids*   This friendly resort has much of what you would find at a pricier Dubai beach hotel, minus the alcohol. Especially good for families, Coral Beach offers two beautiful pools, an excellent kids' club and shaded children's play area, and a lovely beach just in front. Activities include tennis, kayaking, canoeing, windsurfing, snorkeling, water polo, beach volleyball, and water aerobics. Guest rooms are comfortable if fairly simple, colored in blue and yellow tones to lend them a beach feel. There are six restaurants, cafes, and snack shops to choose from, but you'll need to travel to Dubai if you're looking for a sunset cocktail. **Al Dente** (see below), located next to the lobby, is one of the Sharjah's best fine-dining options.

Corniche Rd., P.O. Box 5524, Sharjah. © **6/522-9999**. Fax 6/522-3111. www.coral-international.com. 156 units. AED 870 ($237/£120) and up double. AE, MC, V. Free parking. **Amenities:** 6 restaurants and cafes; 2 outdoor pools; private beach w/watersports; 2 lighted tennis courts; volleyball; soccer; basketball; fitness center; kids' activities; concierge; business center; babysitting; laundry service. *In room:* A/C, TV, dataport, minibar, hair dryer, safe.

Sharjah Rotana Hotel *Value*   If you're planning to stay in Sharjah and want a comfortable night's rest without needless expense, this popular hotel offers a good value. Rotana is known throughout the region as a quality business and leisure hotel chain. This branch sits in the center of Sharjah's commercial district, and in addition to extensive business services offers a temperature-controlled outdoor pool and state-of-the-art fitness center. Guest rooms are well-equipped but lacking in any memorable design; suites feature kitchenettes. Complimentary shuttle service is available for guests who would like to use the hotel's exclusive beach club, just a short drive away.

Al Arouba St., P.O. Box 5734, Sharjah. © **6/563-7777**. Fax 6/563-5000. www.rotana.com. 205 units. AED 625 ($170/£86) and up double. AE, MC, V. Free parking. **Amenities:** Restaurant; lobby cafe; poolside snack bar; outdoor pool; fitness center; steam room; concierge; business center; laundry service; shuttle to beach. *In room:* A/C, TV, dataport, minibar, coffeemaker, hair dryer, safe.

INEXPENSIVE

Beach Hotel *Kids*   This is about as cheap as beachside accommodations in the UAE get. The simple hotel, a three-story block set right on the beach, is especially popular with Germans and Russians. It boasts the largest swimming pool in Sharjah, as well as a kids' pool and playground, beach cafe, and small health club. Don't expect luxury from the guest rooms, which consist of one or two beds, a table and two chairs, and a dresser with a TV. Ask for a room with a balcony overlooking the sea.

Sheikh Sultan Al Awal Rd., P.O. Box 5977, Abu Dhabi. © 2/528-1311. Fax 2/528-5422. www.beachhotel-sharjah. com. 131 units. AED 450 ($123/£62) double; AED 500 ($136/£69) junior suite. AE, MC, V. Free parking. **Amenities:** Restaurant; beach cafe; private beach; outdoor pool and children's pool; small health club; kids' activities; business center; gift shop; salon; laundry service; courtesy shuttle service within Sharjah and to Dubai. *In room:* A/C, TV, dataport, safe.

WHERE TO DINE
MODERATE

Al Dente ✦ ITALIAN   Located off the lobby of the Coral Beach Resort, this is the top Italian restaurant in Sharjah. It's also one of the city's only fine-dining options, with just a handful of tables in a Tuscan-inspired setting and an open kitchen with a glowing brick oven. Begin with the beef carpaccio or fish soup, depending on where your mood is, and continue with the filet of *hammour* (a type of grouper fish) served with a saffron mustard vinaigrette or lamb chops accompanied by hearty vegetables in a tomato basil sauce. If you're willing to stray from the tiramisu, I'd suggest topping off your meal with the *torta de pannini,* a bread pudding with vanilla sauce. No wine is served here, and you'll find the food prices considerably lower than at comparable Dubai restaurants.

Coral Beach Hotel. © 6/522-9999. Reservations recommended. Main courses AED 35–AED 55 ($9.50–$15/£4.80–£7.60). AE, DC, MC, V. Daily noon–3pm and 7–11pm.

Café at the Falls ✦ INTERNATIONAL   This surprising restaurant lies almost hidden within the man-made forest filling up the Radisson SAS atrium lobby. Surrounded by white-lit trees, waterfalls, and koi fish–filled ponds, the visually stunning setting makes for an enchanted meal. Diners can choose from the buffet or an a la carte menu, and there's a terrific selection of salads, sandwiches, pastas, steak, and fish dishes on the latter. Still, the beautifully presented and extensive buffet is the way to go. Although international in scope, regional specialties such as Mongolian barbecue are usually on offer. The guests include a mix of locals and expatriates.

Radisson SAS Resort. © 6/565-7777. Main courses AED 35–AED 95 ($9.50–$26/£4.80–£13); all-you-can-eat buffet AED 85 ($23/£12). AE, DC, MC, V. Daily 6:30–11am, 12:30–3:30pm, and 7–11pm.

Sanobar ✦ LEBANESE   If you're looking for casual Lebanese food in Sharjah, come to Sanobar. The somewhat kitsch dining room is decorated with photos from Lebanon, fishnets hanging from the ceiling, and replica creatures from the sea, including a glass-framed lobster, hanging on the wall. No surprise that the focus, then, is seafood, including *hammour,* salmon, calamari, shrimp, and lobster. The menu shows a photo of each dish, so you'll know exactly what you're in for. All selections are accompanied by hummus, a slice of garlic bread, and a large salad packed with tomatoes, onions, carrots, lettuce, and cucumber. The Sanobar Special is a generously portioned and well-priced plate with fresh fish, shrimp, and lobster. Since no alcohol is served, order one of the refreshing fruit juices to wash it all down.

Al Khan Rd. (near the Big Mosque). © 6/528-3501. All dishes AED 35–AED 65 ($9.50–$18/£4.80–£8.95). MC, V. Sat–Thurs noon–midnight; Fri 1pm–midnight.

INEXPENSIVE

Omar Al Khayyam ARABIC/PERSIAN   This no-nonsense eatery located near the Sharjah Rotana hotel serves first-rate Arabic and Iranian food. Leave any expectations of sophistication at the door, and come here for authentic local cooking. The no-frills ambience is typical of traditional Emirati restaurants. In business for more than

35 years, locals will tell you this is as good as it gets, serving dishes such as mutton kebab with rice, tikka chicken, and steamed rice with any number of meats. All dishes come with salad, soup, curry, and yogurt. As with other establishments in Sharjah, no alcohol is served. You are unlikely to find yourself in the company of many Westerners here.

Al Orooba St. (near Lulu Centre and Sharjah Rotana hotel). ℂ 6/565-4294. All dishes AED 15–AED 30 ($4–$8/ £2.05–£4.15). No credit cards. Daily noon–11pm.

SHOPPING

Sharjah cannot compare with Dubai in terms of the quantity and quality of shopping centers, although there are a few options that come close. **Sharjah City Centre** (ℂ 6/ 532-7700; www.sharjahcitycentre.com), **Mega Mall** (ℂ 6/574-2574; www.sharjah megamall.com), and the **Sahara Centre** (ℂ 6/531-6611; www.sahara-centre.com) all have international and national brand stores, with typically fewer shoppers than Dubai's crowded malls. Sharjah also has excellent traditional markets, including the **Central Souk** (also called the Blue Souk, next to the Khalid Lagoon), which sells jewelry, carpets, perfumes, shawls, and other Arabian goods, and the **Souk Al Arash,** the old bazaar in the Heritage Area where Bedouins once traded charcoal from the desert for goods from Iran and India. Today it, too, offers authentic Arabian products. Both of these covered souks are now air-conditioned, and open from 9am to 1pm and again from 4:30 to 9pm or later.

3 Al Ain ★★

Surrounded by rolling red sand dunes and an imposing mountain range, Al Ain (which means "water spring" in Arabic) is located within the Buraimi Oasis near the Oman border. Not long ago it consisted of no more than a series of sparsely populated villages, but today it's an expanding garden city boasting seven natural oases. Wealthy Emiratis have long made it a summer getaway because of its temperate climate and drier air, while local students continue coming here to study at the UAE's main university. Visitors will also find this charming desert city a welcome change of pace from bustling Dubai. Al Ain was the birthplace of the UAE's late ruler, Sheikh Zayed bin Sultan Al Nahyan, who through a series of greening projects transformed the landscape into something quite beautiful. Lush gardens, parks, date palm plantations, and tree-lined streets fill the city, set next to the Hajar Mountains. Jebel Hafeet is the UAE's second-largest mountain, which can be visited along with the natural hot springs resort of Mubazzarah. Al Ain's tourist sites, including forts, cultural museums, and souks, are clearly marked by brown signs. Al Ain can easily be visited as a day or overnight trip. Travelers can also go to nearby Buraimi town on the Oman side without a visa.

ESSENTIALS
GETTING THERE & DEPARTING
BY CAR Al Ain is about an hour drive from Dubai and 1½ hours from Abu Dhabi. From Dubai, take Sheikh Zayed Road to Interchange 1, and follow the signs to Al Ain. From Abu Dhabi, the road to Al Ain is also clearly marked. From the town center of Al Ain, there's a green sign leading the way to the public hot springs of Mubazzarah and a brown sign for Jebel Hafeet. Jebel Hafeet (the mountaintop) is located up a winding road 13km (8 miles) past Mubazzarah.

CITY LAYOUT   Al Ain is a city of natural springs (oases), parks, and gardens. The main road (Al Ain St.) leading through town is interrupted by a series of roundabouts. The key tourist sites are designated by clearly marked brown or green signs.

EXPLORING AL AIN

Al Ain National Museum ☆   Next to the main oasis in the town center, this museum and fort was the birthplace of the late UAE ruler, Sheikh Zayed bin Sultan Al Nahyan, and was used to protect the oasis from raiders. The museum includes a collection of the gifts he received over the course of his life, photographs, and other exhibitions showcasing the culture and heritage of the Al Ain people. Distinct archaeological and ethnographical sections unveil the pre-oil history of the UAE.

Edge of the main oasis in the town center, near the Al Ain souk. ☎ 3/764-1595. www.aam.gov.ae. Free admission. Sat–Thurs 9am–7:30pm; Fri 3–7:30pm; closed Mon.

Al Ain Oasis ☆☆   The city's largest oasis lies next to the town center, between the main souk area and Al Ain Street. It's home to date palm plantations, some of which are working farms. You can see the ancient Arabian *falaj* irrigation system, in which horizontal underground tunnels are connected to the surface by vertical shafts. Narrow roads on which you can walk or drive lead through the oasis, and you should stick to the pavement when viewing the palm plantations.

Adjacent the town center.

Camel Souk ☆☆   The last camel souk in the UAE is a fascinating look at an age-old trade, where proud owners tout the merits of their desert animals in hopes of selling them for a hefty reward. These even-toed, one-hump creatures will tug at your heartstrings, and this is a great place both to see the camels and to interact with locals. The market is an especially fun place for children, who can sit on the camels in exchange for a tip. It's best to dress conservatively when visiting the camel souk.

5km (3 miles) south of Al Ain in the Meyzad area. Free admission. Open daily in the morning only.

Hili Archaeological Garden ☆   Located 10km (6 miles) north of Al Ain, this open-air archaeological park represents the oldest settlement in the UAE, dating back to the Bronze Age. Inhabitants were involved in agriculture and copper trade. There are several tombs here, including the large round structure surrounded by a moat at the center of the ruins. The two entrances to this grand tomb, where more than 250 skeletons were discovered, are decorated with human and animal relieves.

10km (6¼ miles) north of Al Ain on the Dubai Rd. www.aam.gov.ae. Admission AED 1 (30¢/15p). Daily 4–11pm.

Jebel Hafeet and the Green Mubazzarah ☆☆☆   The UAE's second-highest mountain (1,240m/4,068 ft.) affords a beautiful view of Al Ain and the surrounding desert flat plains. The mountaintop is located up a winding road 13km (8 miles) past the Green Mubazzarah, a popular tourist destination with public hot springs, pools, and chalets that lies at the base of the mountain. There are three viewing points along the beautiful but steep and winding road, and at the top are a large parking area, cafeteria, and the Mercure Hafeet hotel. Bring a camera and some binoculars.

WHERE TO STAY
MODERATE
Hilton Al Ain ☆ *Kids*   This extensive but aging hotel is a good base for families wishing to explore Al Ain, Jebel Hafeet, and the surrounding area. Accommodations

Al Ain

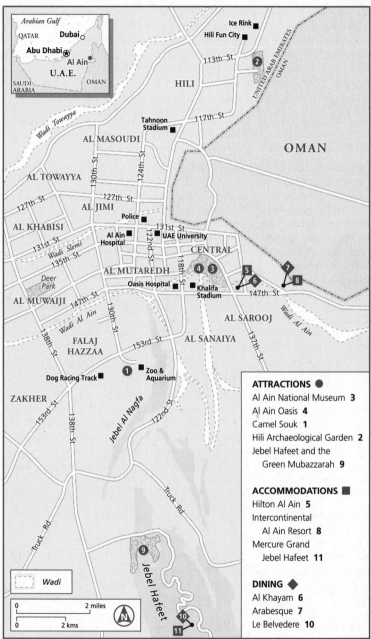

Arabian Gulf

QATAR Dubai

Abu Dhabi ✪
Al Ain •
U.A.E.

SAUDI
ARABIA OMAN

Wadi Towayya

Ice Rink
Hili Fun City

113th St.

HILI

117th St.

Tahnoon
Stadium

AL MASOUDI

OMAN

AL TOWAYYA

130th St.
124th St.

127th St.

127th St.

AL JIMI

Police

131st St.

AL KHABISI

Al Ain
Hospital

122nd St.

UAE University

131st St.

Wadi Slemi
135th St.

CENTRAL

118th St.

AL MUTAREDH

Deer
Park

Oasis Hospital

4 3

5

7

AL MUWAIJI

147th St.

130th St.

Khalifa
Stadium

6

8

147th St.

Wadi Al Ain

FALAJ
HAZZAA

Wadi Al Ain

AL SAROOJ

138th St.

153rd St.

AL SANAIYA

137th St.

1

Zoo &
Aquarium

Dog Racing Track

ZAKHER

153rd St.

138th St.

Jebel Al Nagfa

122nd St.

Truck Rd.

Truck Rd.

9

Jebel Hafeet

Wadi

10

11

0   2 miles

0   2 kms

N

ATTRACTIONS ●

Al Ain National Museum **3**
Al Ain Oasis **4**
Camel Souk **1**
Hili Archaeological Garden **2**
Jebel Hafeet and the
    Green Mubazzarah **9**

ACCOMMODATIONS ■

Hilton Al Ain **5**
Intercontinental
    Al Ain Resort **8**
Mercure Grand
    Jebel Hafeet **11**

DINING ◆

Al Khayam **6**
Arabesque **7**
Le Belvedere **10**

149

include suites, Art Deco–style villas, and regular guest rooms. Some have views of the landscaped gardens and others of Jebel Hafeet. Ask for a room in the hotel's newer wing. Restaurants include Persian, Italian, and Tex-Mex options. Kids will enjoy the waterslide pool, and there's a playground for the smallest family members. Guests also have access to tennis, golf, and spa treatments. The staff will help arrange tours and activities in the surrounding area.

Al Sarooj District, Hilton St., Al Ain. © 800/445-8667 in the U.S. and Canada, or 3/768-6666 in the UAE. Fax 3/768-6888. www.1.hilton.com. 202 units. AED 500 ($136/£69) and up double. AE, DC, MC, V. Free parking. **Amenities:** 5 restaurants and bars; outdoor pool; 4 lighted tennis courts; squash courts; 9-hole golf course; health club; sauna; Jacuzzi; kids' activities; concierge; tour desk; business center; babysitting; laundry service. *In room:* A/C, TV, minibar, safe, Wi-Fi.

Intercontinental Al Ain Resort *Kids*   This resort is the best in the area, a fully refurbished property with beautiful landscaped grounds, modern guest rooms, and extensive amenities. The bulk of daytime activity takes place around the large family pool with its own swim-up bar. Recreational activities include spinning, aqua aerobics, karate, rugby, soccer, tennis, and squash, and there's a lovely spa for guests who prefer to relax. "Time for Tots" is the full-time day-care center, and kids can get their faces painted on weekends. Guest rooms are comfortable but unmemorable in decor, and villas offer separate living rooms and bedrooms. Dining choices include Italian, Asian, Indian, and Arabic restaurants.

Al Nyadat Rd., Al Ain. © 888/424-6835 in the U.S. and Canada, or 3/768-6686 in the UAE. Fax 3/768-6766. www.ichotelsgroup.com. 247 units. AED 500 ($136/£69) and up double. AE, DC, MC, V. Free parking. **Amenities:** 8 restaurants and bars; 3 outdoor pools including 1 for kids; tennis courts; squash courts; spa w/sauna and Jacuzzi; 24-hour fitness center; kids' activities; concierge; tour desk; car rental; business center; gift shop; salon; babysitting; laundry service. *In room:* A/C, TV, minibar, safe.

Mercure Grand Jebel Hafeet Al Ain *Kids*   This mountain resort 2km (1¼ miles) from the top of Jebel Hafeet boasts a spectacular view of Al Ain and the surrounding desert plains below. The self-contained hotel features a health club, minigolf, children's playground, and three swimming pools with water slides. The contemporary guest rooms are bright and airy. Even if you don't stay here, have dinner at **Le Belvedere** (see below), which offers Mediterranean dining with an enchanting view. Lawrence's Bar features live entertainment at night.

Jebel Hafeet (near the mountaintop), Al Ain. © 3/783-8888. Fax 3/783-9000. www.mercure.com. 205 units. AED 500 ($136/£69) and up double. AE, MC, V. Free parking. **Amenities:** 2 restaurants; coffee shop; bar; 3 outdoor pools; 2 tennis courts; health club; minigolf; children's playground; tourist desk; laundry service. *In room:* A/C, TV, minibar, safe.

WHERE TO DINE
MODERATE
Al Khayam *PERSIAN   Authentic Iranian dishes fill the menu, including meat and vegetable grills, charcoal-grilled kebabs, and other house specialties such as the sumac-marinated salmon. Traditional Iranian bread is served freshly baked from Al Khayam's clay oven. The handsome dining room is decorated with traditional *majlis* seating interspersed by wood screens. If you've never tasted Persian food, this is an excellent place to do so.

Hilton Al Ain, Al Sarooj District, Hilton St. © 6/768-6666. Reservations recommended. Main courses AED 35–AED 55 ($9.50–$15/£4.80–£7.60). AE, DC, MC, V. Mon–Sat 12:30–11:30pm.

Arabesque *ARABIC   The quiet buffet-style dining at the Intercon's Arabesque restaurant is a perfect opportunity to sample the great variety of Arabic cuisine. Begin

Musandam

Situated at the northeast tip of the Arabian Peninsula, Musandam makes for a peaceful 1- or 2-day excursion from Dubai. Actually in Oman, the Musandam Peninsula is surrounded by the Gulf of Oman to the east, the Arabian (Persian) Gulf to the west, and the Strait of Hormuz to the north, with Iran just 55km (34 miles) across the strait. The peninsula is punctuated by narrow inlets of deep blue-green water weaving their way between jagged cliffs belonging to the Western Hajar Mountains. Dhow cruises take visitors through these inlets and fjords where swimming, snorkeling, and diving beckon. Rich marine life includes coral reefs, turtles, dolphins, tropical fish, and sometimes whales on the eastern side. This stunningly beautiful area, occasionally referred to as the "Norway of Arabia" because of its fjords, offers some of the best fishing and scuba diving in the Middle East.

Khasab is the laid-back harbor town from which the dhows leave. Visitors can pre-book a dhow tour package with **Khasab Travel & Tours** (© 4/266-9950; www.khasab-tours.com), which also offers mountain safaris, diving trips, and longer Oman excursions. Full-day dhow tours, which include lunch, beverages, and plenty of time for swimming and snorkeling, depart at 9am and return at 4pm; the cost is AED 200 ($55/£28). Half-day dhow trips lasting 4 hours depart at 9am or 1:30pm and cost AED 150 ($41/£21) for adults, half price for children 11 and under. Khasab Travel & Tours handles Oman tourist-visa arrangements. Alternatively, visitors can negotiate the length and price of a private dhow cruise with any of the many local dhow captains working in the Khasab harbor. The scenic town of Khasab also has an old souk, a few restaurants, and a handful of hotels for visitors looking to stay overnight. The best is the **Golden Tulip Hotel** (© 968/2673-0777; www.goldentulip khasab.com), which has its own dive center and will also arrange dhow cruises, mountain safaris, and dolphin-watching excursions.

Allow for about 3 hours to reach Musandam from Dubai. If you are driving yourself, turn right at the Shams Roundabout located 30km (19 miles) north of Ras Al Khaimah, and then follow the road to the UAE exit post. There, you will grab a UAE exit form and then drive a short distance ahead to the Oman point of entry, where you will fill out an entry form and pay for any applicable visa. From there, continue along the coastline until you reach Khasab, the gateway to the Musandam Peninsula. Although driving yourself is feasible (just check with your car-rental agency about insurance policies for entering Oman, which can be expensive), it's easier to visit Musandam through a Dubai-based tour operator who handles transfer and visa arrangements.

with a fresh vegetable salad followed by a sampling of traditional Lebanese meze. Then take your time trying the broad array of dishes from across the Middle East focused on grilled meats, fish, rice, and vegetables. The lunch buffet includes a live cooking station. Don't forget to save room for the sumptuous dessert buffet.

Intercontinental, Al Nyadat Rd. ⓒ 3/768-6686. All-you-can-eat breakfast buffet AED 50 ($14/£6.90); lunch and dinner buffet AED 85 ($23/£12). AE, DC, MC, V. Daily 6:30–11am, 12:30–3:30pm, and 7:30–11:30pm.

Le Belvedere ⭐⭐ MEDITERRANEAN   You'll need to budget about an hour to get here from Al Ain, since the restaurant lies in the Mercure Hotel near the top of Jebel Hafeet. The view of the city below is worth it, and you can easily combine a meal here with a visit to the mountaintop. The brasserie-style restaurant integrates French, Italian, and Moroccan cooking. Fridays bring a popular seafood buffet. Service is relaxed and friendly, and dress is smart-casual. Following dinner, take a walk around the hotel's lush gardens and take in the clean mountain air.

Mercure Grand Jebel Hafeet (near the mountaintop), Al Ain. ⓒ 3/783-8888. All dishes AED 35–AED 65 ($9.50–$18/ £4.80–£8.95). MC, V. Daily 12:30–3pm and 7:30–10:30pm.

Appendix A: Fast Facts, Toll-Free Numbers & Websites

1 Fast Facts: Dubai

Area Codes The country code for the UAE is 971, and the city code for Dubai is 4.

ATM Networks & Cashpoints See "Money & Costs," p. 27.

Automobile Organizations The **Arabian Automobile Association (AAA)** (☎ 4/266-9989 or 800-4900; www.aaauae.com) offers 24-hour recovery service for an annual fee, including basic mechanical repairs, towing service, battery boosting, lockout service, and assistance for vehicles that have a flat tire or run out of gas. The organization is also licensed to issue International Driving Permits.

Business Hours Government offices are typically open Sunday to Thursday from 7:30am to 2:30pm. Private business hours are generally from 9am to 5pm, with some businesses taking an afternoon break and then staying open until later in the evening. Many shops open at 9 or 10am and stay open until 9 or 10pm. The weekend is Friday and Saturday.

Bank hours are Saturday to Wednesday 8am to 1pm, and (for some) again from 4:30 to 6:30pm. They are open Thursday from 8am to noon and are closed Friday.

Car Rentals See "Toll-Free Numbers & Websites," p. 158.

Drinking Laws Alcohol is only available in hotel and club restaurants, bars, and nightclubs. It is not sold in supermarkets or other public places. Technically, drinking or possession of alcohol without a Ministry of Interior liquor permit is illegal except for guests of the hotel. Liquor licenses are issued only to non-Muslim persons who possess UAE residency permits. Drinking alcohol in public is illegal, and there is zero tolerance for drinking and driving; doing so will result in jail and stiff fines.

Driving Rules See "Getting There and Getting Around," p. 24.

Electricity Dubai's electricity is 220–240 volts AC. U.S.-made appliances generally require a transformer to operate here. Bring a **connection kit** of the right power and phone adapters, a spare phone cord, and a spare Ethernet network cable—or find out whether your hotel supplies them to guests.

Embassies & Consulates All embassies are located in the UAE's capital, Abu Dhabi. Many countries also have consulates located in Dubai.

The embassy of **Australia** is on the 14th Floor of the Al Muhairy Center, Sheikh Zayed the First Street, Abu Dhabi (☎ 2/634-6100; www.uae.embassy.gov.ae). The Australian Consulate General in Dubai is on the 25th floor of the Burjuman Business Tower (☎ 4/508-7100).

The embassy of **Canada** is in the Abu Dhabi Trade Towers (Abu Dhabi Mall), West Tower, Abu Dhabi (✆ **2/694-0300;** www.international.gc.ca). The Canadian Consulate in Dubai is on the 7th floor of the Bank Street Building, Khalid bin Waled St. (✆ **4/314-5555**).

The embassy of the **United Kingdom** is on Al Seef Road in Bur Dubai, Dubai (✆ **4/309-4444;** www.britishembassy. gov.uk).

The embassy of the **United States** is at Al Khaleej A. Arabi Street, at 30th Street, Abu Dhabi (✆ **2/414-2200;** abudhabi. usembassy.gov). The U.S. Consulate general in Dubai is in the World Trade Center off Sheikh Zayed Road (✆ **4/311-6000;** dubai.usconsulate.gov).

Emergencies The **Dubai Municipality Emergency Number** is ✆ **4/223-2323.** For police or an ambulance, dial ✆ 999. In case of fire, dial ✆ 997.

Gasoline (Petrol) Gasoline is referred to as petrol in the UAE and is available at stations operated by Emarat, EPPCO, and ENOC. It's sold by the imperial gallon (about 4.5 liters) and costs approximately AED 6.50 ($1.75/90p) per gallon, considerably less than in most Western countries.

Holidays Banks, government offices, post offices, and many stores, restaurants, and other businesses are closed on the following legal national holidays: January 1 (New Year's Day), March 14 (Prophet's Birthday), July 19 (Lailat Al Mi'Raj), September 20 (Eid Al Fitr), November 27 (Eid Al Adha), December 2 (UAE National Day), and December 18 (Islamic New Year). Ramadan in 2009 will be from August 21 to September 19.

For more information on holidays, see "Calendar of Events," p. 22.

Hospitals The best government hospitals include **Al Wasl Hospital** (✆ **4/324-1111;** www.dohms.gov.ae) on Oud Metha Road in Bur Dubai and **Rashid Hospital**

(✆ **4/337-4000;** www.dohms.gov.ae) in downtown Bur Dubai. Both offer emergency services. For private hospitals, the **American Hospital** (✆ **4/336-7777;** www.ahdubai.com) on Oud Metha Road offers excellent emergency services and in-patient and out-patient care, as does **Welcare Hospital** (✆ **4/282-7788;** www. welcarehospital.com) in Al Garhoud, near the Aviation Club. **Dubai Healthcare City** (www.dhcc.ae) also encompasses a selection of hospitals.

Hot lines The toll-free hot line for **Dubai's Tourist Police** is ✆ **800-4438.** The **Dubai Municipality Emergency Number** is ✆ **4/223-2323. Health Call** (✆ **4/363-5343**) offers in-house medical calls 24 hours a day. The team of medical doctors from North America and Europe out of Dubai Healthcare City provide comprehensive primary healthcare.

Insurance Medical Insurance For travel overseas, most U.S. health plans (including Medicare and Medicaid) do not provide coverage, and the ones that do often require you to pay for services upfront and reimburse you only after you return home.

As a safety net, you may want to buy travel medical insurance, particularly if you're traveling to a remote or high-risk area where emergency evacuation might be necessary. If you require additional medical insurance, try **MEDEX Assistance** (✆ **410/453-6300;** www.medex assist.com) or **Travel Assistance International** (✆ **800/821-2828;** www.travel assistance.com; for general information on services, call the company's **Worldwide Assistance Services, Inc.,** at ✆ **800/ 777-8710**).

Canadians should check with their provincial health plan offices or call **Health Canada** (✆ **866/225-0709;** www. hc-sc.gc.ca) to find out the extent of their coverage and what documentation and receipts they must take home in case they are treated overseas.

Travelers from the U.K. should carry their European Health Insurance Card (EHIC), which replaced the E111 form as proof of entitlement to free/reduced cost medical treatment abroad (© **0845 606 2030;** www.ehic.org.uk). Note, however, that the EHIC only covers "necessary medical treatment," and for repatriation costs, lost money, baggage, or cancellation, travel insurance from a reputable company should always be sought (www.travelinsuranceweb.com).

Travel Insurance The cost of travel insurance varies widely, depending on the destination, the cost and length of your trip, your age and health, and the type of trip you're taking, but expect to pay between 5% and 8% of the vacation itself. You can get estimates from various providers through **InsureMyTrip.com**. Enter your trip cost and dates, your age, and other information for prices from more than a dozen companies.

U.K. citizens and their families who make more than one trip abroad per year may find an annual travel insurance policy works out cheaper. Check **www.money supermarket.com**, which compares prices across a wide range of providers for single- and multi-trip policies.

Most big travel agents offer their own insurance and will probably try to sell you their package when you book a holiday. Think before you sign. **Britain's Consumers' Association** recommends that you insist on seeing the policy and reading the fine print before buying travel insurance. The **Association of British Insurers** (© **020/7600-3333;** www.abi.org.uk) gives advice by phone and publishes *Holiday Insurance,* a free guide to policy provisions and prices. You might also shop around for better deals: Try **Columbus Direct** (© **0870/033-9988;** www.columbusdirect.net).

Trip Cancellation Insurance Trip cancellation insurance will help retrieve your money if you have to back out of a trip or depart early, or if your travel supplier goes bankrupt. Trip cancellation traditionally covers such events as sickness, natural disasters, and State Department advisories. The latest news in trip cancellation insurance is the availability of **expanded hurricane coverage** and the **"any-reason"** cancellation coverage—which costs more but covers cancellations made for any reason. You won't get back 100% of your prepaid trip cost, but you'll be refunded a substantial portion. **TravelSafe** (© **888/ 885-7233;** www.travelsafe.com) offers both types of coverage. Expedia also offers any-reason cancellation coverage for its air-hotel packages. For details, contact one of the following recommended insurers: **Access America** (© 866/807-3982; www.accessamerica.com); **Travel Guard International** (© 800/826-4919; www.travelguard.com); **Travel Insured International** (© 800/243-3174; www.travelinsured.com); and **Travelex Insurance Services** (© 888/457-4602; www.travelex-insurance.com).

Internet Access Most Dubai hotels offer Internet access, including business centers with computers. **Al Matrix.com Café** (© 4/343-0000) lies in the Metropolitan Hotel on Sheikh Zayed Road and is open from 10am to midnight. **Formula One Net Café** (© 4/345-1232), in the Palm Strip shopping mall on Jumeirah Beach Road, is open from 10am to 10pm. The **Coffee Bean** (© 4/282-4122) offers Internet access at the Aviation Club in Al Garhoud, and is open from 7am to 11pm. **WorldNet Internet Café** (© 4/332-2913) lies in the Holiday Center on Sheikh Zayed Road and is open from 10am to 11pm.

Language English is widely spoken in Dubai and most public information is written in English as well as Arabic. For a list of common Arabic phrases, see p. 161.

Legal Aid If you run into legal trouble, it's a good idea to contact your country's consulate in Dubai or embassy in Abu Dhabi. They will usually have a list of reputable English-speaking lawyers and contact information. U.S. citizens who are arrested should contact the U.S. Embassy or Consulate General for assistance. The U.S. Consul will provide information on the local judicial system and a list of local attorneys. In Dubai, the U.S. Consul can also arrange for U.S. citizen detainees to meet with an ombudsman from the Human Rights Department of the Dubai police headquarters, if the detainee believes he or she is not being treated fairly. Other embassies and consulates offer similar services.

Lost & Found For lost and found in Dubai, try contacting **Dubai's Tourist Police** (© 800-4438). Be sure to tell all of your credit card companies the minute you discover your wallet has been lost or stolen, and file a report at the nearest police precinct. Your credit card company or insurer may require a police report number or record of the loss. Most credit card companies have an emergency toll-free number to call if your card is lost or stolen; they may be able to wire you a cash advance immediately or deliver an emergency credit card in a day or two. Visa's UAE emergency number is © 4/223-6888. American Express cardholders and traveler's check holders should call © 4/336-5000. MasterCard holders should call © 4/332-2956.

If you need emergency cash over the weekend when all banks and American Express offices are closed, you can have money wired to you via **Western Union** (© 800/325-6000; www.westernunion.com).

Mail UAE mail is reliable and generally takes 6 to 10 days to reach Europe and the U.S., and 8 to 10 days to reach Australia and New Zealand. Letters up to 20 grams cost AED 3 (82¢/40p) to Europe and AED 3.50 (95¢/50p) to the U.S.

Stamps are available for purchase in post offices, supermarkets, and some other shops. Red post boxes for outbound mail are easily distinguishable at post offices and outside many supermarkets. The **main post office** is on Zaabeel Road in Karama, Bur Dubai (© 800-5858).

Newspapers & Magazines Dubai's major English-language newspapers are *Gulf News, Khaleej Times, Emirates Today,* and the *Gulf Today. Seven Days* is an English-language tabloid. Local magazines in English include *Inside Out, TimeOut Dubai, What's On,* and *Connector.* These and some foreign newspapers and magazines are available in bookshops and supermarkets.

Passports The websites listed provide downloadable passport applications as well as the current fees for processing applications. For an up-to-date, country-by-country listing of passport requirements around the world, go to the "International Travel" tab of the U.S. State Department at **http://travel.state.gov**.

For Residents of Australia You can pick up an application from your local post office or any branch of Passports Australia, but you must schedule an interview at the passport office to present your application materials. Call the **Australian Passport Information Service** at © 131-232, or visit the government website at www.passports.gov.au.

For Residents of Canada Passport applications are available at travel agencies throughout Canada or from the central **Passport Office,** Department of Foreign Affairs and International Trade, Ottawa, ON K1A 0G3 (© 800/567-6868; www.ppt.gc.ca). *Note:* Canadian children who travel must have their own passport. However, if you hold a valid Canadian passport issued before December 11, 2001, that bears the name of your child, the passport remains valid for you and your child until it expires.

For Residents of Ireland You can apply for a 10-year passport at the **Passport Office,** Setanta Centre, Molesworth Street, Dublin 2 (© **01/671-1633;** www.irlgov.ie/iveagh). Those 17 and under and 66 and older must apply for a 3-year passport. You can also apply at 1A South Mall, Cork (© **21/494-4700**) or at most main post offices.

For Residents of New Zealand You can pick up a passport application at any New Zealand Passports Office or download it from their website. Contact the **Passports Office** at © **0800/225-050** in New Zealand or 04/474-8100, or log on to www.passports.govt.nz.

For Residents of the United Kingdom To pick up an application for a standard 10-year passport (5-year passport for children 15 and under), visit your nearest passport office, major post office, or travel agency, or contact the **United Kingdom Passport Service** at © **0870/521-0410** or search its website at www.ukpa.gov.uk.

For Residents of the United States Whether you're applying in person or by mail, you can download passport applications from the U.S. State Department website at **http://travel.state.gov.** To find your regional passport office, either check the U.S. State Department website or call the **National Passport Information Center** toll-free number (© **877/487-2778**) for automated information.

Police The emergency number for police or an ambulance is © **999.** The Dubai Police can also be reached at © **800-4438** (www.dubaipolice.gov.ae).

Taxes There's no income or value-added tax (VAT) in Dubai, although a VAT may be coming as soon as 2010. A 10% municipality tax and a 10% service charge are added for hotel and food and beverage bills, but these are usually already incorporated in the price.

Citizens of countries other than those from Gulf Cooperation Council (GCC) countries are required to pay a departure fee of AED 20 ($5.45/£2.75) payable only in the local currency.

Telephones See "Staying Connected," p. 36.

Time Dubai is 4 hours ahead of UCT (formerly known as GMT). It does not observe daylight saving time.

Tipping Many restaurants include a service charge, which will be clearly identified in your bill; for those that do not, a tip of 10% to 15% is appropriate. Your server is generally not allowed to keep the tip, however, which is instead shared with all the staff. Offer AED 5 ($1.35/70p) for valet parking, unless otherwise specified. A few dirhams per bag is an appropriate tip for hotel bell boys. Taxi drivers do not expect to be tipped, although people often round up when paying for the fare.

Toilets Western-style restrooms are widely available in shopping malls, restaurants, and hotel lobbies. Public toilets on the streets are uncommon.

Useful Phone Numbers U.S. Dept. of State Travel Advisory: © **202/647-5225** (staffed 24 hr.)

U.S. Passport Agency: © **202/647-0518**

U.S. Centers for Disease Control International Traveler's Hotline: © **404/332-4559**

Visas Nationals of Australia, Canada, Ireland, New Zealand, the United Kingdom, and the United States (as well as those of a number of other countries) do not require visas to visit the UAE. For more information, visit www.dubaitourism.co.ae.

Water Tap water is desalinated from the Arabian Gulf and is safe to drink, but most visitors prefer bottled mineral water, which is offered in most Dubai hotels and restaurants.

2 Toll-Free Numbers & Websites

MAJOR INTERNATIONAL AIRLINES

Air Canada
© 888/247-2262 (in U.S. and Canada)
www.aircanada.com

Air France
© 800/237-2747 (in U.S.)
© 800/375-8723 (in U.S. and Canada)
© 087/0142-4343 (in U.K.)
www.airfrance.com

Air India
© 212/407-1371 (in U.S.)
© 91 22 2279 6666 (in India)
© 020/8745-1000 (in U.K.)
www.airindia.com

Air New Zealand
© 800/262-1234 (in U.S.)
© 800/663-5494 (in Canada)
© 0800/028-4149 (in U.K.)
www.airnewzealand.com

Alitalia
© 800/223-5730 (in U.S.)
© 800/361-8336 (in Canada)
© 087/0608-6003 (in U.K.)
www.alitalia.com

American Airlines
© 800/433-7300 (in U.S. and Canada)
© 020/7365-0777 (in U.K.)
www.aa.com

British Airways
© 800/247-9297 (in U.S. and Canada)
© 087/0850-9850 (in U.K.)
www.british-airways.com

Continental Airlines
© 800/523-3273 (in U.S. and Canada)
© 084/5607-6760 (in U.K.)
www.continental.com

Delta Air Lines
© 800/221-1212 (in U.S. and Canada)
© 084/5600-0950 (in U.K.)
www.delta.com

Emirates Airlines
© 800/777-3999 (in U.S.)
© 087/0243-2222 (in U.K.)
www.emirates.com

Etihad Airways
© 888/838-4489 (in U.S.)
© 870/241-7121 (in U.K.)
www.etihadairways.com

Finnair
© 800/950-5000 (in U.S. and Canada)
© 087/0241-4411 (in U.K.)
www.finnair.com

Japan Airlines
© 012/025-5931 (international)
www.jal.co.jp

KLM
www.klm.com
(service provided by Northwest Airlines
in U.S.; www.nwa.com)

Korean Air
© 800/438-5000 (in U.S. and Canada)
© 0800/413-000 (in U.K.)
www.koreanair.com

Lufthansa
© 800/399-5838 (in U.S.)
© 800/563-5954 (in Canada)
© 087/0837-7747 (in U.K.)
www.lufthansa.com

Olympic Airlines
© 800/223-1226 (in U.S.)
© 514/878-9691 (in Canada)
© 087/0606-0460 (in U.K.)
www.olympicairlines.com

Qantas Airways
© 800/227-4500 (in U.S.)
© 084/5774-7767 (in U.K. or Canada)
© 13 13 13 (in Australia)
www.qantas.com

South African Airways
© 271/1978-5313 (international)
© 0861 FLYSAA (086/135-9122) (in
   South Africa)
www.flysaa.com

Thai Airways International
© 212/949-8424 (in U.S.)
© 020/7491-7953 (in U.K.)
www.thaiair.com

Turkish Airlines
© 90 212 444 0 849
www.thy.com

CAR-RENTAL AGENCIES

Avis
© 800/331-1212 (in U.S. and Canada)
© 084/4581-8181 (in U.K.)
www.avis.com

Budget
© 800/527-0700 (in U.S.)
© 087/0156-5656 (in U.K.)
© 800/268-8900 (in Canada)
www.budget.com

Dollar
© 800/800-4000 (in U.S.)
© 800/848-8268 (in Canada)
© 080/8234-7524 (in U.K.)
www.dollar.com

MAJOR HOTEL & MOTEL CHAINS

Best Western International
© 800/780-7234 (in U.S. and Canada)
© 0800/393-130 (in U.K.)
www.bestwestern.com

Clarion Hotels
© 800/CLARION or 877/424-6423 (in
   U.S. and Canada)
© 0800/444-444 (in U.K.)
www.choicehotels.com

Courtyard by Marriott
© 888/236-2427 (in U.S.)
© 0800/221-222 (in U.K.)
www.marriott.com/courtyard

Crowne Plaza Hotels
© 888/303-1746
www.ichotelsgroup.com/crowneplaza

United Airlines
© 800/864-8331 (in U.S. and Canada)
© 084/5844-4777 (in U.K.)
www.united.com

US Airways
© 800/428-4322 (in U.S. and Canada)
© 084/5600-3300 (in U.K.)
www.usairways.com

Virgin Atlantic Airways
© 800/821-5438 (in U.S. and Canada)
© 087/0574-7747 (in U.K.)
www.virgin-atlantic.com

Hertz
© 800/645-3131
© 800/654-3001 (for international
   reservations)
www.hertz.com

National
© 800/CAR-RENT (800/227-7368)
www.nationalcar.com

Hilton Hotels
© 800/HILTONS (800/445-8667) (in
   U.S. and Canada)
© 087/0590-9090 (in U.K.)
www.hilton.com

Holiday Inn
© 800/315-2621 (in U.S. and Canada)
© 0800/405-060 (in U.K.)
www.holidayinn.com

Hyatt
© 888/591-1234 (in U.S. and Canada)
© 084/5888-1234 (in U.K.)
www.hyatt.com

InterContinental Hotels & Resorts
© 800/424-6835 (in U.S. and Canada)
© 0800/1800-1800 (in U.K.)
www.ichotelsgroup.com

Marriott
© 877/236-2427 (in U.S. and Canada)
© 0800/221-222 (in U.K.)
www.marriott.com

Radisson Hotels & Resorts
© 888/201-1718 (in U.S. and Canada)
© 0800/374-411 (in U.K.)
www.radisson.com

Ramada Worldwide
© 888/2-RAMADA (888/272-6232)
   (In U.S. and Canada)
© 080/8100-0783 (in U.K.)
www.ramada.com

Renaissance
© 888/236-2427
www.renaissance.com

Ritz-Carlton
© 800/542-8680 (in U.S.)
© 0800/234-000 (in U.K.)
www.ritz-carlton.com

Shangri-La
© 866/565-5050 (in U.S.)
© 0800/028-3337 (in U.K.)
www.shangri-la.com

Sheraton Hotels & Resorts
© 800/325-3535 (in U.S.)
© 800/543-4300 (in Canada)
© 0800/3253-5353 (in U.K.)
www.starwoodhotels.com/sheraton

Westin Hotels & Resorts
© 800/937-8461 (in U.S. and Canada)
© 0800/3259-5959 (in U.K.)
www.starwoodhotels.com/westin

Appendix B:
Useful Terms & Phrases

The official language of Dubai is Arabic, though English is even more widely spoken. With the exception of some local Emiratis, who make up a small percentage of the total population, most everyone living in or traveling to Dubai speaks at least passable English. Street signs and public documents are written in Arabic and English. In hotels, restaurants, shopping centers, beach clubs, sports facilities, entertainment complexes, and other public places, information is usually posted in both Arabic and English (or just English), and the staff invariably speaks English. In some of the city's more traditional areas, particularly Deira and Bur Dubai, you will also hear Hindi, Urdu, and Farsi.

Emiratis (sometimes referred to simply as "locals") speak a Gulf dialect of Arabic. It is similar to the Arabic spoken in Kuwait, Saudi Arabia, Qatar, Bahrain, and parts of Oman. Gulf Arabic tends to be more guttural than classic Arabic and has been influenced by some Persian words. Unique features of Gulf Arabic include pronouncing "k" as "ch" and "j" as "y." The most likely place you will hear it spoken is on television, unless you travel outside Dubai where Arabic is much more common.

Note: When "M/F" is used below, it refers to whether you are speaking to a male or female.

1 Basic Vocabulary

ENGLISH-ARABIC PHRASES

Although you don't need a word of Arabic to get along in Dubai, some familiarization with this rich language will enhance your cultural understanding of the destination. Emiratis will appreciate your efforts to greet them or thank them in Arabic, and it is polite to say *"Salam alaykoom"* to a local before continuing a conversation in English, or *"shukran"* to express appreciation.

ENGLISH	ARABIC
Yes	**Ay-wa/naam**
No	**La'**
Thank you	**Shu-kran**
No thanks	**La shu-kran**
Please	**Min fadlak/min fadliki** (M/F)
Let's go	**Ya-llah**
God willing	**In-sha-la**
Sorry, excuse me	**Af-wan, muta'assif**
Hello	**Salam alaykoom**
Hello (response)	**Wa alaykoom salam**
Good morning	**Sabahh el-kheer**
Good morning (response)	**Sabah in-nuwr**

ENGLISH	ARABIC
Good evening	Massa' el kheer
Good evening (response)	Massa' in-nuwr
Welcome	Ah-hlan wa sah-hlan
Response	Ahh-lan beek/beeki (M/F)
Greetings/Welcome	Mar-haba
How are you?	Kay fah-lak?/Kay fah-lik? (M/F)
Fine, thank you	Zayn, shu-kran/Zayna, shu-kran (M/F)
Praise God	Al hum-duleh-la
Great	Zay al foll
What's your name?	Shuw ismak?/Shuw ismik? (M/F)
My name is	Is-mee [your name]
No problem	Mish-mishkella
Where are you from?	Inta min-ayn/Inti min-ayn? (M/F)
I'm from	Anaa min [country]
America	Ame-ri-ki
Britain	Brai-ta-ni
Europe	O-ro-pi
India	Al hind
It's a pleasure to have met you	Forsa sai-eeda
I'm honored (response)	Ana as-ad
Goodbye	Ma-salama

NUMBERS

0	sifr	16	sittaasher
1	wahed	17	sabataasher
2	itnain	18	tamantaasher
3	talaata	19	tissataasher
4	arbaa'	20	ashreen
5	khamsa	30	tala-teen
6	sitta	40	arba-een
7	saba'	50	khamseen
8	tamanya	60	sitteen
9	tissa	70	saba-een
10	ashera	80	tamaneen
11	hadaasher	90	tissa-een
12	itnaasher	100	mia
13	talataasher	200	mee-tain
14	arabataasher	1,000	alf
15	khamsataasher	2,000	alfayn

DAYS OF THE WEEK, PERIODS OF TIME

The week starts on Sunday, and the weekend is Friday and Saturday. You'll notice if you compare the names of the days to the numbers (above) that they are simply numbered sequentially. Days of the week are usually preceded by the word *yom*, meaning "day."

Sunday	**yom al had**
Monday	**yom al itnayn**
Tuesday	**yom al talaat**
Wednesday	**yom al arba'**
Thursday	**yom al khamees**
Friday	**yom al goma'**
Saturday	**yom as-sebt**
Day/days	**yom/ayam**
Week/weeks	**isbu- a'/asabee-a'**
Month/months	**shahr/shahour**
Today	**an-nahar-da**
Yesterday	**imber-ihh**
Tomorrow	**boukra**
Now	**dil-wa'atee/al-an**
Later	**badayn**

STATEMENTS OF FACT

I understand	**Ana fahim/ana fahma** (M/F)
I don't understand	**Ana mu fa-him/ana mu fahhma** (M/F)
I'm sick	**Ana ay-yan/Ana ay-yana**
I like	**Ana beheb**
I don't like	**Ana mabeh-bish**
I want	**Ana areed**
I want to buy	**Ana areed an ashtaree**
I'm looking for	**Ana badowar**

ASKING QUESTIONS

What?	**Shuw?**
Why?	**Laysh?**
Who?	**Meen?**
When?	**Mata?**
Where?	**Wayn?**
How?	**Kayf?**
May I?	**Mumkin?**
Could you please?	**Mumkin min fadhlak?**

Where is	**Wayn al** [thing]
the grocery store	**ba'ala**
the gas station	**mahattat betrol**
What does that mean?	**Yanni eh?**
Where's the nearest . . . ?	**Wayn aghrab?**
How do I get to	**Ana unzil** [place] **zay?**
the Corniche	**corniche zay?**
What time is it?	**Sa' kam?**
It is . . .	**Sa'** [number]

2 Travel Terms

DIRECTIONS

ala yameen   to the right
ala shi-mel/ala yassar   to the left
fo'   up or above
wara'   behind
wara es-shams   middle of nowhere
uddam al   in front of [thing]
khush   go
ala tool   straight
henna   here
khush yameen min henna   go right here

HOTEL ROOMS

funduq   hotel
ghurfa   room
Andak/andik [thing?] (M/F)   Do you have . . . ?
   ghurfa fadya?   an empty room?
Bikaam?   How much?
tareekh   date
an na-harda   today
Mumkin atfarag-ha?   Can I see it?
takif/mukae-yif   air-conditioning/air-conditioned
ghurfa mukae-yifa   air-conditioned room
marwaha   fan
hamam   toilet
leila wahada   1 night

DESCRIPTORS

Simply tack these adjective after nouns (for example: cheap room = *fundu' arkhees*).

arkhees   cheap

ghalee   expensive

Ghalee giddan!   That's expensive!

hali   free

faadi   empty

kabeer   big

sagheer   small

OTHER USEFUL NOUNS

mataar   airport

sareer   bed

beera   beer

agala   bike

arabeya   car

hes-sab   restaurant check/bill

bab   door

bab al reisi   main door/entrance

saffara   embassy

   saffarat Ameriki   American embassy

   saffarat Canadeya   Canadian embassy

   saffarat Braitani   British embassy

betrol   gas/petrol

mahattat betrol   gas station

moustashfa   hospital

fallous   money

methaf   museum

sayidalaya   pharmacy

mat'am   restaurant

magha   café

ughfa   room

taks   taxi

haga   thing

walla haga   nothing

maiya   water

maiya madaneya   mineral water

3 Hindi Terms & Expressions

Dubai is home to a large number of immigrants from the Indian subcontinent, so a few Hindi phrases can be helpful, whether you're catching a taxi or negotiating the price on your purchase at Meena Bazaar or the Gold Souk.

USEFUL TERMS

Yes	**haanji**
No	**nahin**
Thank you	**dhanyavad**
Hello	**namaste**
How are you?	**Aap kaise hai?**
I am well	**Mai theek hoon**
What is your name?	**Aap ka naam kya hai?**
My name is...	**Mera naam [name] hai**

ASKING QUESTIONS

What?	**Kya?**
Why?	**Kyun?**
Who?	**Kaun?**
When?	**Kab?**
Where?	**Kahan?**
How?	**Kaise?**
How much is this?	**Yeh kitne hai?**

NUMBERS

0	**shunya**
1	**ek**
2	**dho**
3	**theen**
4	**chaar**
5	**paanch**
6	**cheh**
7	**saath**
8	**aath**
9	**nau**
10	**dhus**

DAYS OF THE WEEK, PERIODS OF TIME

Sunday	**ravivar**
Monday	**somvar**
Tuesday	**mangalvar**
Wednesday	**budhvar'**
Thursday	**guruvar**
Friday	**shukravar**
Saturday	**shanivar**
day	**din**
week/weeks	**hafta/hafte**
month	**mahina**
today	**aaj**

| tomorrow | **kaal** |
| now | **ab** |

MENU TERMS

water	**paani**
milk	**doodh**
tea	**chai**
bread	**roti**
rice	**chawal**
hot	**garam**
cold	**tunda**
sugar	**cheeni**
salt	**namak**
drink	**peena**
food	**khanna**
spicy	**teekha**
sweet	**mitha**
potato	**aloo**
tomato	**tamatar**
cucumber	**kheera**
yogurt	**dhay**
onion	**pyaaz**

SHOPPING TERMS

shirt	**kameez**
pants	**patloon**
shoes	**jute**
gold	**sona**
silver	**chandi**
diamond	**hira**
money	**paisa**
ring	**anguthi**
necklace	**mala**
bracelet	**chudi**

Index

See also Accommodations and Restaurant indexes, below.

ACCOMMODATIONS

RESTAURANTS

FROMMER'S® COMPLETE TRAVEL GUIDES

Alaska
Amalfi Coast
American Southwest
Amsterdam
Argentina
Arizona
Atlanta
Australia
Austria
Bahamas
Barcelona
Beijing
Belgium, Holland & Luxembourg
Belize
Bermuda
Boston
Brazil
British Columbia & the Canadian
    Rockies
Brussels & Bruges
Budapest & the Best of Hungary
Buenos Aires
Calgary
California
Canada
Cancún, Cozumel & the Yucatán
Cape Cod, Nantucket & Martha's
    Vineyard
Caribbean
Caribbean Ports of Call
Carolinas & Georgia
Chicago
Chile & Easter Island
China
Colorado
Costa Rica
Croatia
Cuba
Denmark
Denver, Boulder & Colorado Springs
Eastern Europe
Ecuador & the Galapagos Islands
Edinburgh & Glasgow
England
Europe
Europe by Rail

Florence, Tuscany & Umbria
Florida
France
Germany
Greece
Greek Islands
Guatemala
Hawaii
Hong Kong
Honolulu, Waikiki & Oahu
India
Ireland
Israel
Italy
Jamaica
Japan
Kauai
Las Vegas
London
Los Angeles
Los Cabos & Baja
Madrid
Maine Coast
Maryland & Delaware
Maui
Mexico
Montana & Wyoming
Montréal & Québec City
Morocco
Moscow & St. Petersburg
Munich & the Bavarian Alps
Nashville & Memphis
New England
Newfoundland & Labrador
New Mexico
New Orleans
New York City
New York State
New Zealand
Northern Italy
Norway
Nova Scotia, New Brunswick &
    Prince Edward Island
Oregon
Paris
Peru

Philadelphia & the Amish Country
Portugal
Prague & the Best of the Czech
    Republic
Provence & the Riviera
Puerto Rico
Rome
San Antonio & Austin
San Diego
San Francisco
Santa Fe, Taos & Albuquerque
Scandinavia
Scotland
Seattle
Seville, Granada & the Best of
    Andalusia
Shanghai
Sicily
Singapore & Malaysia
South Africa
South America
South Florida
South Korea
South Pacific
Southeast Asia
Spain
Sweden
Switzerland
Tahiti & French Polynesia
Texas
Thailand
Tokyo
Toronto
Turkey
USA
Utah
Vancouver & Victoria
Vermont, New Hampshire & Maine
Vienna & the Danube Valley
Vietnam
Virgin Islands
Virginia
Walt Disney World® & Orlando
Washington, D.C.
Washington State

FROMMER'S® DAY BY DAY GUIDES

Amsterdam
Barcelona
Beijing
Boston
Cancun & the Yucatan
Chicago
Florence & Tuscany

Hong Kong
Honolulu & Oahu
London
Maui
Montréal
Napa & Sonoma
New York City

Paris
Provence & the Riviera
Rome
San Francisco
Venice
Washington D.C.

PAULINE FROMMER'S GUIDES: SEE MORE. SPEND LESS.

Alaska
Hawaii
Italy

Las Vegas
London
New York City

Paris
Walt Disney World®
Washington D.C.

FROMMER'S® PORTABLE GUIDES

Acapulco, Ixtapa & Zihuatanejo
Amsterdam
Aruba, Bonaire & Curacao
Australia's Great Barrier Reef
Bahamas
Big Island of Hawaii
Boston
California Wine Country
Cancún
Cayman Islands
Charleston
Chicago
Dominican Republic

Florence
Las Vegas
Las Vegas for Non-Gamblers
London
Maui
Nantucket & Martha's Vineyard
New Orleans
New York City
Paris
Portland
Puerto Rico
Puerto Vallarta, Manzanillo &
    Guadalajara

Rio de Janeiro
San Diego
San Francisco
Savannah
St. Martin, Sint Maarten, Anguilla &
    St. Bart's
Turks & Caicos
Vancouver
Venice
Virgin Islands
Washington, D.C.
Whistler

FROMMER'S® CRUISE GUIDES

Alaska Cruises & Ports of Call

Cruises & Ports of Call

European Cruises & Ports of Call

FROMMER'S® NATIONAL PARK GUIDES

Algonquin Provincial Park
Banff & Jasper
Grand Canyon

National Parks of the American West
Rocky Mountain
Yellowstone & Grand Teton

Yosemite and Sequoia & Kings
    Canyon
Zion & Bryce Canyon

FROMMER'S® WITH KIDS GUIDES

Chicago
Hawaii
Las Vegas
London

National Parks
New York City
San Francisco

Toronto
Walt Disney World® & Orlando
Washington, D.C.

FROMMER'S® PHRASEFINDER DICTIONARY GUIDES

Chinese
French

German
Italian

Japanese
Spanish

SUZY GERSHMAN'S BORN TO SHOP GUIDES

France
Hong Kong, Shanghai & Beijing
Italy

London
New York
Paris

San Francisco
Where to Buy the Best of Everything.

FROMMER'S® BEST-LOVED DRIVING TOURS

Britain
California
France
Germany

Ireland
Italy
New England
Northern Italy

Scotland
Spain
Tuscany & Umbria

THE UNOFFICIAL GUIDES®

Adventure Travel in Alaska
Beyond Disney
California with Kids
Central Italy
Chicago
Cruises
Disneyland®
England
Hawaii

Ireland
Las Vegas
London
Maui
Mexico's Best Beach Resorts
Mini Mickey
New Orleans
New York City
Paris

San Francisco
South Florida including Miami &
    the Keys
Walt Disney World®
Walt Disney World® for
    Grown-ups
Walt Disney World® with Kids
Washington, D.C.

SPECIAL-INTEREST TITLES

Athens Past & Present
Best Places to Raise Your Family
Cities Ranked & Rated
500 Places to Take Your Kids Before They Grow Up
Frommer's Best Day Trips from London
Frommer's Best RV & Tent Campgrounds in the U.S.A.

Frommer's Exploring America by RV
Frommer's NYC Free & Dirt Cheap
Frommer's Road Atlas Europe
Frommer's Road Atlas Ireland
Retirement Places Rated

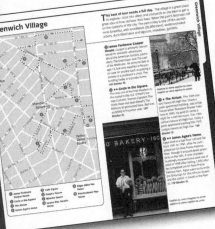

A Guide for Every Type of Traveler

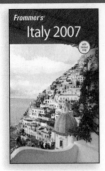

Frommer's Complete Guides

For those who value complete coverage, candid advice, and lots of choices in all price ranges.

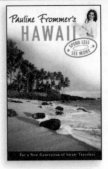

Pauline Frommer's Guides

For those who want to experience a culture, meet locals, and save money along the way.

MTV Guides

For hip, youthful travelers who want a fresh perspective on today's hottest cities and destinations.

Day by Day Guides

For leisure or business travelers who want to organize their time to get the most out of a trip.

Frommer's With Kids Guides

For families traveling with children ages 2 to 14 seeking kid-friendly hotels, restaurants, and activities.

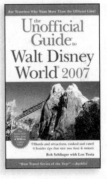

Unofficial Guides

For honeymooners, families, business travelers, and others who value no-nonsense, *Consumer Reports*–style advice.

For Dummies Travel Guides

For curious, independent travelers looking for a fun and easy way to plan a trip.

Visit Frommers.com

WILEY

Now you know.

Explore over 3,500 destinations.

TOKYO — 7766 miles
LONDON — 3818 miles
TORONTO — 4682 miles
SYDNEY — 5087 miles
NEW YORK — 4947 miles
LOS ANGELES — 2556 miles
HONG KONG — 5638 miles

Frommers.com makes it easy.

Find a destination. ✓ Book a trip. ✓ Get hot travel deals.
Buy a guidebook. ✓ Enter to win vacations. ✓ Listen to podcasts. ✓ Check out
the latest travel news. ✓ Share trip photos and memories. ✓ And much more.

Frommers.com

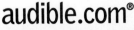

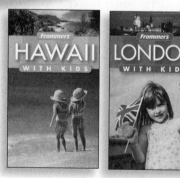